Critical Strategies

German Fiction in the Twentieth Century

Critical Strategies
German Fiction in the Twentieth Century

Elizabeth Boa
and
J. H. Reid

McGILL–QUEEN'S UNIVERSITY PRESS

Montreal
1972

First published 1972 by
Edward Arnold (Publishers) Ltd.,
25 Hill Street, London W1X 8LL

Cloth edition ISBN: 0 7735 0174 6
Paper edition ISBN 0 7735 0175 4

Library of Congress Catalog Card No. 72-90653
Legal deposit 4th quarter

Printed in Great Britain by
Billing & Sons Limited, Guildford and London

Preface

The student of literature has a foot in two worlds, that of his everyday life and that of the novel, play or poem which he is reading, a world whose laws and logic may be quite different from those of the first. Our first two sections concentrate on the internal logic of the work of art. By 'Structures' we understand those formal aspects which emerge only when the novel is viewed as a whole: patterns based, for example, on point of view, changes of time or place, or 'submerged forms'. 'Textural' features, on the other hand, can be isolated and described at any point in the narrative: register, imagery (or its absence), dialogue and tone. The second half of the book turns to the relationship between the fictional world of the work and the real world. Part III examines the materials which the novelist can take from the world of his own experience and incorporate in the fictional world of the novel; it raises the question of meaning and touches on the relationship between fiction and life. The final section suggests some of the ways in which these materials are shaped in the novel. Some novels attempt to create the impression of a world as similar as possible to that of the reader; others depict life less directly, by means of symbols, or discursively, through philosophical analysis. The ironic novel seems so important in German literature that a discussion of it has been included in this section, although the 'ironic mode' is in a different logical category from the others.

It must be emphasized that the individual chapters are not watertight. Long-term structural effects derive, after all, from the accumulation of particular moments in the text. The full value of textural effects may only become evident in the context of the work as a whole. Structure and texture are aspects of the same whole. In particular Chapter 3 (Patterns) and Chapter 4 (Space) may be felt to overlap. This is because the latter is intended to sum up the previous chapters, while examining the concept of structure from a new angle. Cross-references are numerous throughout the book.

The layout of the individual chapters is modelled on Jonathan

Raban's *The Technique of Modern Fiction* (London, 1968). Each chapter contains a discursive essay, followed by an extended extract from one work with a commentary to illustrate in a practical way some of the issues raised more theoretically in the essay. Page references in the text refer to the editions quoted in the first part of the bibliography. Dates of novels have not been given except in the chapter on Politics, History and Utopia, where they seemed most relevant; they can all, however, be found in the Index.

Contents

Acknowledgements

The Publishers' thanks are due to the following for permission to use copyright material:

S. Fischer Verlag, Frankfurt for extracts from Franz Kafka's *Der Prozeß* and *Ein Bericht für eine Akademie*, Thomas Mann's *Der Zauberberg* and *Der kleine Herr Friedemann*; Rowohlt Verlag, Hamburg for an extract from Robert Musil's *Die Verwirrungen des Zöglings Törleß*; Berman-Fischer, Stockholm for an extract from Thomas Mann's *Doktor Faustus*; Suhrkamp Verlag, Frankfurt for extracts from Hermann Hesse's *Das Glasperlenspiel*, Max Frisch's *Homo Faber*, Peter Handke's *Die Hornissen*, Hermann Broch's *Die Schlafwandler* and Hans Erich Nossack's *Das Testament des Lucius Eurinus*; Hermann Luchterhand Verlag, Darmstadt for an extract from Günter Grass's *Die Blechtrommel*; Walter-Verlag, Olten for an extract from Alfred Döblin's *Berlin Alexanderplatz*; Aufbau Verlag, Berlin for an extract from Heinrich Mann's *Der Untertan*; Schocken Books, New York for an extract from Franz Kafka's *Das Schloß*; Kiepenheuer and Witsch, Köln for an extract from Heinrich Boll's *Billard um halbzehn*; Rhein Verlag, Zurich for an extract from Hermann Broch's *Der Versucher*; and Helmut Kossodo AG, Geneva for an extract from Robert Walser's *Der Gehülfe*.

PART I STRUCTURES

1 Point of View

Drama unfolds itself; a novel is narrated. The former is direct and objective: its objects—characters, location, events—speak for themselves and are physically present before the audience. The novel is indirect and subjective; its objects are not experienced by the reader directly, but only by hearsay, through the medium of someone else's mind, from a particular and subjective point of view, whether that of one of the characters or of a fictitious biographer or of some anonymous narrator. There may be narrative elements and therefore points of view in any one drama; but point of view is not a meaningful term in relation to drama as such; it is fundamental to any discussion of the novel.

A practically unlimited variety of points of view is possible, each of which raises its own problems and sheds light on the ultimate meaning of the work. The type of perspective will depend largely upon the distance in space and time between the narrator and his subject-matter: at times he may view it from outside and from afar, at others he may come so close as to identify himself with his hero; sometimes he is looking at events which happened many years previously, sometimes he appears to be experiencing them as they happen.

The least dramatic point of view is that of the anonymous narrator who describes the events and characters of his story in the third person, who often speaks of himself as 'wir' and addresses the reader directly ('geneigter Leser' was the traditional term), and who feels free to comment on what he is describing or to make general philosophical statements or point out to the reader things which are outside the experience of the people in his story.

Um so mehr ist es zu beklagen, daß der übelberüchtigte Zahn der Zeit, dem so viele andere große Werke des Genies und Witzes nicht entgehen konnten, noch künftig entgehen werden, leider! auch der Originale dieser beiden berühmten Reden nicht verschont hat! — wenigstens soviel uns bekannt ist. Denn wer weiß, ob es nicht vielleicht einem künftigen Fourmont, Sevin oder Villoison,

A*

der auf Entdeckung alter Handschriften ausgeht, dereinst gelingen mag, eine Abschrift derselben in irgendeinem bestaubten Winkel einer alten Klosterbibliothek aufzuspüren? (Wieland, *Geschichte der Abderiten*, Book IV, Chapter 12, p. 287)

He is easily confused with the author himself, but it is important to distinguish between them: the narrator is a device, a role which the author has adopted for the time being, in Wieland's case that of the historian—Wieland as author was not really concerned with historical truth but with satirizing contemporary life. This narrator is often called 'omniscient', because he, as distinct from the biographer, knows all there is to be known about his heroes, for the simple reason that he has invented them. 'Eduard, so nennen wir einen reichen Baron im besten Mannesalter ...' is the beginning of Goethe's *Die Wahlverwandtschaften*, and so the narrator makes it clear that the overall perspective from which the novel is to be viewed is not that of Eduard, but that of an outside observer: Eduard is but his creation, to whom he has decided, more or less arbitrarily, to give that name. This is important for a correct understanding of the novel. In this form of narrative the narrator is both in space and time at his farthest from the events he is describing. Indeed he often appears at pains to be closer to his reader than to his story, taking the reader into his confidence to form a conspiracy with him against the characters of the novel. As a result, a frequent feature of this form, from Wieland to Thomas Mann, is irony.

Wieland, as we have seen, was pretending to be a historian. In fact, however, he makes it quite clear that he is poking fun at a literary convention, and he retains all of his narrator's freedom to relate his story as he pleases. When the narrator takes the convention seriously, as in Hesse's *Das Glasperlenspiel*, he will put his own personality further into the background. But he still has a personality. It is clear that the anonymous biographer admires Knecht and accepts his values; he may even be said to vindicate Knecht's decisions. When the narrator steps still further into the background, adopting a camera-like stance, registering, but neither approving nor disapproving, he has abandoned a great deal of his original freedom. This is largely the case in Hauptmann's *Bahnwärter Thiel*.

So far, the overall narrative standpoint has always been one outside the story itself. If, however, the narrator wishes to disappear altogether, he may adopt the standpoint of one of the characters in his novel.

> K. starrte den Aufseher an. Schulmäßige Lehren bekam er hier von einem vielleicht jüngeren Menschen? Für seine Offenheit wurde er mit einer Rüge bestraft? Und über den Grund seiner Verhaftung und über deren Auftrageber erfuhr er nichts? Er geriet in eine gewisse Aufregung, ging auf und ab, woran ihn niemand hinderte, schob seine Manschetten zurück, befühlte die Brust, strich sein Haar zurecht, kam an den drei Herren vorüber, sagte: 'Es ist ja sinnlos', worauf sich diese zu ihm umdrehten und ihn entgegen-kommend, aber ernst ansahen, und machte endlich wieder vor dem Tisch des Aufsehers halt. (Kafka, *Der Prozeß*, Chapter 1, p. 268.)

Not only does the narrator refrain from commenting on the action, as in the previous type; he further restricts his freedom by report-ing nothing which is outside the field of experience of his main character. In *Der Prozeß* we never learn the thoughts of the repre-sentatives of the law, nor of K's acquaintances at the bank or elsewhere, except in so far as they are made known to K. There is no satisfactory, generally accepted term for this type of narration. Robert Humphrey's term 'indirect interior monologue' seems appropriate[1]; the German term *erlebte Rede* denotes more precisely those passages which reproduce the character's thoughts without any kind of external description, but in the preterite indicative, as in the second, third and fourth sentences of the Kafka illustra-tion (cf. also *Dialogue and Narrative*, pp. 61–62). The 'medium' of the narration is normally the central figure of the novel, but need not be so. In space the narrator is very close to him, although not identical with him; in time he may move from reporting events in the past experience of his medium to presenting them as they happen. The relationship with the reader established by the anonymous, omniscient narrator is abandoned completely.

Going one step further in 'dramatizing' his novel, the author can eliminate even the naming of his character—a gesture from outside—and the descriptions of what he does—experienced by the character, therefore in keeping with the single point of view, but nevertheless told from without. This is the case with the 'stream of consciousness' or in Humphrey's terms 'direct interior monologue' technique, which restricts itself to reproducing the workings of the character's mind as they occur.

---

[1] Robert Humphrey, *Stream of Consciousness in the Modern Novel* (Berkeley and Los Angeles, 1954), Chapter 2.

Wie lange wird denn das noch dauern? Ich muß auf die Uhr schauen ... schickt sich wahrscheinlich nicht in einem so ernsten Konzert. Aber wer sieht's denn? Wenn's einer sieht, so paßt er gerade so wenig auf, wie ich, und vor dem brauch' ich mich nicht zu genieren ... Erst viertel auf zehn? ... Mir kommt vor, ich sitz' schon drei Stunden in dem Konzert. (Schnitzler, *Leutenant Gustl*, p. 337)

Expressed in terms of space–time relationships, here the maximum of congruency is obtained: the reader and narrator are in the place of the hero at the same time as the events registered are happening. Where *erlebte Rede* uses the past tense, direct interior monologue uses the present. The language will be uniformly that of the hero, colloquial and banal as in *Leutnant Gustl*, elevated and intellectual as in Goethe's monologue in *Lotte in Weimar*.

At this stage the narrator seems completely to have disappeared. But, as the last example shows, an 'ich' has now entered the scene. In direct interior monologue this 'ich' is not consciously narrating the story; it remains a medium through which the story is told. But it requires only a little more self-awareness and we have a new kind of narrator, the autobiographer. The fictitious diary, for example, is not far from the stream of consciousness technique, as seen in the second part of Max Frisch's *Homo Faber*.

This new kind of narrator, unlike the omniscient narrator, is not anonymous and outside the action of his story, but is himself an actor in the story he is describing. To that extent he too is 'dramatized'. Like the former, however, he can be near or far in time or space from the hero of the novel. In the autobiography he is identical with the hero. It is important here to observe the time relationship between the narrator and the events of his story. In Heinrich Böll's *Ansichten eines Clowns* there is no time-lag between events and their registration; Schnier, the narrator, appears to be writing down the experiences of the few hours covered by the novel as they occur; indeed one would at times be inclined to describe it as a 'stream of consciousness' novel. A much more frequent point of view in time is that of the mature man looking back on the events of his life. But even here subtle changes of emphasis are common: a description of youthful escapades solely from the point of view of the sadder and wiser man would often be tedious. The 'Ich-Erzähler' need not himself be the centre of interest. In Broch's *Der Versucher* he stands somewhat apart from the community he describes and plays a minor role in events. He may be a friend or admirer of the hero, as in several novels of Raabe and in *Doktor Faustus*. Again interesting shifts in time and space are possible.

Ultimately this type of narration merges more or less imperceptibly with that of the anonymous, omniscient narrator discussed at the beginning. For the biographer will often have to invent conversations of which he can in all probability have no recollection or even scenes at which he may not have been present. And it may not make very much difference whether the narrator is named or anonymous: in both cases he is a convention, a literary fiction, an individual voice belonging to a person possessed of identifiable qualities and values, which are just as much part of the society shown in the novel as are those of any of the characters proper.

The points of view so far outlined are neither exclusive nor mutually exclusive. Very few novels can have been written from first to last from the standpoint of the outside, omniscient narrator. 'Dramatization', at least in the form of dialogue, will frequently be necessary if only for the sake of liveliness; to create suspense, the narrator may withhold information from the reader by adopting a limited viewpoint. The narrative standpoint in such novels as Max Frisch's *Mein Name sei Gantenbein* is highly complex and difficult to fit into any one of the categories outlined. Of importance are, firstly, the appropriateness of the narrative standpoint to the subject-matter and, secondly, the wider implications of perspectives or changes in perspective.

The anonymous, omniscient, talkative narrator has not completely disappeared from the twentieth-century novel, as is frequently stated, but has been considerably modified. One reason for this is mainly technical. The anonymous narrator speaking from a kind of limbo between the real world of the author and the fictional world of the plot could seem artificial and unsatisfactory. The drama had always been a much more respectable genre than the novel, especially in Germany, and one of the most striking developments in these two genres in the twentieth century has been the way in which they have affected each other: novelists have tried to 'dramatize' their novels, while dramatists have been writing 'epic' theatre, discounting dialogue and introducing a point of view extraneous to that of the characters by means of film projections, placards and even, as in Brecht's *Der kaukasische Kreidekreis*, a 'narrator'.

The traditional narrator might also be considered inappropriate to the subject-matter of modern novels. In general, the eighteenth- and nineteenth-century narrator was the one fixed point in his novel to which all else could be related. His values were the ultimate values. In terms of ideas he was comparable to the theist god, in terms of social relationships he resembled the monarch. In both ways he had an integrating function, and his disappearance may reflect both social and ideological disorientation. Nowhere is this clearer than in the works of Franz Kafka. What then, one must ask, is the function of the apparently old-fashioned narrator in Thomas Mann's *Der Zauberberg*? Is he the fixed point to which all is related and in which all has its meaning? Is he to be trusted? Is, for example, his judgment on Hans Castorp reliable? (See Chapter 16.)

The difference between the dramatized narrator and the fictional autobiographer is also worth examining in more detail. A test for the consistency of the former point of view is to substitute an 'ich' for an 'er' throughout, making the appropriate grammatical changes. In terms of realism one obvious impossibility in the autobiography is the death of the narrator. Gottfried Keller's struggle with *Der grüne Heinrich* bears witness to this difficulty. *Der Prozeß*, on the other hand, narrated throughout as indirect interior monologue, can without any change in perspective end in the death of Josef K. A more far-reaching difference concerns the personality of the narrator. The autobiography demands great self-awareness, the ability to reflect on one's career and make judgments on it. Leutnant Gustl could not be expected to relate his own story: it is precisely his lack of self-awareness that Schnitzler is caricaturing. And Josef K.? Felix Krull, the confidence-trickster, makes a credible attempt at autobiography. But, like all confidence-tricksters, he makes mistakes from time to time; the bombast of his language lets him down, and the reader is able to see through him. On the whole *erlebte Rede* and the related stream of consciousness technique seem particularly appropriate and effective at grasping life at the moment of its being lived. But this directness is often accompanied by a lack of complexity. The first person narrative offers great scope for the play of perspectives in space and time within a single novel: the subtle changes of emphasis in a mature man writing his memoirs or the clash of personalities between the biographer and his hero which has been so important in the German novel from Raabe's *Die Akten des Vogelsangs* to Thomas Mann's *Doktor Faustus.*

Finally, two points which have been alluded to and which will be discussed in more detail later are worth mentioning: realism and parody. Many of the developments in the history of the narrator can be traced to an attempt to awaken in the reader the illusion of experiencing life as he would experience it in reality. Since the omniscient, personal but anonymous narrator is the most intrusive reminder to the reader that he is not experiencing reality, this is the standpoint most likely to be attacked in the name of realism. But, since in effect *every* narrative standpoint is a fiction in any case—a convention, part of the 'rhetoric' of the novel—the pendulum may swing back at any time and the author, while ostensibly adopting the conventions of the realist mode, make it clear that he is quite aware of their conventional nature. The result is parody. Wieland, as we have seen, parodies the narrator-as-historian convention. At one point in *Hundejahre* Günter Grass is clearly parodying the convention that the biographer-actor should himself have experienced what he is relating, when he has Harry Liebenau, his narrator, perform superhuman feats of athletics in order to observe two separate activities going on simultaneously at different ends of a mountain. The constant dualism in the novel between realism and fantasy is nowhere clearer than in the history of narrative perspectives.

The following extended extract from Robert Musil's first novel *Die Verwirrungen des Zöglings Törleß* provides an opportunity to examine in greater detail some points of view in context. Törleß is a pupil at a boarding school in a remote region of the Austro-Hungarian Empire. He is intelligent and sensitive but passive, and has fallen under the influence of two more mature boys, Beineberg and Reiting. Having escorted his parents to the railway station after a short visit he spends the rest of the day with Beineberg, ending up in the company of Božena, a prostitute, who claims to have been formerly in the service of Beineberg's mother.

Während Božena sprach, fühlte sich Törleß ihren gemeinen Anspielungen fast wehrlos preisgegeben.

Was sie schilderte, sah er lebendig vor sich. Beinebergs Mutter wurde zu seiner eigenen. Er erinnerte sich der hellen Räume der elterlichen Wohnung. Der gepflegten, reinen, unnahbaren Gesichter, die ihm zu Hause bei den Diners oft eine gewisse Ehrfurcht eingeflößt hatten. Der vornehmen, kühlen Hände, die sich selbst beim Essen nichts zu vergeben schienen. Eine Menge solcher Einzelheiten fiel ihm ein, und er schämte sich, hier in einem kleinen, übelriechenden Zimmer zu sein und mit einem Zittern auf die demütigenden Worte einer Dirne zu antworten. Die Erinnerung an die vollendete Manier dieser nie formvergessenen Gesellschaft wirkte stärker auf ihn als alle moralische Überlegung. Das Wühlen seiner dunklen Leidenschaften kam ihm lächerlich vor. Mit visionärer Eindringlichkeit sah er eine kühle, abwehrende Handbewegung, ein chokiertes Lächeln, mit dem man ihn wie ein kleines unsauberes Tier von sich weisen würde. Trotzdem blieb er wie festgebunden auf seinem Platze sitzen.

Mit jeder Einzelheit, deren er sich erinnerte, wuchs nämlich neben der Scham auch eine Kette häßlicher Gedanken in ihm groß. Sie hatte begonnen, als Beineberg die Erläuterung zu Boženas Gespräch gab, worauf Törleß errötet war.

Er hatte damals plötzlich an seine eigene Mutter denken müssen, und dies hielt nun fest und war nicht loszubekommen. Es war ihm nur so durch die Grenzen des Bewußtseins geschossen — blitzschnell oder undeutlich weit — am Rande — nur wie im Fluge gesehen — kaum ein Gedanke zu nennen. Und hastig war darauf eine Reihe von Fragen gefolgt, die es verdecken sollten: 'Was ist es, das es ermöglicht, daß diese Božena ihre niedrige Existenz an die meiner Mutter heranrücken kann? Daß sie sich in der Enge desselben Gedankens an jene herandrängt? Warum berührt sie nicht mit der Stirne die Erde, wenn sie schon von ihr sprechen muß? Warum ist es nicht wie durch einen Abgrund zum Ausdruck gebracht, daß hier gar keine Gemeinsamkeit besteht? Denn, wie ist es doch? Dieses Weib ist für mich ein Knäuel aller geschlechtlichen Begehrlichkeiten; und meine Mutter ein Geschöpf, das bisher in wolkenloser Entfernung, klar und ohne Tiefen, wie ein Gestirn jenseits alles Begehrens durch mein Leben wandelte …'

Aber alle diese Fragen waren nicht das Eigentliche. Berührten es kaum. Sie waren etwas Sekundäres; etwas, das Törleß erst nachträglich eingefallen war. Sie vervielfältigten sich nur, weil keine das Rechte bezeichnete. Sie waren nur Ausflüchte, Umschreibungen der Tatsache, daß vorbewußt, plötzlich, instinktiv ein seelischer Zusammenhang gegeben war, der sie vor ihrem Entstehen schon in bösem Sinne beantwortet hatte. Törleß sättigte sich mit den Augen an Božena und konnte dabei seiner Mutter nicht vergessen; durch ihn hindurch verkettete die beiden ein Zusammenhang: Alles andere war nur ein sich Winden unter dieser Ideenverschlingung. Diese war die einzige Tatsache. Aber durch die Vergeblichkeit, ihren Zwang abzuschütteln, gewann sie eine fürchterliche, unklare Bedeutung, die wie ein perfides Lächeln alle Anstrengungen begleitete.

· · · · · ·

Törleß sah im Zimmer umher, um dies loszuwerden. Aber alles hatte nun schon diese eine Beziehung angenommen. Der kleine eiserne Ofen mit den Rostflecken auf der Platte, das Bett mit den wackligen Pfosten und der gestrichenen Lade, von der die Farbe an vielen Stellen abblätterte, das Bettzeug, das schmutzig durch die Löcher des abgenutzten Lakens sah; Božena, ihr Hemd, das von der einen Schulter geglitten war, das gemeine, wüste Rot ihres Unterrockes, ihr breites, schwatzendes Lachen; endlich Beineberg, dessen Benehmen ihm im Vergleich zu sonst wie das eines unzüchtigen Priesters vorkam, der, toll geworden, zweideutige Worte in die ernsten Formen eines Gebetes flicht ...: all das stieß nach der einen Richtung, drängte auf ihn ein und bog seine Gedanken gewaltsam immer wieder zurück.

Nur an einer Stelle fanden seine Blicke, die geschreckt von einem zum andern flüchteten, Frieden. Das war oberhalb der kleinen Gardine. Dort sahen die Wolken vom Himmel herein und reglos der Mond.

Das war, als ob er plötzlich in die frische, ruhige Nachtluft hinausgetreten wäre. Eine Weile wurden alle Gedanken ganz still. Dann kam ihm eine angenehme Erinnerung. Das Landhaus, das sie letzten Sommer bewohnt hatten. Nächte im schweigenden Park. Ein sternzitterndes, samtdunkles Firmament. Die Stimme seiner Mutter aus der Tiefe des Gartens, wo sie mit Papa auf den schwach schimmernden Kieswegen spazierenging. Lieder, die sie halblaut vor sich hinsang. Aber da, ... es fuhr ihm kalt durch den Leib, ... war auch wieder dieses quälende Vergleichen. Was mochten die beiden dabei gefühlt haben? Liebe? Nein, der Gedanke kam ihm jetzt zum erstenmal. Überhaupt war das etwas ganz anderes. Nichts für große und erwachsene Menschen; gar für seine Eltern. Nachts am offenen Fenster sitzen und sich verlassen fühlen, sich anders fühlen als die Großen, von jedem Lachen und von jedem spöttischen Blick mißverstanden, niemandem erklären können, was man schon bedeute, und sich nach einer sehnen, die das verstünde, ... das ist Liebe! Aber dazu muß man jung und einsam sein. Bei ihnen mußte es etwas anderes gewesen sein; etwas Ruhiges und Gleichmütiges. Mama sang einfach am Abend in dem dunklen Garten und war heiter ...

Aber gerade das war es, was Törleß nicht verstand. Die geduldigen Pläne, welche für den Erwachsenen, ohne daß er es merkt, die Tage zu Monaten und Jahren zusammenketten, waren ihm noch fremd. Und ebenso jenes Abgestumpftsein, für das es nicht einmal mehr eine Frage bedeutet, wenn wieder ein Tag zu Ende geht. Sein Leben war auf jeden Tag gerichtet. Jede Nacht bedeutete für ihn ein Nichts, ein Grab, ein Ausgelöschtwerden. Das Vermögen, sich jeden Tag sterben zu legen, ohne sich darüber Gedanken zu machen, hatte er noch nicht erlernt.

Deswegen hatte er immer etwas dahinter vermutet, das man ihm verberge. Die Nächte erschienen ihm wie dunkle Tore zu geheimnis-

vollen Freuden, die man ihm verheimlicht hatte, so daß sein Leben
leer und unglücklich blieb.

Er erinnerte sich an ein eigentümliches Lachen seiner Mutter und
sich wie scherzhaft fester an den Arm ihres Mannes Drücken, das er
an einem jener Abende beobachtet hatte. Es schien jeden Zweifel
auszuschließen. Auch aus der Welt jener Unantastbaren und Ruhigen
mußte eine Pforte herüberführen. Und nun, da er wußte, konnte er
nur mit jenem gewissen Lächeln daran denken, gegen dessen böses
Mißtrauen er sich vergeblich wehrte – – –

Božena erzählte unterdessen weiter. Törleß hörte mit halber
Aufmerksamkeit hin. Sie sprach von einem, der auch fast jeden
Sonntag kam ... 'Wie heißt er nur? Er ist aus deinem Jahrgang.'

'Reiting?'

'Nein.'

'Wie sieht er aus?'

'Er ist ungefähr so groß wie der da', Božena wies auf Törleß, 'nur
hat er einen etwas zu großen Kopf.'

'Ah, Basini?'

'Ja, ja, so nannte er sich. Er ist sehr komisch. Und nobel; er trinkt
nur Wein. Aber dumm ist er. Es kostet ihm eine Menge Geld, und
er tut nichts, als mir erzählen. Er renommiert mit den Liebschaften,
die er zu Hause haben will; was er nur davon hat? Ich sehe ja doch,
daß er zum erstenmal in seinem Leben bei einem Frauenzimmer ist.
Du bist ja auch noch ein Bub, aber du bist frech; er dagegen ist
ungeschickt und hat Angst davor, deswegen erzählt er mir lang und
breit, wie man als Genußmensch — ja, so hat er gesagt — mit Frauen
umgehen müsse. Er sagt, alle Weiber seien nichts anderes wert; woher
wollt ihr denn das schon wissen?'

Beineberg grinste sie zur Antwort spöttisch an.

'Ja lach nur!' herrschte ihn Božena belustigt an, 'ich habe ihn
einmal gefragt, ob er sich denn nicht vor seiner Mutter schämen würde.
"Mutter? ... Mutter?" sagt er drauf, "was ist das? Das existiert
jetzt nicht. Das habe ich zu Hause gelassen, bevor ich zu dir ging ..."
Ja, mach nur deine langen Ohren auf, so seid ihr! Nette Söhnchen,
ihr feinen jungen Herren; eure Mütter könnten mir beinahe leid tun!...'

Bei diesen Worten bekam Törleß wieder die frühere Vorstellung
von sich selbst. Wie er alles hinter sich ließ und das Bild seiner Eltern
verriet. Und nun mußte er sehen, daß er damit nicht einmal etwas
fürchterlich Einsames, sondern nur etwas ganz Gewöhnliches tat. Er
schämte sich. Aber auch die anderen Gedanken waren wieder da.
Sie tuen es auch! Sie verraten dich! Du hast geheime Mitspieler!
Vielleicht ist es bei ihnen irgendwie anders, aber das muß bei ihnen
das gleiche sein: eine geheime, fürchterliche Freude. Etwas, in dem
man sich mit all seiner Angst vor dem Gleichmaß der Tage ertränken
kann ... Vielleicht wissen sie sogar mehr ...?! ... Etwas ganz Unge-

wöhnliches? Denn sie sind am Tage so beruhigt; ... und dieses Lachen seiner Mutter? ... als ob sie mit ruhigem Schritte ginge, alle Türen zu schließen.

(pp. 40—3)

As the title suggests, the focus of our attention throughout the novel, with few exceptions, is the hero Törleß. In the passage quoted everything relates to him or is experienced by him. Nevertheless, a detailed examination shows that there is no single narrative standpoint. Sometimes we view Törleß from outside, sometimes we experience life from his point of view, and we do this with varying degrees of closeness.

The first five paragraphs are concerned exclusively with Törleß's unexpressed reflections and emotions. At first they are narrated rather than reproduced. The narrative standpoint is very close to but not identical with that of Törleß. This is clearest in the sentence: 'Die Erinnerung an die vollendete Manier dieser nie formvergessenen Gesellschaft wirkte stärker auf ihn als alle moralische Überlegung.' (paragraph 2) The comparison at once betrays the standpoint of a commenting narrator. The narrator abridges Törleß's thoughts in the words 'Eine Menge solcher Einzelheiten fiel ihm ein' (paragraph 2). The adverbs 'trotzdem' (paragraph 2) and especially 'nämlich' (paragraph 3) do not belong to the consciousness of Törleß but to the narrator, who is arranging and explaining Törleß's thoughts to us. Narrative is further revealed in the verbs used: 'fühlte', 'sah', 'erinnerte sich', 'fiel ihm ein', 'kam ihm vor', 'denken müssen'. True inner monologue reproduces the thoughts without explaining that they are thoughts. The fourth paragraph does then introduce Törleß's reflections directly, not as *erlebte Rede*, but as direct interior monologue, in the present tense and the first person singular. Musil's stream of consciousness technique, however, is somewhat different from that of Schnitzler: he puts the thoughts of his hero into quotation marks as if it were direct speech, and the careful construction of the sentences—especially the last—suggests that he is not really attempting to reproduce thought processes. Once again, therefore, a certain distance can be detected. In fact paragraph 5 has greater immediacy. Here for the first time in our extract is what appears to be *erlebte Rede*. In sentences such as 'Aber alle diese Fragen waren nicht das Eigentliche' and 'Diese war die einzige Tatsache' there is no narrative voice interposing itself between the reader and Törleß's thoughts. But are they

Törleß's thoughts? Are they not too articulate for an adolescent boy? Earlier, at the beginning of the previous paragraph, the narrator has pointed out that what is going on in Törleß's psyche can hardly be called 'thoughts'. This is a basic technical difficulty to which we shall return later.

The two paragraphs which follow concern the external world as it appears to Törleß. The point of view is his; especially at the beginning we experience it with him. Nevertheless, the voice of a narrator can be heard, albeit softly, in phrases such as 'im Vergleich zu sonst', 'vorkam', 'nur an einer Stelle'.

Paragraph 8 is one of the most interesting. Once more we are concerned with Törleß's reflections. At first we are still viewing them, as it were, from outside: 'Das war, als ob ...'; he thinks, he remembers. The next sentences, lacking verbs, are clearly intended to reproduce directly the images in Törleß's mind as inner monologue. And yet there is a barely perceptible change of perspective within one sentence: 'Die Stimme seiner Mutter aus der Tiefe des Gartens' implies the external narrator ('seiner Mutter' rather than 'der Mama', as he would undoubtedly think of her; this is the word used at the end of the paragraph), while 'wo sie mit *Papa* ... spazierenging' can only be part of Törleß's inner monologue—here vocabulary determines the point of view. A further explanatory interpolation from the narrator ('es fuhr ihm kalt durch den Leib') then precedes the most extended piece of inner monologue of the whole extract.

Paradoxically it is followed by the longest and most obvious piece of narrator's commentary. The next two paragraphs are told from the standpoint of an older man pointing out what Törleß does not understand: 'noch nicht'—the standpoint is distant in space and time.

Paragraph 11 returns to Törleß's present experience. Once more we find an alternation of narrative standpoints. The first sentence implies the outside narrator; the following are from Törleß's point of view; the last is indeterminate.

The passage of dialogue is less interesting for our purposes—dialogue is dramatic and therefore normally lacks point of view. Nevertheless, since this dialogue is in a narrative context the reader is mainly concerned with its effect on Törleß—listens to it, as it were, with his ears—and we note that Musil ensures that we do not forget this point of view, as we might do in a protracted conversation, by having Törleß mentioned in the middle of it.

The final paragraph has nothing new to offer as regards technique. After some initial hesitation, the point of view becomes that of Törleß and the *erlebte Rede* technique is apparent.

The question arises: is the lack of consistency in Musil's treatment of point of view a defect? It was his first novel; perhaps we can attribute it to immaturity? *Törleß* appeared in 1906, at a time when the technique of reproducing the inner workings of the mind by means of *erlebte Rede* was only beginning to become widespread. Perhaps *Törleß* betrays defects analogous to those of a primitive aeroplane? Neither of these explanations seems satisfactory. There is no immutable law which demands unity of perspective in the novel, any more than one would nowadays insist on unity of place in the drama. Musil's narrative is so controlled, his alternation of perspectives so consistent that we must look elsewhere.

Törleß's 'confusions' are due to the irrationality of so much of human experience. He is fascinated by the 'otherness' of people who, nevertheless, are 'the same' as he is. Basini is a boy like himself: yet he has stolen money. Božena is a woman like his mother: but how can his mother possibly have anything in common with a prostitute? Later he finds himself confused by the irrational numbers used in mathematics: infinity and the square root of minus one. Mathematics can make use of the irrational as a link between two perfectly rational clauses. Life, Törleß discovers, is very largely a question of *perspective*; one tries to understand other people by imagining oneself in their position, but this is never completely possible. Musil's treatment of narrative perspectives reflects this basic theme of the novel. But beyond this, and perhaps more simply, Törleß's experiences are themselves irrational in the sense that his thoughts are 'kaum ein Gedanke zu nennen' (paragraph 4); later when he 'discovers infinity', he finds himself tormented by the realization that words cannot express his experience. In this area the conventional stream of consciousness or interior monologue technique breaks down, for it can only express the expressible, the formulated thoughts of an individual. Musil's narrator is not the hearty, jocular or ironic narrator of traditional fiction, but one who is at pains to come as close to his subject as possible in a scientific dissection of what is itself quite unscientific. His method—varying points of view shifting in a scarcely perceptible manner—is highly appropriate.

2 Time

'Die Zeit ist das Element der Erzählung, wie sie das Element des Lebens ist—unlösbar damit verbunden, wie mit den Körpern im Raum.' So writes Thomas Mann in *Der Zauberberg* (*Strandspaziergang*, p. 748). Time, the metrics of change, is one of the main instruments we use to order and shape our existence. As in life so too in fiction, with one essential difference. In life time and tide may wait for no man, but in the fictional world the author, God of his creation, may slow down or quicken, arrest, even reverse the flow of time.

The sense of a time-dimension in the novel, of fictional time, depends on the amount of space the author devotes to each part of his narrative. Two main factors are involved: the 'time' the events narrated in the novel purport to cover, the *narrative-time*, and the *author-time*, that is the 'time' or rather space the author devotes to each part of the narrative-time. The relationship between these two constitutes the time-structure of a novel. German criticism uses the terms *Erzählzeit* and *erzählte Zeit* for author-time and narrative-time respectively. 'Narration-time' and 'narrated-time' seem somewhat too alike in English and thus liable to cause confusion.

Time in a play often moves at a more or less regular pace, sometimes even maintaining a coincidence between dramatic-time and audience-time: a play lasting three hours, for example, whose action also purports to cover three hours. The flow of time in a novel, however, is seldom if ever regular. In *Der Zauberberg*, for example, the narrative-time is seven years, but far more author-time is given to the first few *weeks* of Hans Castorp's stay in the sanatorium than to the last five *years*. The time-structure of *Der Zauberberg* does not ape the regularity of the clock but shows a very varied rhythm. There might seem to be exceptions to the rule that the novelist does not work by the metronome. The author-time in Hermann Broch's *Tod des Vergil* is divided fairly evenly among the forty-eight hours in which Virgil lies dying. (And no doubt it might take about forty-eight hours to read the book, were one participating in a reading marathon. The question of reader-time is, however, trivial.) But within each hour of the forty-eight the pace changes.

The reasons for the shifts in the relationship between author-time and narrative-time are as many as there are novels. Certain formal categories can be abstracted however. The basic constituents of the novel are events, characters and places. In simpler kinds of novel like the adventure story where event is all-important, the time-structure follows the demands of the plot. The most exciting events are expanded, the unimportant bits hurried over. We should be so absorbed that we are 'scarcely aware of time passing'. Of course, in basing his time-structure on events an author may have many different aims apart from the creation of suspense. In *Die Blechtrommel*, for example, Günter Grass juxtaposes long accounts of trivial events in his hero Oskar's private life with the briefest mention of vast historical events to grotesque satirical effect.

As well as, or instead of, events, characters may determine the time-structure. *Der Zauberberg* may again serve as an example. Its time-structure is based on the hero's sense of time and aware-ness of change. Thus the early part of Hans's stay is expanded because he is very conscious of his new milieu and every event brings significant changes. As his life in the sanatorium settles into a routine, he becomes less aware of the passage of time. Mann uses his author-time to mirror this process, devoting proportionately far more author-time to the early period of the narrative-time. What we might call psychological-time, that is a character's sense of time, is perhaps the most important time category in a genre so centrally concerned with individual experience. Here the questions of time-structure and point of view overlap. Kafka's *Das Schloß* is an example of how the point of view of one character, K., determines the time-structure of a whole novel so that psychological-time virtually swallows up all sense of an objective passage of time and succession of events. The short days, the constant winter, the ever-impending darkness are the 'objective correlative' to K.'s state of mind. If time is the measure-ment of change, then the tendency of time to be assimilated into undifferentiated night reflects K.'s sense of futility. His situation is not marked by change, he makes no progress. Futility, conveyed through the time relationships, determines the structure of the individual sections with their viciously circular movement, and of the novel as a whole which, as many critics have said, could be continued indefinitely.

Time as the succession of events and psychological-time, the character's inner sense of time, are the two basic ingredients in the time-structure of novels. When a lot of author-time is devoted to description of place or milieu, or as commonly happens in the German novel to discursive digressions, fictional time becomes less important as a structural element.

There are two main trends in the treatment of time in the novel. The two kinds of novel might be called *linear* and *fugal*. In the linear novel the movement is basically in a forward direction, though the rhythm of this movement may vary enormously depending on the different use of psychological- and event-time. The author's main aim is to convey through the medium of words a sense of time passing analogous to our sense of time in reality as succession and change.

In the fugal novel the author uses time as a means of ordering his fictional world to a degree beyond what is possible in reality. The ultimate aim of the fugal novel is not so much to present a succession as to show past and present at once, to be here and there simultaneously, to overcome the limitations of time and space. The final effect of the fugal novel as compared with the linear novel is of a spatial network of relationships rather than a temporal succession of states and events. Proust's search for lost time, for total recall, was at the same time an aesthetic quest for the fugal novel. To use a musical metaphor from Mann's *Doktor Faustus*, in the fugal novel the horizontal melodic line with its succession of notes is transformed into the vertical chord of simultaneous notes. But the novel, unless it be reduced to some unimaginable magic formula, cannot achieve perfect simultaneity. Joyce's *Finnegans Wake* represents the culmination but also the final failure of the fugal novel when it seeks to sever all connections with linear time. Thus the categories of fugal and linear novel overlap, since the linear novel too, if it has any artistic merit, will to some extent invite us to see past and present, beginning and end as a unity. The difference is one of emphasis.

Authors have used many different devices to bring together parts of their narrative separate in time. The most radical, since the most removed from reality, is a reversal of the order of events so that what follows in narrative-time is narrated before what precedes it. An author may use this device to show how the past affects the present, for example, or to produce ironic or otherwise striking juxtapositions. Uwe Johnson's *Mutmaßungen über Jakob*, for instance, begins with the death of the hero. A similar but less radical technique is to move back in time through the memory of a character, a special use of psychological-time. Perhaps the most striking example of this device in modern German literature is Broch's *Tod des Vergil*; this vast reverie of a dying man whose mind wanders back even beyond birth into a prenatal, indeed prehuman sphere and forward into a vision of the Christian future which will succeed the Roman present. Two or more narrative strands following each other in narrative-time may be interwoven in author-time. A special form of this device is the extended use in the novel of the narrative framework common in the *Novelle*, as in *Doktor Faustus*, for example, or in Grass's *Die Blechtrommel*, where the story of Oskar as narrator moves forward in time parallel with his account of his past history.

Besides manipulating the time-structure itself an author may use many means to draw together areas of his narrative separate in time. Thomas Mann's use of the *leitmotiv* recalls earlier parts of his narrative in later contexts, so bringing into conjunction past and present in his fictional world. Like a rock in a stream of water the *leitmotiv* causes an eddy in the flow of fictional time. The movement forward is checked by memory of the past. Similar in effect can be the use of location, like the mountain landscape in Broch's *Der Versucher* or the great city in Döblin's *Berlin Alexanderplatz*, which remains the same despite the changing fates of the characters, and so binds together past and present in a unity.

So far we have been discussing how the world of fiction with its fictional characters and events also has a fictional time-dimension. Time, of perennial concern to all cultures and ages, may also be a theme in novels. But this is a different question and there is no reason in principle why fictional time should be used to illuminate the nature of real time. In practice, however, the novel strives to dramatize wherever possible. For example, if an author has views on psychology he may express these in many ways, but it is most likely that he will dramatize them through the characters in his novel. And so it is with time. Novelists from Laurence Sterne and the German Romantics onwards have used fictional time to make statements about real time. The works of Sterne or a novel such as Brentano's *Godwi* are extreme examples of the fugal novel and go far beyond imitation of reality in their treatment of time. This is not surprising, since direct imitation obviously does not so much illuminate as *reflect*. However, even the linear mimetic novel may surprise our attention and illuminate without breaking the links with life. Thomas Mann's work hardly comes into the category of the extreme experimental novel, but he is never humdrumly straightforward. In *Der Zauberberg*, as we have seen, he uses the time-structure of his novel to illuminate the difference between the subjective sense of time of a character and the objective passage of mechanical clock-time, and so adds to our understanding of the workings of time.

In real life we have various frames of reference by which we 'tell the time' apart from our own subjective sense of time or the clock. So it is in the novel. For example, a novelist may wish to contrast or integrate the world of man with the natural world by playing off psychological-time against the natural revolution of the seasons as Goethe does in *Die Wahlverwandtschaften*. In Broch's *Der Versucher* the distribution of author-time among events, natural description and characterization creates a tension such as we often experience in real life, between natural change and evolution and perverted, historically determined convulsions in the human sphere. Equally, social, political or cultural frames of reference may serve to dramatize some of the significant complexities of time which are latent in our experience. On the other hand a novel may convey the opposite sort of experience we sometimes have, of timelessness, as in the mystic experiences of Ulrich in Musil's *Mann ohne Eigenschaften*.

In Thomas Mann's *Doktor Faustus* a complex time-structure is used both explicitly and symbolically to throw light on the nature of time and change. The following extract may serve as illustration. It comes half-way through the book and follows on the chapter describing the interview between the musician Adrian Leverkühn, the modern Faustus, and the Devil. The narrator, Serenus Zeitblom, takes up his narrative again which he had interrupted to present Adrian's own written account of the interview.

Es ist tröstlich, mir sagen zu können, daß der Leser den außerordentlichen Umfang des vorigen Abschnitts, der ja die beunruhigende Seitenzahl des Kapitels über Kretzschmars Vorträge noch beträchtlich übertrifft, nicht mir wird zur Last legen dürfen. Die damit verbundene Zumutung liegt außer meiner Autorenverantwortung und darf mich nicht kümmern. Adrians Niederschrift irgendeiner erleichternden Redaktion zu unterwerfen; das 'Zwiegespräch' (man beachte die protestierenden Gänsefüßchen, mit denen ich dies Wort versehe, ohne mir freilich zu verhehlen, daß sie ihm nur einen Teil des ihm inne-wohnenden Grauens zu entziehen vermögen) — dies Gespräch also in einzeln bezifferte Paragraphen aufzulösen, konnte keine Rücksicht auf die ermüdbare Rezeptionsfähigkeit des Publikums mich bewegen. Mit leidvoller Pietät hatte ich ein Gegebenes wiederzugeben, es von Adrians Notenpapier in mein Manuskript zu übertragen; und das habe ich nicht nur Wort für Wort, sondern, ich darf wohl sagen: Buchstaben für Buchstaben getan, — oft die Feder niederlegend, oft zu meiner Erholung mich unterbrechend, um mit gedankenschweren Schritten mein Arbeitszimmer zu durchmessen oder mich, die Hände über der Stirn gefaltet, aufs Sofa zu werfen, sodaß mir tatsächlich wie sonderbar das klingen möge, ein Kapitel, das ich nur zu kopieren hatte, nicht schneller von der so manches Mal zitternden Hand gegangen ist, als irgend ein früheres eigener Komposition.

Ein sinn- und gedankenvolles Abschreiben ist in der Tat (wenigstens für mich; aber auch Monsignore Hinterpförtner stimmt mir hierin bei) eine ebenso intense und zeitverzehrende Beschäftigung, wie das Niederlegen eigener Gedanken, und wie schon an früheren Punkten der Leser die Zahl der Tage und Wochen, die ich der Lebensgeschichte meines verewigten Freundes schon gewidmet hatte, unterschätzt haben mag, so wird er auch jetzt in seiner Vorstellung hinter dem Zeitpunkt zurückgeblieben sein, zu dem ich die gegenwärtigen Zeilen abfasse. Möge er meine Pedanterie belächeln, aber ich halte es für richtig, ihn wissen zu lassen, daß, seit ich diese Aufzeichnungen begann, schon fast ein Jahr ins Land gegangen und über der Abfassung der jüngsten Kapitel der April 1944 herangekommen ist.

Selbstverständlich meine ich mit diesem Datum dasjenige, unter dem ich selbst mit meiner Tätigkeit stehe, — nicht das, bis zu welchem meine Erzählung fortgeschritten ist, und das ja auf den Herbst 1912, zwanzig Monate vor Ausbruch des vorigen Krieges, lautet, als Adrian mit Rüdiger Schildknapp von Palestrina nach München zurückkehrte und für sein Teil zunächst in einer Schwabinger Fremdenpension (Pension Gisella) Wohnung nahm. Ich weiß nicht, warum diese doppelte Zeitrechnung meine Aufmerksamkeit fesselt, und weshalb es mich drängt, auf sie hinzuweisen: die persönliche und die sachliche, die Zeit, in der der Erzähler sich fortbewegt, und die, in welcher das Erzählte sich abspielt. Es ist dies eine ganz eigentümliche Verschrän-kung der Zeitläufe, dazu bestimmt übrigens, sich noch mit einem Dritten zu verbinden: nämlich der Zeit, die eines Tages der Leser sich zur geneigten Rezeption des Mitgeteilten nehmen wird, sodaß dieser es also mit einer dreifachen Zeitordnung zu tun hat: seiner eigenen, derjenigen des Chronisten und der historischen.

Ich will mich in diese Spekulationen, die in meinen eigenen Augen das Gepräge einer gewissen erregten Müßigkeit tragen, nicht weiter verlieren und nur hinzufügen, daß das Wort 'historisch' mit weit düsterer Vehemenz auf die Zeit zutrifft, *in* welcher —, als auf die, *über* welche ich schreibe. In den letzten Tagen wütete der Kampf um Odessa, eine verlustreiche Schlacht, die mit dem Fall der berühmten Stadt am Schwarzen Meer in die Hände der Russen geendet hat, ohne daß freilich der Gegner vermocht hätte, unsere Ablösungs-operationen zu stören.

(Chapter XXVI, pp. 386–8)

Through the medium of Zeitblom Mann introduces an ironic internal commentary on the problems of composition, including that of time-structure. The narrative-time spans the period between the 1880s and 1945. It is divided into two main strands. The narrative proper concerns Adrian's life from his birth in 1885 till his collapse from the effects of syphilis in 1930, with a small postscript bringing us up to his death in 1940. The second strand covers the time from 1943 to 1945, in which Zeitblom is writing down his account of his friend's life. The progress of the war figures largely in this strand. By interweaving these two strands of time, Mann invites us to look at Leverkühn's life history from two points of view. We see it from inside as it unfolds but at the same time we see it backwards, as it were, always in relation to the political events which followed Adrian's collapse. This underlines Adrian's symbolic role as a representative German and points to one of the main themes of the novel: how far were the German intellectual tradition and the German intellectuals of the inter-war period responsible for the catastrophe of the Third Reich? We experience immediately *and* with hindsight simultaneously, and so are perhaps invited to judge but not finally condemn. We share the perplexities of an individual. But we see them also as symptomatic of a historical crisis for which individuals were finally responsible but which no single individual could transcend.

Mann thus gets the best of both worlds. The novel is basically linear in structure with the corresponding solid, traditional values of clarity and suspense. Yet the extended use of the narrator's time-strand brings juxtapositions just as striking and awakens our sense of time as thoroughly as many a more obviously 'experimental' structure. Rather than overtly breaking the illusion of reality by disrupting the forward movement of fictional time, Mann prefers to ironize. We are never allowed to forget that we are reading a novel, that its time-structure is part of a fictional world. We can see this from our extract. Zeitblom's naïve worry about the inordinate length of some sections of his account points to the fundamental problem of time-structure: the relationship between author-time and narrative-time. The effect of these remarks is to remind us of the fictionality of the whole. They recall to us the existence of an author behind the ostensible author, Zeitblom, an author who is using *his* author-time to achieve certain effects. Indeed they remind us that we are reading Thomas Mann, whose work has a tendency to be overweightily intellectual so that time in his novels does not pass quickly enough but occasionally hangs heavy.

We may enjoy this ironic apology for its own sake as part of a witty play with the conventions of the novel form. Yet it is more than a game with the reader. By constantly reminding us that we are reading a story, not history, that we are in a fictional world, Mann causes his novel to question itself, as it were, to question its own legitimacy. The legitimacy or not of art, of the beautiful autonomous work, in an age of political disaster and immense human suffering is one of the main themes of the novel. The time-structure which plays off the *story* of Adrian against the *history* of the years in which Zeitblom is supposedly writing, and the constant reminders that we are reading fiction, enact in themselves this theme. Is there any place in the barbarity of the twentieth century for the work of art? The answer is neither art for art's sake nor art as documentary, but an in-between position. Zeitblom's projection of a reader in the future, towards the end of our extract, invites us in our historical world of real time to judge the story of Leverkühn against our own experience of the history of our age. The time-structure of this novel is, then, open-ended rather than closed. It supports a coherent fictional world, but at the same time points beyond itself into the real world.

It remains to point out a few of the other devices Mann uses to link time in his novel with real time, with history. The proliferation of sixteenth-century references—names, places, Adrian's use of sixteenth-century German, the Faust legend itself—suggest a parallel between the upheavals of the wars of religion which ushered in the 'bürgerliches Zeitalter' and the upheavals of the twentieth century which are perhaps witness to its end. Such a parallelism might suggest that history repeats itself in a cyclic movement. This is counteracted, however, by a sense of history as a dialectical movement in which each period is unique and not simply a repetition of an earlier situation. Yet each new situation contains elements of the past, the problems humanity must face remain basically the same, though the forms they assume are ever-changing and ever more complex. The reader thus has a sense of various layers of time linked together by analogy or as part of one great development: Zeitblom the narrator's time from 1943 to 1945; the life-span of Adrian from 1885 to 1940; the sixteenth century; the development between the sixteenth century and the twentieth century. These reverberations of the past into the present are conjured up through musical history, including a history of musical instruments, and through the different types of language in the novel from the early Middle High German of the little boy Echo's prayers, the Lutheran German Adrian uses, up to the twentieth-century jargon of the Munich aesthetes. Above all there are the descriptions of Adrian Leveкühn's music with their parodistic borrowings from earlier styles, ranging from barbarous glissandi representative of the primitive howl of premusical, prehistoric man to the sophisticated idioms of a late stage in musical culture. Time past and time present thus meet and interact in the human mind and its creations: in Thomas Mann's novel as in Adrian Leverkühn's compositions.

3 Patterns

Every novel has a structure based on narrative point of view; every novel has a time-structure. Sometimes, however, there are two further types of structure. Both may be called 'patterns', since the term 'pattern' can mean on the one hand the distinctive, more or less regular constellation of certain features (such as the abstract patterns of Celtic art), on the other hand the predetermined model on which a piece of work is based (the sewing-pattern, for example). The first is an 'intrinsic' pattern, the second is 'extrinsic' and can be appreciated only by the person who recognizes the model on which it is based.

One kind of intrinsic pattern is based on the *leitmotiv*. This term is used in two senses in German criticism. In the first place it denotes the central motif or symbol of a literary work, a kind of extended metaphor (see *Imagery*); in this sense it is commonly used in connection with the *Novelle*. The other sense is more immediately relevant. The term is borrowed from musical criticism; it denotes a characteristic succession of notes repeated each time a person or idea is to be evoked, a technique developed especially by Richard Wagner. Thomas Mann, the most prominent technician of the *leitmotiv* in German literature, admitted to having learned his craft from a study of Wagner. In his lecture on *Der Zauberberg* for students at Princeton University he distinguishes between the 'naturalistisch-charakterisierende, sozusagen mechanische Weise' of his early works and the 'symbolische Art' of *Der Zauberberg* (*Der Zauberberg*, p. x). Christian Buddenbrook's 'ziemlich kleine, runde und tiefliegende Augen' and his 'gebogene Nase', which are mentioned almost every time he appears, are a purely characterizing *leitmotiv*. This type is developed and given more depth in later novels. In *Lotte in Weimar* Lotte's shaking head is not merely descriptive but indicates weakness and the distance separating present from past. In this way it approaches the symbolic kind of *leitmotiv*. For example, in *Der Zauberberg* the number seven plays an important role. The thermometer has to be retained in the mouth for seven minutes, there are seven tables in the dining-room of the sanatorium where Hans Castorp spends seven years. Seven is thus associated with disease. But it is also associated with love, for Madame Chauchat's room is No. 7, and the seventh day, seventh week and seventh month of Hans's sojourn at the sanatorium mark important stages in the development of his passion for her. Love and disease, moreover, are linked elsewhere in the novel, notably in the lectures of Dr. Krokowski. And the unfortunate Settembrini, who castigates the mentality of the inmates of the sanatorium, is none the less associated with it, not only by his illness but also by his name, which once more incorporates the number seven. Settembrini is further linked with Madame Chauchat in the reader's mind since he lodges in the house of her dressmaker. And so on. The *leitmotiv* patterns in *Der Zauberberg* imply a structure behind that created by points of view and time shifts, implying hidden relationships and deeper meanings in the novel.

Thomas Mann is not the only novelist to employ this technique. In *Berlin Alexanderplatz* three groups of *leitmotivs* stand out. The words of *Die Wacht am Rhein* with their mixture of unthinking patriotism and quietism ('Lieb Vaterland, magst *ruhig* sein') evoke much of what is wrong with Biberkopf's outlook, while the lines of *Es ist ein Schnitter* point to the ultimate futility of purely individual effort in view of the overriding fact of death. The most important *leitmotiv*, however, is the comparison of man and the animals; it undergoes many transformations in the course of the novel, from the idea of passive submission (in the slaughterhouse scenes) through the values of collectivity (the herd) down to the final assertion of the characteristic which distinguishes man from the animals, his 'Vernunft', his ability to judge the occasions on which to identify himself with the herd and those when he should not. In contemporary literature *leitmotivs* are prominent in the novels of Heinrich Böll and Günter Grass.

Lessing stressed in his *Laokoon* the relationship between music and literature as 'time arts', as opposed to the 'spatial' forms of painting and sculpture. It is appropriate in this context that music and literature should employ similar devices in pursuit of similar ends. For if Wagner's *leitmotivs* were born of the necessity to find new ways of giving form and unity to a piece of music after the traditional, classical forms had been dissolved by the Romantic composers, so the *leitmotiv* in the modern novel can serve as a substitute for the more traditional unifying features of the 'omniscient' narrator and the plot with its clear-cut beginning, middle and denouement. It is notable, for example, that *leitmotivs* are of greater importance in third-person narratives, such as the examples quoted, than in first-person narratives, to which the person of the fictitious biographer or autobiographer lends a basic unity. And, as mentioned in the previous chapter, since each time they occur they evoke all other occurrences of the same motif they are important in relation to time-structure (see *Time*).

Leitmotiv patterns on the whole adhere to the concept of the novel as a 'musical', i.e. time form. Another type of intrinsic pattern, that based on the montage technique, represents a more radical break with traditional structures: instead of the novel of the 'nacheinander' we have the novel of the 'nebeneinander', simultaneity rather than successivity. Montage is a technical term from film-making, reflecting the influence of this new art form on the novel from the beginning of the century onwards. It denotes the cutting and joining together of strips of continuous film in the final editing of the material used. The 'real' time sequence may thereby be disturbed, even reversed; the juxtaposition of temporally or even thematically unrelated lengths of material—story, narrative, dialogue, description—results in an effect resembling that of collage, and the novel thus approaches the spatial or visual arts. Alfred Döblin's early novels largely run true to his theory that the novel, like the earthworm, should be capable of being cut into pieces while each piece remains viable.[1] *Wallenstein*, for example, could hardly be less like the traditional historical biography implied in the title. It consists rather of disconnected scenes, descriptions, conversations, a minority of which directly concern Wallenstein himself. Even *Berlin Alexanderplatz*, with its subtitle 'Die Geschichte vom Franz Biberkopf', frequently 'cuts' the biography in order to insert extracts from newspaper reports, weather forecasts, descriptions of Berlin slaughterhouses, Bible stories and the like. While the purpose of some of these 'digressions' may be to illuminate by comparison the life story of the central character, the overall result is the creation of a remarkable and on the whole static picture of life in its totality, something which would not have been possible had the author restricted himself to Biberkopf's adventures. The third part of Hermann Broch's *Schlafwandler* trilogy shows another

---

[1] Bemerkungen zum Roman,[1] in *Aufsätze zur Literatur*, ed. Walter Muschg (Olten/Freiburg i. Br; 1963), p. 21.

B

type of montage. Not only does it interweave a large number of quite independent stories, but it introduces in ten instalments a philosophical discussion of the 'Zerfall der Werte' which Broch sees as characteristic of his age.

'Extrinsic' patterns can be either thematic or formal. The retelling of an archetypal story in contemporary guise or with contemporary implications is common in twentieth-century literature: Joyce's *Ulysses* and Mann's *Joseph und seine Brüder* at once spring to mind (see *Symbolism*). Besides any universality of theme in such models, their structure gives shape in an age lacking in forms. 'Formal' patterns, sometimes called 'submerged forms', are rather more important for our purposes. The detective story, for example, has a clearly defined shape and tradition: a mystery is stated, a series of attempts made to solve it, an unexpected turning point brings the solution. Examples of its adaptation in serious literature include Doderer's *Ein Mord, den jeder begeht,* Bergengruen's *Der Großtyrann und das Gericht,* and Dürrenmatt's *Der Richter und sein Henker.* The picaresque novel too, with its frequent change of location and the large number of loosely connected adventures that befall its anti-hero, the 'Schelm' or 'picaro', has a structure which can be recognized in such works as Mann's *Felix Krull,* Döblin's *Babylonische Wandrung* and Grass's *Die Blechtrommel.* In these examples of 'detective-stories' and 'picaresque' novels the term 'extrinsic' pattern is justified, since their authors are not writing *in* a tradition but consciously copying, adapting and possibly parodying one for their own rather different purposes. An interpretation of such novels will therefore ask why the pattern is being used and to what extent the author deviates from it.

A work which unites both kinds of extrinsic pattern, formal and thematic, is Alfred Döblin's last novel, *Hamlet.* It also exemplifies the montage technique in so far as it consists of a number of stories told within the framework of the story of the Allison family. Each of these stories in turn—*King Lear, Pluto and Proserpine, Jaufie Rudel,* etc.—is a model intended to shed light on the relationships within the family and to suggest some answers to Edward Allison's questions. The title of the novel points to one thematic model. The war has led Edward to question current attitudes to society and family life; he gradually discovers that relationships between his parents are not as stable as he had imagined; the disintegration but final reconciliation of the family is the result. As in the model the instability of family relationships is seen as the reflection of a 'rottenness' in society in the wider sense. The submerged pattern, however, is that of the detective story in its variant form of the psychoanalytical case history: Edward's search for the truth, his uncovering of the past, his probings in his own subconscious form the structure of this novel.

But the most important submerged form in German narrative literature is that of the *Entwicklungsroman* or *Bildungsroman*. The former is the more general term; the latter denotes more specifically those works in which cultural influences play an important role; the basic pattern, however, is common to both. Three structural characteristics may be isolated. In the first place, it is a biographical novel, dealing with the major part of the life-history of one individual; as distinct from the novel of manners, the social or historical novel, it does not attempt to depict a whole age or society except insofar as the latter is reflected in the experience of the hero. Nevertheless, the hero's environment *is* important since in the second place the novel is concerned not merely with tracing his biography, but with finding meaning in it, by showing how the rough diamond is polished by life, how the hero comes to terms with himself and outside reality and becomes an integrated and useful member of society—more or less strong didactic undertones are a feature of the narrator's relation to his reader. Indeed, it may be claimed that the most memorable features of *Simplicissimus*, *Wilhelm Meisters Lehrjahre* and *Der Nachsommer* are not the heroes, who tend to be pale and passive figures, but the events, the times, the Thirty Years War, the theatre ensemble, Risach's rose garden. The third feature of the *Entwicklungsroman* is organic progression in time: man, as an integral part of nature and subject to nature's laws, 'develops' in accordance with these laws. This is nowhere clearer than in Stifter's *Der Nachsommer*, but the influence of Goethe's ideas on metamorphosis is obvious. The motif of the garden, park or other natural setting is fundamental to this kind of novel, and paradoxically it is in the question of the relation between man and nature (the beasts going to the slaughterhouse) that such an apparently urban novel as *Berlin Alexanderplatz* can be seen to reflect (albeit uneasily) the tradition.

There are few major German novels prior to the end of the nineteenth century for which the term *Entwicklungsroman* has not been claimed, none for which it has not been disputed. This is due partly no doubt to the influence of Goethe's *Wilhelm Meister*, which can scarcely be over-estimated, partly to the political, social and literary conditions peculiar to pre-1870 Germany, which favoured an introspective literature concerned more with the individual than with society as a whole. Since the emergence of Germany as a modern, unified and industrialized state, however, the German novel has tended to turn outwards in the main tradition of the European social novel, as witness the works of Fontane and Raabe, Thomas and Heinrich Mann. Nevertheless, the tradition of the peculiarly 'German' novel has remained strong enough for traces of it to be discovered in such apparently disparate novels as *Der Zauberberg, Berlin Alexanderplatz, Das Glasperlenspiel* and *Die Blechtrommel*. All of these novels provide a portrait of a society, all show the hero coming to terms with it in some way, all are more or less didactic. Other characteristics of the pattern are, for example, the spiritual mentor (Settembrini in *Der Zauberberg*) and the importance of cultural influences on the development of the hero (Goethe and Rasputin in *Die Blechtrommel*—here we at once see an ironic relationship to the pattern). Such novels cannot be completely appreciated without some understanding of this underlying pattern, whether it is being adopted, adapted or even parodied.

Hermann Hesse's *Das Glasperlenspiel* is a rather more conventional example of the latterday *Entwicklungsroman*. *Wilhelm Meister* was an obvious influence: traces of it are to be seen in the reference to Castalia as 'die pädagogische Provinz', a term taken from the *Wanderjahre*, and especially in the name of the hero, Knecht, an allusion to the name of Goethe's hero; here already, however, we see a change in emphasis. At the beginning of his anecdote *Der Bettler*, written shortly after *Das Glasperlenspiel*, Hesse remarks on the difficulty of story-telling today owing to the purely private nature of so much of our experience: 'daß das Erzählen eine Kunst sei, deren Voraussetzungen uns Heutigen, oder doch mir, fehlen und deren Ausübung darum nur noch das Nachahmen überkommener Formen sein kann, ist mir inzwischen immer klarer geworden ...'[2] Such a 'Nachahmen überkommener Formen' can be seen in *Das Glasperlenspiel*; nevertheless it too shows some striking deviations from the pattern and it is such deviations that make it so important to appreciate the model.

The following passage occurs at the beginning of the final chapter of the novel. During a distinguished career which has

[2] *Gesammelte Schriften* (Frankfurt a.M., 1957), Volume 4, p. 844.

brought him to the height of success in Castalia, the position of Magister Ludi, Josef Knecht has felt increasingly uneasy about the Republic of Letters itself. The only hope of preserving the spiritual values which he holds dear is to turn outwards, to go out into the world and to teach. Accordingly he asks to be relieved of his post and sent to an ordinary school outside Castalia, from which he hopes, somewhat on the model of the monks of the Dark Ages, to be able to infiltrate and convert the world. The administration refuses to grant his request.

Nachdem der Meister den Brief gelesen hatte, in welchem die Behörde sein Gesuch abschlägig beschied, spürte er ein leises Schaudern, ein Morgengefühl von Kühle und Nüchternheit, das ihm anzeigte, die Stunde sei gekommen, und es gebe nun kein Zögern und Verweilen mehr. Dies eigene Gefühl, das er 'Erwachen' nannte, war ihm von den entscheidenden Augenblicken seines Lebens her bekannt, es war ein belebendes und zugleich schmerzliches; eine Mischung von Abschied und Aufbruch, tief im Unbewußten rüttelnd wie Frühlingssturm. Er sah nach der Uhr, in einer Stunde hatte er eine Kurslektion zu halten. Er beschloß, diese Stunde der Einkehr zu widmen, und begab sich in den stillen Magistergarten. Auf dem Wege dahin begleitete ihn eine Verszeile, die ihm plötzlich eingefallen war:

Denn jedem Anfang ist ein Zauber eigen …

die sagte er vor sich hin, nicht wissend, bei welchem Dichter er sie einst gelesen habe, aber der Vers sprach ihn an und gefiel ihm und schien dem Erlebnis der Stunde ganz zu entsprechen. Im Garten setzte er sich auf eine mit ersten welken Blättern bestreute Bank, regelte die Atmung und kämpfte um die innere Stille, bis er geklärten Herzens in Betrachtung versank, in der die Konstellation dieser Lebensstunde sich in allgemeinen, überpersönlichen Bildern ordnete. Auf dem Rückwege zum kleinen Hörsaal aber meldete sich schon wieder jener Vers, er mußte ihm wieder nachsinnen und fand, er müsse etwas anders lauten. Bis plötzlich sein Gedächtnis sich erhellte und ihm zu Hilfe kam. Leise sprach er vor sich hin:

Und jedem Anfang wohnt ein Zauber inne,
Der uns beschützt und der uns hilft, zu leben.

Aber erst gegen Abend, als längst die Kursstunde gehalten und allerlei andere Tagesarbeit getan war, entdeckte er die Herkunft jener Verse. Sie standen nicht bei irgendeinem alten Dichter, sie standen in einem seiner eigenen Gedichte, die er einst als Schüler und Student geschrieben hatte, und das Gedicht endete mit der Zeile:

Wohlan denn, Herz, nimm Abschied und gesunde!

Noch an diesem Abend beschied er seinen Stellvertreter zu sich und eröffnete ihm, daß er morgen für unbestimmte Zeit verreisen müsse. Er übergab ihm alles Laufende mit kurzen Anweisungen und verabschiedete sich freundlich und sachlich wie sonst vor einer kurzen Amtsreise.

Daß er den Freund Tegularius verlassen müsse, ohne ihn einzuweihen und ihn mit einem Abschiednehmen zu belasten, war ihm schon früher klargeworden. Er mußte so handeln, nicht nur um den so empfindlichen Freund zu schonen, sondern auch um seinen ganzen Plan nicht zu gefährden. Mit einer vollzogenen Handlung und Tatsache würde sich der andre vermutlich schon abfinden, während eine überraschende Aussprache und Abschiedsszene ihn zu unliebsamen Unbeherrschtheiten hinreißen konnte. Knecht hatte eine Weile sogar daran gedacht, abzureisen, ohne ihn überhaupt noch einmal zu sehen. Nun er dies überlegte, fand er aber doch, daß es einer Flucht vor dem Schwierigen allzu ähnlich sein würde. So klug und richtig es sein mochte, dem Freunde eine Szene und Aufregung und eine Gelegenheit zu Torheiten zu ersparen, so wenig durfte er sich selbst eine solche Schonung gönnen. Es war noch eine halbe Stunde bis zur Zeit der Nachtruhe, er konnte Tegularius noch aufsuchen, ohne ihn oder sonst jemanden zu stören. Es war schon Nacht auf dem weiten Innenhofe, den er überschritt. Er klopfte an seines Freundes Zelle, mit dem eigentümlichen Gefühl: zum letztenmal, und fand ihn allein. Erfreut begrüßte ihn der beim Lesen Überraschte, legte sein Buch beiseite und hieß den Besucher sitzen.

'Ein altes Gedicht ist mir heute eingefallen', fing Knecht zu plaudern an, 'oder doch einige Verse daraus. Vielleicht weißt du, wo das Ganze zu finden ist?'

Und er zitierte: 'Denn jedem Anfang wohnt ein Zauber inne ...'

Der Repetent brauchte sich nicht lange zu bemühen. Er erkannte das Gedicht nach kurzem Nachdenken wieder, stand auf und holte aus einem Pultfach das Manuskript von Knechts Gedichten, die Urhandschrift, welche dieser ihm einst geschenkt hatte. Er suchte darin und zog zwei Blätter heraus, welche die erste Niederschrift des Gedichtes trugen. Er reichte sie dem Magister hin.

'Hier', sagte er lächelnd, 'der Ehrwürdige möge sich bedienen. Es ist das erstemal seit vielen Jahren, daß Ihr Euch dieser Dichtungen zu erinnern geruhet.'

Josef Knecht betrachtete die Blätter aufmerksam und nicht ohne Bewegung. Als Student, während seines Aufenthaltes im ostasiatischen Studienhaus, hatte er diese beiden Blätter einst mit Verszeilen beschrieben, eine ferne Vergangenheit blickte ihn aus ihnen an, alles sprach von einem beinahe vergessenen, nun mahnend und schmerzlich wieder erwachenden Ehemals, das schon leicht angegilbte Papier, die jugendliche Handschrift, die Streichungen und Korrekturen im

Texte. Er meinte sich nicht nur des Jahres und der Jahreszeit zu
erinnern, in welchen diese Verse entstanden waren, sondern auch des
Tages und der Stunde, und zugleich jener Stimmung, jenes starken
und stolzen Gefühls, das ihn damals erfüllt und beglückt hatte und
dem die Verse Ausdruck gaben. Er hatte sie an einem jener besonderen
Tage geschrieben, an welchen das seelische Erlebnis ihm zuteil
geworden war, das er Erwachen nannte.

Sichtlich war die Überschrift des Gedichtes, noch vor dem Gedichte
selbst, als dessen erste Zeile entstanden. Mit großen Buchstaben in
stürmischer Handschrift war sie hingesetzt und lautete:
'Transzendieren!'

Später erst, zu einer anderen Zeit, in anderer Stimmung und
Lebenslage, war diese Überschrift samt dem Ausrufezeichen gestrichen
und war in kleineren, dünneren, bescheideneren Schriftzeichen dafür
eine andere hingeschrieben worden. Sie hieß: 'Stufen.'

Knecht erinnerte sich jetzt wieder, wie er damals, vom Gedanken
seines Gedichtes beschwingt, das Wort 'Transzendieren!' hingeschrieben hatte, als einen Zuruf und Befehl, eine Mahnung an sich
selbst, als einen neu formulierten und bekräftigten Vorsatz, sein Tun
und Leben unter dies Zeichen zu stellen und es zu einem Transzendieren, einem entschlossen-heitern Durchschreiten, Erfüllen und
Hintersichlassen jedes Raumes, jeder Wegstrecke zu machen. Halblaut
las er einige Strophen vor sich hin:

> Wir sollen heiter Raum um Raum durchschreiten,
> An keinem wie an einer Heimat hängen,
> Der Weltgeist will nicht fesseln uns und engen,
> Er will uns Stuf' um Stufe heben, weiten.

'Ich hatte die Verse viele Jahre vergessen', sagte er, 'und als einer
von ihnen mir heute zufällig einfiel, wußte ich nicht mehr, woher ich
ihn kenne und daß er von mir sei. Wie kommen sie dir heute vor?
Sagen sie dir noch etwas?'

Tegularius besann sich.

'Mir ist es gerade mit diesem Gedicht immer eigentümlich gegangen',
sagte er dann. 'Das Gedicht gehört zu den wenigen von Euch, die ich
eigentlich nicht mochte, an denen irgend etwas mich abstieß oder
störte. Was es sei, wußte ich damals nicht. Heute glaube ich es zu
sehen. Euer Gedicht, Verehrter, das Ihr mit dem Marschbefehl
"Transzendieren!" überschrieben und dessen Titel Ihr später, Gott
sei Dank, durch einen sehr viel besseren ersetzt habet, hat mir nie so
recht gefallen, weil es etwas Befehlendes, etwas Moralisierendes oder
Schulmeisterliches hat. Könnte man ihm dieses Element nehmen oder
vielmehr diese Tünche abwaschen, so wäre es eines Eurer schönsten
Gedichte, das habe ich soeben wieder bemerkt. Sein eigentlicher Inhalt
ist mit dem Titel "Stufen" nicht schlecht angedeutet; Ihr hättet aber

ebensogut und noch besser "Musik" oder "Wesen der Musik" darüber schreiben können. Denn nach Abzug jener moralisierenden oder predigenden Haltung ist es recht eigentlich eine Betrachtung über das Wesen der Musik, oder meinetwegen ein Lobgesang auf die Musik, auf ihre stete Gegenwärtigkeit, auf ihre Heiterkeit und Entschlossenheit, auf ihre Beweglichkeit und rastlose Entschlossenheit und Bereitschaft zum Weitereilen, zum Verlassen des eben erst betretenen Raumes oder Raumabschnittes. Wäre es bei dieser Betrachtung oder diesem Lobgesang über den Geist der Musik geblieben, hättet Ihr nicht, offenbar schon damals von einem Erzieherehrgeiz beherrscht, eine Mahnung und Predigt daraus gemacht, so könnte das Gedicht ein vollkommenes Kleinod sein. So wie es vorliegt, scheint es mir nicht nur zu lehrhaft, zu lehrerhaft, sondern es scheint mir auch an einem Denkfehler zu kranken. Es setzt, lediglich der moralischen Wirkung wegen, Musik und Leben einander gleich, was mindestens sehr fragwürdig und bestreitbar ist, es macht aus dem natürlichen und moralfreien Motor, der die Triebfeder der Musik ist, ein "Leben", das uns durch Zurufe, Befehle und gute Lehren erziehen und entwickeln will. Kurz, es wird in diesem Gedicht eine Vision, etwas Einmaliges, Schönes und Großartiges zu Lehrzwecken verfälscht und ausgenutzt, und dies ist es, was mich schon immer dagegen eingenommen hat.'

(*Die Legende*, pp. 480–84)

Two motifs of this passage are especially relevant to the tradition of the *Entwicklungsroman*. The first is the idea of gradual, organic development expressed in terms of 'Erwachen', 'Stufen' or 'Transzendieren'. The second is the relation of this, by Fritz Tegularius but implicit throughout the novel, to musical structures. 'Erwachen' and 'Transzendieren' can be viewed as two different aspects of the 'Stufen' in Knecht's development. The first implies the passive, unconscious process in which the stimulus comes from without, the second the active, deliberate will of the subject, whose inner conviction spurs him to change his position. The terms themselves and their synthesis thus reflect the major conflict of the novel, that between the *vita activa* and the *vita comtemplativa*. Knecht is by nature more inclined to the latter than to the former: in this he is a representative member of Castalia, for which, as he says in his letter to the administration, 'Betrachtung' is more important than 'Tat' (*Das Rundschreiben* p. 466). His development throughout the major part of the novel occurs on the lines rather of 'Erwachen' than of a deliberate policy on his part. In this the 'Erziehergestalten' of the traditional *Entwicklungsroman* play a vital role, guiding his energies in the right paths; a key figure is the

Music Master who early in the novel expresses a similar concept of personality in the words: 'Jeder von uns ist nur ein Mensch, nur ein Versuch, ein Unterwegs' (*Die Berufung* p. *156*). Up to the end of the novel Knecht's development is unproblematic; although from earliest times he sees more clearly than the others the limitations of Castalia, he makes no serious attempt to break away from it. In this acceptance of his surroundings he resembles rather the hero of *Der Nachsommer* than the Meister of the *Lehrjahre*. His 'awakening' is his gradual achievement of awareness of himself, his position in Castalia and the position of Castalia with regard to the outside world. His final decision to leave Castalia and devote himself to the active service of humanity, however, is a deliberate break with the past, a 'transcending', but one which is none the less organic and logical, as it is based on the 'awakening' to the full realization of the shaky moral and political foundations of the province. That the development is organic is underlined, as in the traditional models, by the role played by nature in the novel. In our extract it is not fortuitous that Knecht meditates in a garden; a wilder natural setting is later the scene of his death.

The basic idea of the novel is expressed in a poem; this poem itself is, according to Tegularius, really about the essence of music, and Knecht does not disagree. The idea of the individual human life as a work of art echoes in this case the *Bildungsroman* rather than the *Entwicklungsroman*. This is, of course, already implied by the role of the guides and mentors who 'shape' the life of the fortunate individual who falls into their hands. Cultural influences have always been important in this kind of novel, and discussions of works of literature or the other arts have taken up a prominent position in their textures—one need only think of the discussions of *Hamlet* in *Wilhelm Meisters Lehrjahre*. In Knecht's life music is a primary influence from the first visit of the Music Master to his school. Elsewhere he is reported to have described the basic tendency of classical music as 'Wissen um die Tragik des Menschentums, Bejahen des Menschengeschicks, Tapferkeit, Heiterkeit' (*Einführung*, p. 116). These are clearly terms which likewise describe his ideal personality, and in this awareness Knecht goes out into the world and meets his fate. And yet even in music the ideal is perhaps transient, and must be capable of being developed. For Tito's dance before the fatal swim is dionysian, non-classical, orgiastic, and it is in Tito that hopes for the future are invested.

B*

As with the traditional *Entwicklungsroman* the society in which Knecht lives is described in great detail and is indeed in many ways more memorable than the hero himself. There are, however, some important differences. Knecht's development ultimately leads him in the opposite direction from that taken by the type, away from society—Castalia—into what is ultimately an individualistic end—the personal encounter of tutor with pupil. It is true that Knecht's departure from Castalia is an attempt at integration with society in the wider sense. But this is really a different story, since the novel has not been concerned with the presentation of *this* society in any depth. Either way the 'überkommene Form' has been broken. Moreover, that the encounter with Tito, the representative of the outside world, should lead to Knecht's death, is a much more pessimistic conclusion than that of the type. Self-fulfilment in self-sacrifice, the radical abandonment of self—the balance between individual and society sought, for example, by Wilhelm Meister, has been lost. We are led to believe that Knecht's example will transform Tito; but it must be noted that Tito's education is thus given a quite irrational basis, not that of discussion and logical argument. All this in turn no doubt points to the problematic nature of 'Bildung' in the twentieth century. *Das Glasperlenspiel*, in spite of the allusions to and reflections of a traditional structure, remains a novel of its age.

4   Space

In life we are always at some time—and somewhere. Chapter 2 considered narrative-time, the representation of real time. The first part of this chapter will look at *location*, the representation of place. Just as novels can be analysed in terms of their own peculiar time-structure, some other aspects of structure, such as montage, are more easily described by analogy with the visual or plastic arts. The second part of the chapter will take this approach a little further and consider the novel as a 'spatial' form in a metaphorical sense of space.

Location can be examined from two points of view, the structural and the textural. What structural role may the location of a novel play in its overall economy? On the other hand, how, at any particular moment of his text, does the author go about conjuring up location? It is in the first aspect that the two senses of space may overlap: the treatment of physical space or location may contribute to a sense of the novel as a metaphorical space, as, say, a canvas filled with patterns. Perhaps the most striking example of such an overlap in the history of the European novel is Tolstoy's *War and Peace*. The vastness of Russia, the huge yet organized cast of characters, the complex interweaving of different narrative strands, the mighty historical events, all mirror each other. The sense of the physical space of Russia coalesces with the sense of the novel as a metaphorical space filled out with significant patterns. Tolstoy's novel is spacious in every sense. A converse example is Kafka's *Das Schloß*. Here physical space expands and contracts in a most alarming way. Sense of space depends largely on a sense of the distance between objects and between ourselves and these objects. K. seems unable to establish these relations with any certainty. As a result, the outdoor scenes are if anything more suffocating than those set in even the narrowest of interiors. Space is, as it were, replaced by a vacuum inimical to life. As in *War and Peace*, here an author's use of physical space mirrors the total effect of the novel as a metaphorical space, but in the opposite way. Kafka's novel is spatial, but far from spacious. The shifting quality of space pervades the whole of *Das Schloß* and is difficult to show briefly. Perhaps Kafka's *Kleine Fabel* may serve instead to illustrate a similar effect.

> 'Ach', sagte die Maus, 'die Welt wird enger mit jedem Tag. Zuerst war sie so breit, daß ich Angst hatte, ich lief weiter und war glücklich, daß ich endlich rechts und links in der Ferne Mauern sah, aber diese langen Mauern eilen so schnell aufeinander zu, daß ich schon im letzten Zimmer bin, und dort im Winkel steht die Falle, in die ich laufe.' — 'Du mußt nur die Laufrichtung ändern', sagte die Katze und fraß sie. (*Erzählungen*, p. 326)

A description of location, which as texture appears quite realistic, may assume symbolic significance if seen in relation to the structure. This is certainly so of the two examples just mentioned. The meaning of such symbolism may be more or less easy to paraphrase apart from the concrete symbol depending on the nature of the work. In a novel of ideas, such as Thomas Mann's *Zauberberg*, the mountain location has a symbolic meaning more readily separable from immediate textural descriptions than is the case with Tolstoy's Russian landscape or Kafka's oppressive corridors and landscapes. There the meaning is too intimately joined to the effect these locations have on the characters and indeed on the reader. Yet Thomas Mann does not present us simply with a 'meaning' wrapped up in a cardboard mountain; an overlap between metaphorical and physical space is present in his novel as well. Part of its spatial effect derives from the sheer illusion of physical space he conjures up in his mountain descriptions. This is less true of Broch's triangular 'Bahnhofsplatz' in *Die Schuldlosen*. As one of a series of triangular motifs it is clearly integrated into the structure of the novel. It evidently has symbolic significance. But in this case the symbolic meaning so overshadows the physical location that it takes on a certain abstraction. Metaphorical space, rather than overlapping with, completely swallows up physical space. The final effect is allegorical rather than symbolic.

When location is structurally important it is often symbolic as well. But this need not be so. In a modern picaresque novel like Grass's *Blechtrommel*, the shifts of scene brought about by the vicissitudes of war and the post-war division of Germany are part of a total structure dramatizing the changes and dislocations in an individual life and in the life of a whole people in a period of upheaval. Yet the places themselves are not symbolic. The Vienna of Doderer's *Strudlhofstiege* is a unifying structural element in a shifting kaleidoscope of people and times, yet it too is scarcely symbolic.

So far we have been looking at location as an aspect of structure. But of course many questions arise as to the techniques an author may use at any point in the texture of his novel to create a sense of physical space. From what point of view will he work? Will he, as does Doderer, create an area which exists solidly and independently of any of the characters? Here we find a celebration of the very bricks and stones of Vienna, of its busy narrow alleys and broader spaceous prospects. Or will he, like Kafka, leave us with no objective standpoint at all so that the outer world remains uncertain in its contours? (See *Realism*.)

Location is a matter of objects within space. Will an author concentrate on objects as such or will he aim through his treatment of objects to create a three-dimensional effect? Again Kafka provides many brilliant examples of how to conjure up through words something as intangible as space itself. On the other hand Thomas Mann, in handling, for example, the descriptions of interiors in *Buddenbrooks*, concentrates on certain key objects which catch the eye, and produces a somewhat flatter, less three-dimensional effect than Kafka.

Finally it might be added that just as time may become a subject of concern in the novel, either dramatized in the time-structure or dealt with in other ways, so too with space. The relation between man and the physical world he inhabits is of basic human concern. The values with which he invests the space he inhabits and the objects surrounding him are perhaps second in importance only to his relationships with other human beings in determining how he understands himself and his existence. Two trends can be distinguished. Some works celebrate the world of objects outside man; some, more typically perhaps in our time, describe the alienation of man from the world around him. The natural and the man-made environment are both important here and indeed one major theme of twentieth-century literature is the contrast between them. (See *Nature*.) Such concerns may be fully dramatized through the treatment of space and location, as in Kafka's work. Or again they may be partly dramatized, partly rendered more discursively through conversations of the characters or directly by the narrator.

Here is a passage from Alfred Döblin's *Berlin Alexanderplatz*, a novel in which, as its title suggests, the location is of supreme importance.

Der Rosenthaler Platz unterhält sich.

Wechselndes, mehr freundliches Wetter, ein Grad unter Null. Für Deutschland breitet sich ein Tiefdruckgebiet aus, das in seinem ganzen Bereich dem bisherigen Wetter ein Ende bereitet hat. Die geringen vor sich gehenden Druckveränderungen sprechen für langsame Ausbreitung des Tiefendruckes nach Süden, so daß das Wetter weiter unter seinem Einfluß bleiben wird. Tagsüber dürfte die Temperatur niedriger liegen als bisher. Wetteraussichten für Berlin und weitere Umgebung.

Die Elektrische Nr. 68 fährt über den Rosenthaler Platz, Wittenau, Nordbahnhof, Heilanstalt, Weddingplatz, Stettiner Bahnhof, Rosenthaler Platz, Alexanderplatz, Straußberger Platz, Bahnhof Frankfurter Allee, Lichtenberg, Irre anstalt Herzberge. Die drei Berliner Verkehrsunternehmen, Straßenbahn, Hoch- und Untergrundbahn, Omnibus, bilden eine Tarifgemeinschaft. Der Fahrschein für Erwachsene kostet 20 Pfennig, der Schülerfahrschein 10 Pfennig. Fahrpreisermäßigung erhalten Kinder bis zum vollendeten 14. Lebensjahr, Lehrlinge und Schüler, unbemittelte Studenten, Kriegsbeschädigte, im Gehen schwer behinderte Personen auf Ausweis der Bezirkswohlfahrtsämter. Unterrichte dich über das Liniennetz. Während der Wintermonate darf die Vordertür nicht zum Ein- und Aussteigen geöffnet werden, 39 Sitzplätze, 5918, wer aussteigen will, melde sich rechtzeitig, die Unterhaltung mit den Fahrgästen ist dem Wagenführer verboten, Auf- und Absteigen während der Fahrt ist mit Lebensgefahr verbunden.

Mitten auf dem Rosenthaler Platz springt ein Mann mit zwei gelben Paketen von der 41 ab, eine leere Autodroschke rutscht noch grade an ihm vorbei, der Schupo sieht ihm nach, ein Straßenbahnkontrolleur taucht auf, Schupo und Kontrolleur geben sich die Hand: Der hat aber mal Schwein gehabt mit seine Pakete.

Diverse Fruchtbranntweine zu Engrospreisen, Dr. Bergell, Rechtsanwalt und Notar, Lukutate, das indische Verjüngungsmittel der Elefanten, Fromms Akt, der beste Gummischwamm, wozu braucht man die vielen Gummischwämme.

Vom Platz gehen ab die große Brunnenstraße, die führt nördlich, die AEG. liegt an ihr auf der linken Seite vor dem Humboldthain. Die AEG. ist ein ungeheures Unternehmen, welches nach Telefonbuch von 1928 umfaßt: Elektrische Licht- und Kraftanlagen, Zentralverwaltung, NW 40, Friedrich-Karl-Ufer 2–4, Ortsverkehr, Fernverkehr Amt Norden 4488, Direktion, Pförtner, Bank Elektrischer Werte A.G., Abteilung für Beleuchtungskörper, Abteilung Rußland

Abteilung Metallwerke Oberspree, Apparatefabriken Treptow, Fabriken Brunnenstraße, Fabriken Hennigsdorf, Fabrik für Isolierstoffe, Fabrik Rheinstraße, Kabelwerk Oberspree, Transformatoren-Fabrik Wilhelminenhofstraße, Rummelsburger Chaussee, Turbinenfabrik NW 87, Huttenstraße 12–16.

Die Invalidenstraße wälzt sich linksherum ab. Es geht nach dem Stettiner Bahnhof, wo die Züge von der Ostsee ankommen: Sie sind ja so berußt — ja hier staubts. — Guten Tag, auf Wiedersehn. — Hat der Herr was zu tragen, 50 Pfennig. — Sie haben sich aber gut erholt. — Ach die braune Farbe vergeht bald. — Woher die Leute bloß das viele Geld zu verreisen haben. — In einem kleinen Hotel da in einer finstern Straße hat sich gestern früh ein Liebespaar erschossen, ein Kellner aus Dresden und eine verheiratete Frau, die sich aber anders eingeschrieben haben.

Vom Süden kommt die Rosenthaler Straße auf den Platz. Drüben gibt Aschinger den Leuten zu essen und Bier zu trinken, Konzert und Großbäckerei. Fische sind nahrhaft, manche sind froh, wenn sie Fische haben, andere wieder können keine Fische essen, eßt Fische, dann bleibt ihr schlank, gesund und frisch. Damenstrümpfe, echt Kunstseide, Sie haben hier einen Füllfederhalter mit prima Goldfeder.

In der Elsasser Straße haben sie den ganzen Fahrweg eingezäunt bis auf eine kleine Rinne. Hinter dem Bauzaun pufft eine Lokomobile. Becker-Fiebig, Bauunternehmer A.G., Berlin W 35. Es rumort, Kippwagen liegen bis zur Ecke, wo die Commerz- und Privatbank ist, Depositenkasse L., Aufbewahrung von Wertpapieren, Einzahlung von Banksparkonten. Fünf Männer knien vor der Bank, Arbeiter, schlagen kleine Steine in die Erde.

(Book II, pp. 51–3)

This passage is typical of the 'montage' technique Döblin uses to convey the vast complexity of a great modern city. The rich visual confusion of shops, tram-cars, lights, crowds, advertisements, the sense of bustling disorganized movement are brought out by short phrases: pieces of advertisement, statistical information, weather forecasts, snatches of song, fleeting thoughts passing through the mind of one of the crowd, or of the central character Franz Biberkopf or indeed of the narrator himself. These phrases, couched in the ludicrously contrasting styles appropriate to advertiser, bureaucrat, worker or educated bourgeois are a stylistic kaleidoscope mirroring the confusion of the city. So much for the texture with its multiplicity of view-points, objects and its other spatial effects, now of narrow bustling streets, now of the wind whipping across an empty square.

Structurally these impressions of Berlin play a vital role in the counterpoint of chaos and order which Döblin builds up through the course of his novel. The outer chaos of the city has its counterpart in the mental and moral confusion of the principal character, Franz Biberkopf. The interpenetration of milieu and individual is most vividly expressed by the interpenetration of language mentioned above, so that it is not always clear whether we are inside or outside Franz's head, whether the confused phrases are his thoughts or the narrator's presentation of Berlin. Döblin thus builds up a correspondence between the location, the psychology of his principal character and the language of the novel. This might suggest that Döblin has carried his method too far, and that in trying to convey a confusing city and a confused mind he has written a confusing and confused novel. However, he provides a clear framework for his pointillistic canvas by making strong chapter divisions and preceding each chapter with a summary of the main point it sets out to make. In the end the great bulk of the novel itself and the confusion of its two protagonists, Berlin and Franz Biberkopf, are as it were corseted in these moral sentences. Thus a clear shape emerges from the confusion, a shape which finds its formal focus-point in the chapter headings, its psychological focus-point in the emergent (if only *in potentio*) moral will of Franz Biberkopf and its physical focus-point in Alexanderplatz, the changing yet unchanging heart of Berlin.

Let us turn now in more detail to the novel as a metaphorical 'space'. A novel may be apprehended spatially, not in the trivial and literal sense of the book as an object in space or of the page covered with print, but metaphorically, as a verbal artefact in which part relates to part within a whole in a way analogous to the relationship of objects within real space. In reality our sense of space depends very much on our perception of the relationship of objects to each other: the sea is vast in relation to the ship on the horizon or the observer looking at it. In an analogous way, the more the reader can perceive the novel simultaneously, can see its various parts in relation, the more he may be said to see it spatially.

Of all modern literary forms, the novel is the one that has been most concerned with Life and least with Art. The formal development of the novel up to the beginning of the twentieth century has been largely the development of ever more subtle devices to render the novel life-like, to conceal art, to make the reader forget he is reading fiction and feel involved in the 'reality' of what he is reading. In this way the reader is invited to enter into the physical space of the novel, into its location. But he is seduced into forgetting that the novel is a metaphorical space, a verbal artefact and not life itself. Any device which on the contrary tends to remind the reader that he is reading a work of art with its own shape and form, rather than drawing him into the illusion that he is involved in a slice of life, is likely to intensify appreciation of the spatial form of the work. Such devices may not derive from any aesthetic intent, yet one effect is often to create the necessary distance for aesthetic appreciation.

A novel is most obviously a structure of parts adding up to a whole by virtue of the usual division of novels into chapters. In early forms such divisions were just a series of episodes more or less complete in themselves, a string of stories perhaps connected by a central character or joined by a framework like the *Decameron*. A later development is the use of chapter divisions to create suspense, no doubt partly the effect of publishing novels in serial form in newspapers and partly in imitation of the drama. The division now comes not at the end of an episode but at a point calculated to make the reader curious as to what happens next. Thus part is more closely bound to part than in the episodic chronicle. The corresponding overall structure is the novel with a plot, where suspense is sustained not just between single sections, but is carried over the whole parabola of the novel. The end is related to the beginning by solving the mystery or problem posed at the start, while the intervening sections are steps on the way to a denouement. Such a form clearly gives unity of a sort. On the other hand, suspense may be so involving that the reader does not have the critical distance necessary to appreciate formal qualities. The story-novel, though it sacrifices the unity provided by a plot clearly linking beginning and end, may develop other, subtler means of creating an aesthetic unity, means the reader may see more clearly since he is not so involved in the suspense of plot.

Twentieth-century novels offer many variations of these three basic types: the episodic chronicle, the plot-novel and the story-novel. The last chapter considered the detective-story pattern, necessarily plot-novel, and the picaresque or *Schelmenroman*, necessarily chronicle. In serious literature these patterns often become, so to speak, self-conscious. They are highlighted or varied in some way so that they can be appreciated as *form*. In Dürrenmatt's *Der Richter und sein Henker*, a 'serious' detective story, the identity of the criminal is clear from fairly early on. Since the reader is no longer driven by simple curiosity to reach the denouement, he is not too involved to admire the inexorable logic of the edifice Dürrenmatt builds up. In *Die Blechtrommel*, Günter Grass lends the pattern of the *Schelmenroman* more unity than the original type by his skilful playing-off of Oskar the narrator against Oskar the rascally hero. The judgment of Oskar-narrator on his earlier self is a unifying theme in the otherwise rather loosely strung episodes. The moral distance from Oskar as rascally hero results also in a degree of aesthetic distance; we are made aware that the rascality of the hero is a literary convention and are therefore able to enjoy it as such, while making at the same time a moral judgment on it. (See *Irony*.) No typical structure of chapters can be laid down for the story-novel, but many interesting effects are possible here too. The story itself may form a satisfying shape, like that of *Buddenbrooks* with its crisscross development: the falling line of the social and physical decline of the Buddenbrook family crossed by the rising line of the heightened sensibility of some of its members. Or the single chapters may follow a repeated pattern, like the spiralling movement of episodes in Kafka's novels.

Apart from structural divisions into chapters or episodes, many other narrative techniques may draw attention to the 'how' as well as the 'what' of the novel and so contribute to a sense of the work as an aesthetic space. Most important of all may be the effect of the time-structure. As far as it is possible to generalize about something as protean as the novel, it is true to say that the more fugal a novel becomes, the more spatial it will be. Indeed an alternative label for the fugal novel might well be the spatial novel. The reason is evident. By bringing into conjunction events separated in narrative-time, the author can throw into sharp relief a pattern of relationships or ironies in the events he is narrating. Time, as it were, does not so much pass as collide. Linear succession in time is converted into spatial pattern. Spatial is a broader term, however, than fugal, which refers only to the time-structure. Many novels may be highly spatial in effect without a fugal time-structure, thanks to the various patterning devices discussed here and in the previous chapter.

Broch's novel *Die Schuldosen* may serve as an example of a highly spatial novel, while at the same time showing some of the drawbacks of an excess of formalism. Without the buoyancy of a realistic core, the essentially realistic genre of the novel tends to sink under a weight of patterns and symbolism.

Die Schuldlosen is concerned with the responsibility for the cataclysms of the twentieth century of the apparently guiltless but criminally apathetic majority of Europeans. The hero Andreas and his like are guilty precisely through their 'innocence', that is through their refusal to become involved in action, their refusal of responsibility.

At first sight the novel has a linear time-structure. On closer reading it emerges that each section of the Andreas story follows a similar pattern: a trial of Andreas and his subsequent failure to face some test of responsibility. The climax of each section always occurs at eleven minutes past five in the afternoon. The series culminates in his suicide, an act through which he accepts his guilt and tries to atone by self-sacrifice. This too occurs at the same magic hour. Bearing this series in mind, the opening rather obscure section of the Andreas story now suggests that what follows is not a straight portrayal in linear succession, but Andreas's final vision, in the moment of death, of the course of his own life. Its significant pattern of trial and failure is perceptible now to the dying man and shines through the confusions of his mind at the time when the events were first happening. A double perspective is thus present throughout. This structure represents a very radical attempt to 'turn time into space'. The successive stages of Andreas's life are spread out like pictures superimposed on each other before the inner eye of the dying man. And only if we as readers can achieve a simultaneous vision of the author-time, just as Andreas telescopes the narrative-time, can we understand the novel as a whole.

Perhaps it should be emphasized that, as the word 'understand' suggests, this is at least as much a question of symbolic *meaning* as of spatial *form*, as far as these can be separated. However, Broch makes use of repeated images and motifs which act as verticals connecting and giving depth to these two-dimensional photographic layers. In this way he creates the effect or feeling of space we have been talking about, this time in depth. One such motif is that of the triangle: the triangle of the Bahnhofsplatz where Andreas comes to live; three-cornered relationships between characters; the cipher of the eye of God set in a triangle; a musical triad, and so on. These motifs have 'meaning', but for the moment we are concerned with the feeling of triangularity, a spatial feeling, which pervades the whole novel and carries the symbolic meaning. Something like these symbolic meanings could have been conveyed by quite different means, dramatized more fully through actions and events, acted out by more rounded characters, rather than condensed into abstract shapes. The novel gains in concision and multiplicity of meaning. On the other hand Broch has perhaps rather overdone it. So abstract are his geometrical patterns that he is forced, in order to render his meaning clear, to introduce obtrusively didactic poems *ex cathedra* and to put sermons into the mouths of his characters. What he gains in new angles he loses in old-fashioned density.

PART II   TEXTURES

---

5   Register

While structures become apparent only when the novel is viewed as a whole, there are other aspects which can be appreciated in isolation, or as reading proceeds. These we propose to call 'textural' aspects. Some of them can be sensed from the opening sentence of the work:

> Indem ich die Feder ergreife, um in völliger Muße und Zurück-gezogenheit — gesund übrigens, wenn auch müde, sehr müde (so daß ich wohl nur in kleinen Etappen und unter häufigem Ausruhen werde vorwärtsschreiten können), indem ich mich also anschicke, meine Geständnisse in der sauberen und gefälligen Handschrift, die mir eigen ist, dem geduldigen Papier anzuvertrauen, beschleicht mich das flüchtige Bedenken, ob ich diesem geistigen Unternehmen nach Vorbildung und Schule denn auch gewachsen bin. (Thomas Mann, *Bekenntnisse des Hochstaplers Felix Krull,* p. 9)

At once the attentive reader is struck by the 'register' of this passage, which characterizes both the writer and his relationship to his audience.

Register has been described as 'a variety of a language defined with reference to the circumstances in which it is used, and to the purposes for which it is used, as opposed to a dialect, which is a variety defined with reference to the set of people who use it.'[1] However, as dialect will frequently be adopted according to the circumstances in which the speaker finds himself, it too may be treated as a variety of register. Thus Joe Bloggs will describe his ailments in different terms according to the person to whom he is talking, whether it is his doctor, his boss, his wife or his friends at work, and in German-speaking Switzerland an educated person will automatically switch from Schwyzerdütsch to Hochdeutsch if he encounters a foreigner. Register is closely associated with role and situation and this distinguishes it from the more traditional and vaguer term 'style'. 'Style' can refer both to features

---

[1] A. R. Meetham, *Encyclopaedia of Linguistics. Information and Control* (Oxford, 1969) p. 695.

of a writer's work which mark it as belonging to him alone ('X has, or lacks, style'), and to features which relate it to the work of other people ('Y writes in the expressionist style'); 'register' has a purely generalizing connotation—there is, as it were, a stock of registers from which any writer or speaker can draw to fit the situation. Where 'style' can be diachronic in import, referring to one historical fashion later succeeded by another ('the Baroque style'), 'register' is always synchronic, relating to the possibilities available at a given moment. Where 'style' can be inward-looking, referring to the language best suited to what the writer wishes to say, 'register' is outward-looking, relating to the external situation, the context in which he wishes to say it. Where 'style' may be the largely spontaneous expression of an individual personality ('le style, c'est l'homme même'), 'register' draws attention to a more or less conscious role-playing. Style in the senses outlined is, of course, also important for the analysis of the novel as of other genres, and the methods for describing style and register are similar. Nevertheless, in a genre in which the voice of the narrator, who may don various guises, is of paramount importance, and whose main material is social situation and responses to them (see *Man and Society*), it is register which must be considered first; moreover, role-playing is a key concept in the twentieth-century attitude to character (see *Character*).

A number of features combine to give Krull's first sentence its particular register. In the first place the length of the sentence is striking, also its complexity, the hypotaxis being intensified by the artificial repetition of the opening idea, which the two successive parenthetical statements have obscured. Clearly this is an attempt at the old-fashioned period; the writer is trying hard to imitate a style—trying too hard, perhaps, for the pedantry of the two interpolations creates a fussy effect out of keeping with the rest. The semi-tautological doubling of nouns and adjectives is another obvious feature: 'Muße und Zurückgezogenheit', 'in kleinen Etappen und unter häufigem Ausruhen', 'sauber und gefällig', 'Vorbildung und Schule'; it points to an attempt to create a pleasing impression through rhythm rather than to express an idea. The language approaches the precious: 'die Feder ergreife' (a cliché), 'mich anschicke', 'dem geduldigen Papier', 'beschleicht mich das flüchtige Bedenken'. Few nouns are allowed to stand without at least one adjective. And if we look beyond the language at what is actually said, we find, apart from the literary cliché of the writer's modesty, the highly revealing, complacent allusion to his 'saubere und gefällige Handschrift'. Outward appearances then are the main thing, precisely the hallmark of the confidence-trickster whom we know he is from the novel's title, and we may justifiably assume that his 'Muße und Zurückgezogenheit' are the enforced ones of life in prison! The register of the sentence is the literary, non-colloquial, slightly archaic and undoubtedly elevated; Krull is playing here the role of the *littérateur*, which can be seen through by anyone who is not prepared to take him on his own terms.

Registers can be classified in various ways. In the first place, one adopts a particular register according to the topic one is discussing, a football match or the behaviour of molecules in an experiment, for example. Neo-classical and Renaissance criticism distinguished three styles, high, medium and low, which had to be used according to the subject treated, high style for tragedy, low for comedy. Inasmuch as these 'styles' were situational, they parallel our conception of register. Incongruity of register and subject-matter is still a favourite device for humour, as in Döblin's description of the murder of Agamemnon:

> Wie ihn das Weib zu Haus hat, steckt sie ihn ins Bad. Sie zeigt im Augenblick, daß sie ein beispielloses Luder ist. Sie schmeißt im Wasser ein Fischnetz über ihn, daß er nichts machen kann, und dann hat sie schon ein Beil mitgebracht wie zum Holzhacken. Er ächzt: 'Weh mir, getroffen!' Draußen fragen sie: 'Wer schreit da über sich?' 'Weh mir und wieder!' Die antike Bestie murkst ihn ab, zuckt nicht mit der Wimper, sie reißt noch draußen das Maul auf: 'Vollendet hab ichs, ein Fischnetz warf ich ihm um und schlug zweimal, und mit zwei Seufzern streckte er sich, und dann schickte ich ihm noch einen dritten Hieb zum Hades nach.' Worauf die Senatoren bekümmert sind, immerhin aber die treffende Bemerkung finden: 'Wir staunen deiner Rede Kühnheit an.' Diese Frau also wars, diese antike Bestie, die gelegentlich eines ehelichen Amüsements mit Agamemnon Mutter eines Knaben geworden war, welcher bei seiner Geburt den Namen Orestes erhielt. Sie wurde später von dieser Frucht ihrer Freuden gekillt, und ihn plagen dann die Erinnyen. (*Berlin Alexanderplatz*, Book II, p. 107)

There is a double incongruence here. The narrative register is that of the Berlin underworld ('Luder', 'schmeißen', 'abmurksen', 'killen') and conflicts with the content of the classical myth. The burlesque effect is intensified by the juxtaposition of the narrated passages with passages in direct speech which are taken in part from a German translation of Aeschylus's play and whose register is the elevated, poetic, archaic ('Weh mir und wieder!', 'Vollendet hab ichs'). The matter-of-fact description of the chorus's reaction (they are 'bekümmert', but find nonetheless the 'treffende Bemerkung') likewise contrasts with the poetic content of their words, an iambic pentameter ('Wir staunen deiner Rede Kühnheit an').

The burlesque effect is heightened in that the spoken words are in the elevated register, while the narrative is in the colloquial. Normally the reverse might have been expected. In fact the most obvious distinction of registers is between the written and the spoken language, and within these two groups various subdivisions can be made. Compare for example the schoolchildren's slang of Ditta's description of the photograph taken at the end-of-term ball:

> Alle stehen sie da aufgebaut. Was hatten wir doch für Tüten in unserer Tanzstunde. Lustige Tüten. Die da, das sind die Klöppler und Blecher, alle auf einem Haufen. Sehe ich sie da stehen, so meine ich gleich, ich höre sie auch, ich stünde mit ihnen am Schelmeck und höre sie durcheinanderreden: 'Kleine Sauferei machen' — 'Der Kurszettel' — 'Mal was vom Konto abheben.' (Gerd Gaiser, *Schlußball*, Chapter 3, p. 29)

with the political clichés of Diederich Heßling's speeches:

> 'Aus dem Lande des Erbfeindes', schrie Diederich, 'wälzt sich immer wieder die Schlammflut der Demokratie her, und nur deutsche Mannhaftigkeit und deutscher Idealismus sind der Damm, der sich ihr entgegenstellt. Die vaterlandslosen Feinde der göttlichen Weltordnung aber, die unsere staatliche Ordnung untergraben wollen, die sind auszurotten bis auf den letzten Stumpf, damit, wenn wir dereinst zum himmlischen Appell berufen werden, daß dann ein jeder mit gutem Gewissen vor seinen Gott und seinen alten Kaiser treten kann, und wenn er gefragt wird, ob er aus ganzem Herzen für des Reiches Wohl mitgearbeitet habe, er an seine Brust schlagen und offen sagen darf: "Ja!"' (Heinrich Mann, *DerUnt ertan*, Chapter 6, p. 489)

These are but two possibilities within the spoken register Within the written register there are even more. Consider the grandly poetic opening of Hermann Broch's *Der Tod des Vergil*, with its dactylic rhythms, alliterations, metaphors, circumlocutions and archaic vocabulary, all attempting to recapture the atmosphere of ancient epic appropriate to the central figure:

Stahlblau und leicht, bewegt von einem leisen, kaum merklichen
Gegenwind, waren die Wellen des adriatischen Meeres dem kaiser-
lichen Geschwader entgegengeströmt, als dieses, die mählich
anrückenden Flachhügel der kalabrischen Küste zur Linken, dem
Hafen Brundisium zusteuerte, und jetzt, da die sonnige, dennoch
so todesahnende Einsamkeit der See sich ins friedvoll Freudige
menschlicher Tätigkeit wandelte, da die Fluten, sanft überglänzt
von der Nähe menschlichen Seins und Hausens, sich mit vielerlei
Schiffen bevölkerten, mit solchen, die gleicherweise dem Hafen
zustrebten, mit solchen, die aus ihm ausgelaufen waren, jetzt, da
die braunsegeligen Fischerboote bereits überall die kleinen Schutz-
molen all der vielen Dörfer und Ansiedlungen längs der weißbe-
spülten Ufer verließen, um zum abendlichen Fang auszuziehen,
da war das Wasser beinahe spiegelglatt geworden; perlmuttern
war darüber die Muschel des Himmels geöffnet, es wurde Abend,
und man roch das Holzfeuer der Herdstätten, sooft die Töne des
Lebens, ein Hämmern oder ein Ruf von dort hergeweht und
herangetragen wurden. (p. 9)

or the officialese of long stretches of Kafka's novels:

Man ist unwillkürlich geneigt, in der Nacht die Dinge von einem
mehr privaten Gesichtspunkt zu beurteilen, die Vorbringungen
der Parteien bekommen mehr Gewicht, als ihnen zukommt, es
mischen sich in die Beurteilung gar nicht hingehörige Erwägungen
der sonstigen Lage der Parteien, ihrer Leiden und Sorgen, ein; die
notwendige Schränke zwischen Parteien und Beamten, mag sie
äußerlich fehlerlos vorhanden sein, lockert sich, und wo sonst, wie
es sein soll, nur Fragen und Antworten hin- und wiedergingen,
scheint sich manchmal ein sonderbarer, ganz und gar unpassender
Austausch der Personen zu vollziehen. (*Das Schloß*, Chapter 18,
p. 714)

or the pedantic style of Serenus Zeitblom with his humanist
education:

Nun ist dieses Wort, 'Genie', wenn auch über-mäßigen, so doch
gewiß edlen, harmonischen und human-gesunden Klanges und
Charakters, und meinesgleichen, so weit er von dem Anspruch
entfernt ist, mit dem eigenen Wesen an diesem hohen Bezirke
teilzuhaben und je mit divinis influxibus ex alto begnadet gewesen
zu sein, sollte keinen vernünftigen Grund sehen, davor zurück-
zubangen, keinen Grund, nicht mit freudigem Aufblick und ehrer-
bietiger Vertraulichkeit davon zu sprechen und zu handeln. So
scheint es. Und doch ist nicht zu leugnen und ist nie geleugnet
worden, daß an dieser strahlenden Sphäre das Dämonische und
Widervernünftige einen beunruhigenden Anteil hat, daß immer

eine leises Grauen erweckende Verbindung besteht zwischen ihr
und dem unteren Reich, und daß eben darum die versichernden
Epitheta, die ich ihr beizulegen versuchte, 'edel', 'human-gesund'
und 'harmonisch', nicht recht darauf passen wollen, — selbst dann
nicht — mit einer Art schmerzlichen Entschlusses stelle ich diesen
Unterschied auf — selbst dann nicht, wenn es sich um lauteres
und genuines, von Gott geschenktes oder auch verhängtes Genie
handelt und nicht um ein akquiriertes und verderbliches, um den
sünd- und krankhaften Brand natürlicher Gaben, die Ausübung eines
gräßlichen Kaufvertrages ... (Thomas Mann, *Doktor Faustus*, Chapter 1, p. 11)

or the language of the physics text-book which Döblin uses to
describe the way in which Ida was killed:

Das erste Newtonsche [njutensche] Gesetz, welches lautet: Ein
jeder Körper verharrt im Zustand der Ruhe, solange keine Kraft-
wirkung ihn veranlaßt, seinen Zustand zu ändern [bezieht sich auf
Idas Rippen]. Das zweite Bewegungsgesetz Njutens: Die Bewe-
gungsänderung ist proportional der wirkenden Kraft und hat mit
ihr die gleiche Richtung [die wirkende Kraft ist Franz, beziehungsweise sein Arm und seine Faust mit Inhalt]. (*Berlin
Alexanderplatz*, Book II, p. 105)

Berlin Alexanderplatz indeed provides examples of most possible
registers and in this respect at least approaches the totality of
Joyce's *Ulysses*. In each of the cases quoted the function of the
register should be analysed for a full appreciation of the novel. A
further interesting task would be to compare the examples from
the novels by Thomas Mann in order to determine how they
differ.

Clearly register will normally be related to point of view.
Indeed, one might describe register as the textural aspect of point
of view. As we have seen, Felix Krull betrays his social status (or
lack of it) in the language he uses, and much the same could be
said of the traditional third-person, 'omniscient' narrator. But
since register has essentially a characterizing function, it is much
more difficult to define it in the case of the more 'objective'
narrative techniques, whether these are based on a position inside
or outside the narrative. In the latter case the register will often
be described as 'neutrally scientific', that is to say, avoiding jargon
while remaining detached and matter-of-fact. The famous description of typhus in *Buddenbrooks* is almost of clinical text-book quality
(although few text-book authors have the *style* of Thomas Mann):

Mit dem Typhus ist es folgendermaßen bestellt: Der Mensch fühlt eine seelische Mißstimmung in sich entstehen, die sich rasch vertieft und zu einer hinfälligen Verzweiflung wird. Zu gleicher Zeit bemächtigt sich seiner eine physische Mattigkeit, die sich nicht allein auf Muskeln und Sehnen, sondern auch auf die Funktionen aller inneren Organe erstreckt, und nicht zuletzt auf die des Magens, der die Aufnahme von Speise mit Widerwillen verweigert. Es besteht ein starkes Schlafbedürfnis, allein trotz äußerster Müdigkeit ist der Schlaf unruhig, oberflächlich, beängstigt und unerquicklich ... (Part II, Chapter 3, p. 751)

But even the Naturalist descriptions of external reality—and Naturalist theory claimed that its method was 'scientific'—and later dissections of inner realities in the manner, for example, of Musil's *Törleß*, may be described in these terms. The language in all these cases is clear, unemotional and frequently concrete, as befits the 'objective' description. A further difficulty is posed by the *erlebte Rede* form of narrative: on the one hand, since the perspective is that of the protagonist one might expect the register to be his also; but on the other hand, to do this consistently (as in fact the stream of consciousness technique does) would be to sacrifice one of the advantages of this form, the duality of vision provided by the narrator and his medium. In practice a compromise is adopted: the language is coloured sufficiently with the register appropriate to the medium, while at the same time remaining distinct from it. Böll's *Haus ohne Hüter* provides some good examples. It is narrated from five different viewpoints, two of which are illustrated in the following passages:

Wenn die Mutter in der Nacht den Ventilator laufen ließ, wurde er wach, obwohl die Gummiflügel dieser Luftmühle nur ein weiches Geräusch erzeugten: fluppendes Surren und manchmal ein Stocken, wenn die Gardine zwischen die Flügel geriet. Dann stand die Mutter auf, zog leise fluchend die Gardine aus dem Getriebe und klemmte sie zwischen die Türen des Bücherschranks. Aus grüner Seide war der Schirm von Mutters Stehlampe: wasserhelles Grün, gelb unterstrahlt, und das Glas roten Weins, das auf dem Nachttisch stand, erschien ihm fast wie Tinte: dunkles, träge aussehendes Gift, das die Mutter in kleinen Schlucken nahm. (Chapter 1, p. 7)

Sie spürte schon seit einigen Minuten, daß jemand sie von hinten anstarrte mit der Beharrlichkeit des sieghaften Typs, der sicher war, erhört zu werden. Es gab Unterschiede; sie konnte sogar spüren, wenn jemand sie von hinten mit den schmerzlichen Augen des schüchternen Verehrers ansah. Aber dieser hier war seiner selbst sicher, ein Blick ohne Melancholie, und sie beschäftigte sich eine halbe Minute lang damit, ihn sich vorzustellen: dunkel, elegant, ein wenig angesnobt; vielleicht hatte er eine Wette abgeschlossen: 10:1, daß ich in drei Wochen mit ihr gepennt habe. (Chapter 3, p. 28)

In the first extract the simple syntax, the repetition of 'Mutter', the metaphor of the 'Luftmühle' clearly belong to the child's world and at least indicate, without reproducing, the childish register; in the second, the social clichés 'sieghafter Typ', 'schüchterner Verehrer', 'angesnobt' belong to the register of the society woman.

The following longer passage from the opening pages of Max Frisch's novel *Homo Faber* is worth examining in some detail for the register of its language and the importance of this register for the understanding of the novel.

Wir starteten in La Guardia, New York, mit dreistündiger Verspätung infolge Schneestürmen. Unsere Maschine war, wie üblich auf dieser Strecke, eine Super-Constellation. Ich richtete mich sofort zum Schlafen, es war Nacht. Wir warteten noch weitere vierzig Minuten draußen auf der Piste, Schnee vor den Scheinwerfern, Pulverschnee, Wirbel über der Piste, und was mich nervös machte, so daß ich nicht sogleich schlief, war nicht die Zeitung, die unsere Stewardeß verteilte, *First Pictures Of World's Greatest Air Crash In Nevada*, eine Neuigkeit, die ich schon am Mittag gelesen hatte, sondern einzig und allein diese Vibration in der stehenden Maschine mit laufenden Motoren — dazu der junge Deutsche neben mir, der mir sogleich auffiel, ich weiß nicht wieso, er fiel auf, wenn er den Mantel auszog, wenn er sich setzte und sich die Bügelfalten zog, wenn er überhaupt nichts tat, sondern auf den Start wartete wie wir alle und einfach im Sessel saß, ein Blonder mit rosiger Haut, der sich sofort vorstellte, noch bevor man die Gürtel geschnallt hatte. Seinen Namen hatte ich überhört, die Motoren dröhnten, einer nach dem andern auf Vollgasprobe —
Ich war todmüde.
Ivy hatte drei Stunden lang, während wir auf die verspätete Maschine warteten, auf mich eingeschwatzt, obschon sie wußte, daß ich grundsätzlich nicht heirate.
Ich war froh, allein zu sein.
Endlich ging's los —
Ich habe einen Start bei solchem Schneetreiben noch nie erlebt, kaum hatte sich unser Fahrgestell von der weißen Piste gehoben, war von den gelben Bodenlichtern nichts mehr zu sehen, kein Schimmer,

später nicht einmal ein Schimmer von Manhattan, so schneite es. Ich sah nur das grüne Blinklicht an unsrer Tragfläche, die heftig schwankte, zeitweise wippte; für Sekunden verschwand sogar dieses grüne Blinklicht im Nebel, man kam sich wie ein Blinder vor.

Rauchen gestattet.

Er kam aus Düsseldorf, mein Nachbar, und so jung war er auch wieder nicht, anfangs Dreißig, immerhin jünger als ich; er reiste, wie er mich sofort unterrichtete, nach Guatemala, geschäftlich, soviel ich verstand —

Wir hatten ziemliche Böen.

Er bot mir Zigaretten an, mein Nachbar, aber ich bediente mich von meinen eignen, obschon ich nicht rauchen wollte, und dankte, nahm nochmals die Zeitung, meinerseits keinerlei Bedürfnis nach Bekanntschaft. Ich war unhöflich, mag sein. Ich hatte eine strenge Woche hinter mir, kein Tag ohne Konferenz, ich wollte Ruhe haben, Menschen sind anstrengend. Später nahm ich meine Akten aus der Mappe, um zu arbeiten; leider gab es gerade eine heiße Bouillon, und der Deutsche (er hatte, als ich seinem schwachen Englisch entgegenkam mit Deutsch, sofort gemerkt, daß ich Schweizer bin) war nicht mehr zu stoppen. Er redete über Wetter, beziehungsweise über Radar, wovon er wenig verstand; dann machte er, wie üblich nach dem zweiten Weltkrieg, sofort auf europäische Brüderschaft. Ich sagte wenig. Als man die Bouillon gelöffelt hatte, blickte ich zum Fenster hinaus, obschon nichts andres zu sehen war als das grüne Blinklicht draußen an unsrer nassen Tragfläche, ab und zu Funkenregen wie üblich, das rote Glühen in der Motor-Haube. Wir stiegen noch immer —

Später schlief ich ein.

Die Böen ließen nach.

Ich weiß nicht, warum er mir auf die Nerven ging, irgendwie kannte ich sein Gesicht, ein sehr deutsches Gesicht. Ich überlegte mit geschlossenen Augen, aber vergeblich. Ich versuchte, sein rosiges Gesicht zu vergessen, was mir gelang, und schlief etwa sechs Stunden, überarbeitet wie ich war — kaum war ich erwacht, ging er mir wieder auf die Nerven.

Er frühstückte bereits.

Ich tat, als schliefe ich noch.

Wir befanden uns (ich sah es mit meinem rechten Auge) irgendwo über dem Mississippi, flogen in großer Höhe und vollkommen ruhig, unsere Propeller blinkten in der Morgensonne, die üblichen Scheiben, man sieht sie und sieht hindurch, ebenso glänzten die Tragflächen, starr im leeren Raum, nichts von Schwingungen, wir lagen reglos in einem wolkenlosen Himmel, ein Flug wie hundert andere zuvor, die Motoren liefen in Ordnung.

'Guten Tag!' sagte er —

Ich grüßte zurück.

'Gut geschlafen?' fragte er —

Man erkannte die Wasserzweige des Mississippi, wenn auch unter Dunst, Sonnenglanz drauf, Geriesel wie aus Messing oder Bronze; es war noch früher Morgen, ich kenne die Strecke, ich schloß die Augen, um weiterzuschlafen.

Er las ein Heftlein, rororo.

Es hatte keinen Zweck, die Augen zu schließen, ich war einfach wach, und mein Nachbar beschäftigte mich ja doch, ich sah ihn sozusagen mit geschlossenen Augen. Ich bestellte mein Frühstück ... Er war zum ersten Mal in den Staaten, wie vermutet, dabei mit seinem Urteil schon fix und fertig, wobei er das eine und andere (im ganzen fand er die Amerikaner kulturlos) trotzdem anerkennen mußte, beispielsweise die Deutschfreundlichkeit der meisten Amerikaner.

Ich widersprach nicht.

Kein Deutscher wünsche Wiederbewaffnung, aber der Russe zwinge Amerika dazu, Tragik, ich als Schweizer (Schwyzzer, wie er mit Vorliebe sagte) könne alldies nicht beurteilen, weil nie im Kaukasus gewesen, er sei im Kaukasus gewesen, er kenne den Iwan, der nur durch Waffen zu belehren sei. Er kenne den Iwan! Das sagte er mehrmals. Nur durch Waffen zu belehren! sagte er, denn alles andere mache ihm keinen Eindruck, dem Iwan —

Ich schälte meinen Apfel.

Unterscheidung nach Herrenmenschen und Untermenschen, wie's der gute Hitler meinte, sei natürlich Unsinn; aber Asiaten bleiben Asiaten —

Ich aß meinen Apfel.

Ich nahm meinen elektrischen Rasierapparat aus der Mappe, um mich zu rasieren, beziehungsweise um eine Viertelstunde allein zu sein, ich mag die Deutschen nicht, obschon Joachim, mein Freund, auch Deutscher gewesen ist ... In der Toilette überlegte ich mir, ob ich mich nicht anderswohin setzen könnte, ich hatte einfach kein Bedürfnis, diesen Herrn näher kennenzulernen, und bis Mexico-City, wo mein Nachbar umsteigen mußte, dauerte es noch mindestens vier Stunden. Ich war entschlossen, mich anderswohin zu setzen; es gab noch freie Sitze. Als ich in die Kabine zurückkehrte, rasiert, so daß ich mich freier fühlte, sicherer — ich vertrage es nicht, unrasiert zu sein — hatte er sich gestattet, meine Akten vom Boden aufzuheben, damit niemand drauf tritt, und überreichte sie mir, seinerseits die Höflichkeit in Person. Ich bedankte mich, indem ich die Akten in meine Mappe versorgte, etwas zu herzlich, scheint es, denn er benutzte meinen Dank sofort, um weitere Fragen zu stellen.

Ob ich für die *Unesco* arbeite?

Ich spürte den Magen — wie öfter in der letzten Zeit, nicht schlimm, nicht schmerzhaft, ich spürte nur, daß man einen Magen hat, ein blödes Gefühl. Vielleicht war ich drum so unausstehlich. Ich setzte

mich an meinen Platz und berichtete, um nicht unausstehlich zu sein, von meiner Tätigkeit, *technische Hilfe für unterentwickelte Völker*, ich kann darüber sprechen, während ich ganz anderes denke. Ich weiß nicht, was ich dachte. Die *Unesco*, scheint es, machte ihm Eindruck, wie alles Internationale, er behandelte mich nicht mehr als Schwyzzer, sondern hörte zu, als sei man eine Autorität, geradezu ehrfürchtig, interessiert bis zur Unterwürfigkeit, was nicht hinderte, daß er mir auf die Nerven ging.
Ich war froh um die Zwischenlandung.
Im Augenblick, als wir die Maschine verließen und vor dem Zoll uns trennten, wußte ich, was ich vorher gedacht hatte: Sein Gesicht (rosig und dicklich, wie Joachim nie gewesen ist) erinnerte mich doch an Joachim. —
Ich vergaß es wieder.
Das war in Houston, Texas.
Nach dem Zoll, nach der üblichen Schererei mit meiner Kamera, die mich schon um die halbe Welt begleitet hat, ging ich in die Bar, um einen Drink zu haben, bemerkte aber, daß mein Düsseldorfer bereits in der Bar saß, sogar einen Hocker freihielt — vermutlich für mich! — und ging gradaus in die Toilette hinunter, wo ich mir, da ich nichts andres zu tun hatte, die Hände wusch.

(pp. 7–12)

If we look first at the vocabulary used, probably the most striking feature is the abundance of technical words belonging to the jargon of international air travel: 'starten', 'Start', 'Strecke', 'Piste', 'Stewardeß' 'Maschine', 'Vollgasprobe'. This is the vocabulary of a man used to air travel and familiar with the terminology. He likes, moreover, to give precise details of geographical locations (Mississippi, La Guardia, Houston, Texas) and brand names ('rororo', later his Hermes Baby typewriter), whether these are relevant to our understanding of the report or not: this is a characteristic of a man used to dealing with facts, concrete information, rather than essences or ideas. We note also the mixture of *Papierdeutsch* ('beispielsweise', 'beziehungsweise') and modern slang or colloquialisms ('Drink', 'Bar', 'so jung war er auch wieder nicht', 'der Deutsche war nicht mehr zu stoppen', 'machte sofort auf europäische Brüderschaft'). There is then no attempt at a literary style; Walter Faber writes as he speaks and calls a spade a spade. He much prefers concrete nouns to abstractions; the only idea mentioned, that of 'europäische Bruderschaft', he evidently despises; otherwise the only abstract nouns are un-problematic ones like 'Verspätung', 'Neuigkeit', 'Höhe'. Nor does he use words that are in any way emotionally charged: 'Tragik' is used by the German, not by Faber; even his irritation and restlessness are expressed more as physiological sensations ('er ging mir auf die Nerven', 'Ich spürte nur, daß man einen Magen hat, ein blödes Gefühl'; he is 'nervös', not 'ängstlich'). In striking contrast with the language used by Felix Krull quoted earlier, adjectives are used very sparingly indeed and almost invariably merely for factual information: 'die verspätete Maschine', 'in großer Höhe', otherwise mainly colours, visual impressions translated exactly into words. The significant exception is the word 'üblich', which occurs no less than five times in this opening passage and contributes decisively to our impression of a man whom nothing can surprise, who has calculated all the risks, has seen it all before.* Not only is the language concrete, but the emphasis is on the technological rather than the natural, a feature which is the more striking in that the snowstorm might well have provided an opportunity for meditations on nature; however, the snow is always seen in conjunction with man-made objects: 'Piste', 'Scheinwerfer', 'Fahrgestell', 'Bodenlichter'. Even the simile used to describe the Mississippi reflects the man-made: 'Geriesel wie aus Messing oder Bronze'. Otherwise what little imagery there is hardly strikes one as such, so outworn have the expressions become: 'Man kam sich wie ein Blinder vor', 'die Höflichkeit in Person'. Again we find the mentality of the technologist, the engineer, the man who has to do with man-made objects rather than with nature or ideas.

The sentence construction underlines this. Most of the sentences are short, going straight to the point: 'Wir hatten ziemliche Böen', 'Die Böen ließen nach'. Longer sentences are generally paratactical in construction and asyndeton is common: 'Ich richtete mich sofort zum Schlafen, es war Nacht.' 'Er kam aus Düsseldorf, mein Nachbar, und so jung war er auch wieder nicht.' When verbs are not essential they are frequently omitted: 'meinerseits keinerlei Bedürfnis nach Bekanntschaft.' The occasional long sentence is constructed in a perfectly clear manner, so that there is no need to look back to the beginning again, as was the case with the first sentence of *Felix Krull*: the 'so daß' construction of sentence four is much easier to follow than a 'da ... deshalb ... ' construction

---

* Here our analysis is touching on the question of *tone*, a concept which will be dealt with later. In fact the passage takes on a quite different tone when viewed in the light of the events which take place between what is described here and the time of writing.

would would have been, and the 'nicht … sondern … ' type of sentence is likewise simple to understand.

Walter Faber is an engineer. Things, rather than people or ideas, are his province. In fact his relationships with people are very unsatisfactory, as can be seen from the passage quoted. Before the war he was in love with a Jewish girl, Hanna Landsberg. They drifted apart, and when he learned that she was expecting their child he arranged for her to have an abortion, without himself going back to see her. Some twenty years later, through a series of coincidences beginning with the flight described in the passage quoted, he meets a girl on the boat from America to Europe, falls in love with her, and has an affair with her. While they are sunbathing on a lonely beach in Greece she is bitten by a snake. He manages to get her to hospital, but she dies, not from the snake bite but from the head injuries which she sustained when she fell, startled by his sudden appearance. At her death-bed he meets Hanna, who reveals that the girl was their daughter.

Retold in this manner the story sounds highly improbable—though no less plausible than the story of Oedipus, with which it is clearly analogous. What raises it above the melodramatic is the characterization of Faber, whom Frisch presents as the proto-type of Technological Age man. Faber believes that man is master of the world, or that he can at least calculate dangers so accurately as to know whether or not to disregard them. The air disaster in Nevada fails to shake him, for the probability of a similar disaster happening to him is calculably small. In the same way he rejects the thought that the girl might be his own daughter, even when the indications make it appear more and more possible: the coincidences necessary for it to be the case are too great. In the characterization of Walter Faber register plays a decisive role. The language is colloquial, concrete, matter-of-fact, far removed from the atmosphere of Greek mythology. And yet 'it happens' to this sober, unemotional technologist. Had Frisch chosen to tell the story from a different viewpoint in a more emotional, literary manner, the effect would have been unbearably melodramatic. In this respect the distancing function of register in *Homo Faber* is similar to that of the interpolation of the scandal-ized humanist Serenus Zeitblom as narrator in Thomas Mann's *Doktor Faustus*.

C

6 Dialogue and Narrative

Eine Gattung, die beschreibende Teile verbindet mit erzählenden und redende mit handelnden, zu schweigen von der Schaubarkeit der Welt, die aus dem allen wird, und von den Klängen der Sprache, himmlischen oder armen: wahrhaftig, der Roman, wie das große 19. Jahrhundert ihn hinterlassen hat, ist das erreichte Gesamtkunstwerk, oder es gäbe keins.[1]

In the course of this hymn to the novel Heinrich Mann draws attention to further important textural elements. What gives an individual novel its peculiar 'weave' is very largely the relative proportions it contains of dialogue and narrative, and within narrative of description (whether of actions or states), summary and commentary. A predominance of dialogue and description is characteristic of the 'scenic' or 'dramatic' novel; when summary and commentary prevail we have the 'panoramic' or 'philosophical' novel. These elements are not exclusive; for example, they take no account of the segments of undigested 'reality' which contribute to the montage of *Berlin Alexanderplatz*—the newspaper cuttings at the beginning of Book II—or the poems which the Romantic authors liked to insert in their novels. These latter, however, may conveniently be understood in relation to the wider terms 'scenic' or 'panoramic'.

Mann himself looked to nineteenth-century models for his textures; the influence of Flaubert is apparent in his treatment of the 'scene'. A novel like *Der Untertan* is clearly scenic: comparatively brief sections of summary or commentary invariably lead into large dramatic sections, set-pieces in which the characters reveal themselves through their own words and actions. What one immediately remembers about *Der Untertan* are such scenes, limited in number but often of some considerable length; the pub politics, the evening of the amateur theatricals, the climactic unveiling of Kaiser Wilhelm's memorial, at which the pompous speeches are punctuated by claps of thunder and the assembly eventually

---

[1] Heinrich Mann, *Ein Zeitalter wird besichtigt* (Berlin, 1947), p. 249.

scattered by a tremendous downpour of rain. Other authors place much less emphasis on the scene. Large stretches of *Der Mann ohne Eigenschaften* consist mainly of commentary or meditation; Döblin's *Giganten*, the shortened version of his *Berge, Meere und Giganten*, consists very largely of summary and contains little dialogue. Kafka's novels are scenic, but the link passages of summary are reduced to a minimum and there is no commentary at all. Many contemporary novels lack dialogues, although they do not necessarily lack the scene. This is true of the novels of Heinrich Böll, where the effect is to underline the breakdown in communication between the characters, each isolated in his own monadological and monological cell.

For Alice before her entry to Wonderland, 'conversations' came immediately after 'pictures' as the prerequisite of a 'useful' book, and she could tell at a glance the 'uselessness' of the book her sister was reading. Dialogue in the novel lends vividness and interest. Robert Musil's widow reports the provisional nature of some of the posthumous chapters of *Der Mann ohne Eigenschaften*: 'Er wollte sie auflockern und leichter machen, in Gespräche zwischen Ulrich und Agathe aufteilen ...' (p. 1659) One of the rare passages to arouse the reader of *Der Tod des Vergil* from his metaphysical slumbers occurs when the meditations of the dying Virgil are disturbed by a drunken altercation outside his window (pp. 118 ff.). The obscene concreteness of the language underlines the contrast with the abstract reflections preceding. 'Der Sinn erweitert, aber lähmt; die Tat belebt, aber beschränkt', wrote Goethe.[2] Too much reflection not only paralyses the thinker; it may also send the reader to sleep. Dialogue is itself a form of action, the only form which the novel can directly reproduce. It can, therefore, play an important part in the advancement of the plot. It is further a means of characterizing the speaker directly, as in the following passage from *Der Untertan*. Guste Daimchen has just been told that her fiancé has left her; Diederich suggests that he had in any case been bound to her only by her money.

Da rang es sich los aus Guste. 'Haben Sie 'ne Ahnung! Das ist es ja, das kann und kann ich ihm nicht verzeihen, daß ihm immer *alles* wurscht war, sogar mein Geld!'
  Diederich war erschüttert. 'Mit so einem soll man sich nicht einlassen', stellte er fest. 'Die haben keinen Halt und laufen einem

[2] *Wilhelm Meisters Lehrjahre*, Book VIII, Chapter 5.

durch die Finger.' Er nickte gewichtig. 'Wem das Geld wurscht ist, der versteht das Leben nicht!' (Chapter 5, p. 357)

The novel which depends on the personality of the narrator or of a single dramatized consciousness will often be monolithic. Dialogue introduces the possibility of the dialectical. This can be seen clearly in Thomas Mann's *Der Zauberberg*. By dividing himself into Naptha and Settembrini the narrator not only makes a philosophical argument livelier but also forces the reader to see the relativity of the standpoint of each; the balance between the humanist and the absolutist pervades the novel. This type of dialogue, in which a genuine clash of personalities and ideas occurs, must be distinguished from the trivial conversation of society, which, if reproduced, will usually be the object of satire:

> Susanne war auch im Krankenhaus, sagte er.
> Aber nur drei Wochen, sagte sie rasch.
> Ach, sagte ich.
> Und Sie?
> Elf, sagte ich. Sagte es aber so, als sei das nicht der Rede wert.
> Ich danke für Obst und Südfrüchte, sagte sie.
> Oh, ich finde das Krankenhaus gar nicht so übel, sagte ich ...

(Martin Walser, *Halbzeit*, Part I, Chapter 2, p. 297)

Indeed, in such satire lies the real strength of *Halbzeit*. The author lays bare the artificiality of social small-talk, in which the participants posture before an applauding audience and frequently find themselves forced by the rules of the game into expressing views contrary to what they actually believe. Perhaps even more significant is pseudo-dialogue, in which communication does not take place at all. This is almost invariably the case in Kafka's novels, in which the characters are so preoccupied with themselves that they are unable to hear what the other is saying:

> 'Einleitungen überhöre ich immer', sagte Fräulein Bürstner. 'Das erleichtert meine Aufgabe', sagte K. 'Ihr Zimmer ist heute früh, gewissermaßen durch meine Schuld, ein wenig in Unordnung gebracht worden, es geschah durch fremde Leute gegen meinen Willen und doch, wie gesagt, durch meine Schuld; dafür wollte ich um Entschuldigung bitten.' 'Mein Zimmer?' fragte Fräulein Bürstner und sah statt des Zimmers K. prüfend an. 'Es ist so', sagte K., und nun sahen beide einander zum erstenmal in die Augen, 'die Art und Weise, in der es geschah, ist an sich keines Wortes wert.'

'Aber doch das eigentlich Interessante', sagte Fräulein Bürstner. 'Nein', sagte K. 'Nun', sagte Fräulein Bürstner, 'ich will mich nicht in Geheimnisse eindrängen, bestehen Sie darauf, daß es uninteressant ist, so will ich auch nichts dagegen einwenden. Die Entschuldigung, um die Sie bitten, gebe ich Ihnen gern, besonders da ich keine Spur einer Unordnung finden kann.' Sie machte, die flachen Hände tief an die Hüften gelegt, einen Rundgang durch das Zimmer. Bei der Matte mit den Photographien blieb sie stehen. 'Sehen Sie doch!' rief sie. 'Meine Photographien sind wirklich durcheinandergeworfen. Das ist aber häßlich. Es ist also jemand unberechtigterweise in meinem Zimmer gewesen.' K. nickte und verfluchte im stillen den Beamten Kaminer, der seine öde, sinnlose Lebhaftigkeit niemals zähmen konnte. 'Es ist sonderbar', sagte Fräulein Bürstner, 'daß ich gezwungen bin, Ihnen etwas zu verbieten, was Sie sich selbst verbieten müßten, nämlich in meiner Abwesenheit mein Zimmer zu betreten.' (*Der Prozeß*, Chapter 1, pp. 278–9)

Not all dialogue in the novel is reproduced in direct speech. Kafka frequently uses indirect speech, and since German normally uses for this purpose the subjunctive, what is being reported often becomes even more hypothetical and shadowy. The distancing effect of indirect speech as compared to the more dramatic direct form is illustrated humorously in the following passage from Peter Handke's *Die Hornissen*. The subject is the loss of a key; having scolded his wife, the husband turns to his sons:

Meiner Treu, hatte sich der Mann mit gleichen Worten vor den Söhnen aufgeplustert, wir würden den heutigen Tag nicht so bald vergessen! Mit Verlaub, schimpfte er weiter, wenn es nach ihm ginge, so würde uns jetzt anders werden! Wir unterstünden uns, stocherte er in seinem Zorn, ihm unter die Augen zu treten? Das werde uns noch reuen! schürte er fort. Ihr vermaledeites Gesindel! verkehrte er den eigenen Namen. Ihr Schelme! Daß wir ihm aus den Augen gingen! Und sofort! ordnete er an. Ob wir wüßten, was wir seien? fragte er. Schurken und Bösewichter! gab er sich selber die Antwort, Tagediebe, Strauchräuber und Wegelagerer! Nachtmahre! widersprach er sich: Mischlinge, Bastarde! Er werde uns noch eines anderen belehren! Kein Stein, verkündete er, werde auf dem anderen bleiben! (pp. 131–2)

The wrath of the father is grotesquely muted by the indirect way in which it is reported.

Indirect speech must be distinguished from *erlebte Rede*, mentioned in our first chapter in connection with the dramatized consciousness technique. The following passage, also from Kafka's *Der Prozeß*, is worth examining from this point of view:

> Heute wußte K. nichts mehr von Scham, die Eingabe mußte gemacht werden. Wenn er im Büro keine Zeit für sie fand, was sehr wahrscheinlich war, dann mußte er sie zu Hause in den Nächten machen. Würden auch die Nächte nicht genügen, dann mußte er einen Urlaub nehmen. Nur nicht auf halbem Wege stehenbleiben, das war nicht nur in Geschäften, sondern immer und überall das Unsinnigste. Die Eingabe bedeutete freilich eine fast endlose Arbeit. … Und wie traurig war eine solche Arbeit überdies. Sie war vielleicht geeignet, einmal nach der Pensionierung den kindisch gewordenen Geist zu beschäftigen und ihm zu helfen, die langen Tage hinzubringen. Aber jetzt, wo K. alle Gedanken zu seiner Arbeit brauchte, wo jede Stunde, da er noch im Aufstieg war und schon für den Direktor-Stellvertreter eine Drohung bedeutete, mit größter Schnelligkeit verging und wo er die kurzen Abende und Nächte als junger Mensch genießen wollte, jetzt sollte er mit der Verfassung dieser Eingabe beginnen. (Chapter 7, pp. 361–2)

The most remarkable features of this passage are possibly the temporal adverbs 'heute' and 'jetzt' in the first and last sentence respectively. Both refer to present time and yet both are used with past tenses. This apparently illogical combination is possible only in fiction and sheds an interesting light on what the novel can do. Reported speech would not only require the subjunctive; it would also replace 'heute' with 'an jenem Tage' and 'jetzt' with 'zu diesem Zeitpunkt'. *Erlebte Rede* has the contrary effect to that of reported speech: the latter creates distance in space and time, the former brings events and people closer. The preterite tense, as the adverbs of present time indicate, does not put events into the past; it is a purely fictional, timeless tense.[3] The passage quoted might almost as well have been written in the present tense; indeed, in the stage directions for plays the present tense is invariably used. Here then we have another example in the novel of what is inherently dramatic.

With indirect speech and *erlebte Rede* we have left dialogue and begun to discuss aspects of narrative. Descriptive narrative may be subdivided according to the object of the description, whether a blow-by-blow report of an action or series of actions, or the evocation of a setting, landscape or state of mind. The former will evidently play an important role in the adventure story or novel

[3] Cf. Käte Hamburger, *Die Logik der Dichtung* (Stuttgart, 1957), pp. 27 ff.

of action, the latter dominates the lyrical novel, where it gives the novelist great scope for special poetic effects (see *Imagery*). Description is thus very often concerned with space or location, also with characterization. Summary, on the other hand, is important in relation to time and tempo: the narrator can swiftly pass over the less important events in order to concentrate on the important ones. Summary is thus also an important aspect of plot. Commentary, the third feature of narrative, is an especially important element in the German novel and will be examined in detail in *Essayism*. It ranges from speculation on what might have happened through the traditional moralizing of the eighteenth- and nineteenth-century novel to the 'Essayismus' of Musil, Thomas Mann and Broch, in which social, metaphysical, scientific and theological questions may be expounded without any apparent regard for the needs of plot and character on which the English novel so largely depends. It must, however, be clearly distinguished from the philosophical dialogues of *Der Zauberberg*, in which the arguments are dramatized and at the same time relativized by reference to the character of the person expounding them.

The textural elements of dialogue and narrative have an important relationship to the structural elements discussed earlier, especially point of view and tempo. Dialogue, as the element most properly belonging to the drama, generally emphasizes the here and now rather than the there and then; the longer it is the more the reader will lose sight of any outside point of view there may be. Description may or may not be part of the dramatized consciousness of one of the characters; but with it the narrative is clearly moving into the realm of the outside observer. Summary is the province of a narrator with an overall point of view, able to look back on events and detect a pattern in them. But again the effect of distance whether in space or time may easily be blurred. Consider the beginning of Chapter 4 of *Der Prozeß*:

> In der nächsten Zeit war es K. unmöglich, mit Fräulein Bürstner auch nur einige wenige Worte zu sprechen. Er versuchte auf die verschiedenste Weise an sie heranzukommen, sie aber wußte es immer zu verhindern. (p. 318)

This cannot be treated as an extract from K.'s impressions: somebody must be summarizing them. And yet, since the point of view remains that of K., we do not read it as the statement of an external narrator. Even the novel of the stream of consciousness does not report *every* detail for *all* the time. Commentary, however, is the narrative element which belongs most clearly to the outside narrator; it is completely absent from Kafka's novels.

Similar conclusions may be drawn regarding tempo. Dialogue most clearly approximates to 'real' tempo, and it is logical that Arno Holz, the arch-theorist of Naturalist 'Sekundenstil', should place such emphasis on reproducing 'die Sprache des Lebens',[4] that is to say, the conversations of everyday life. Description of events too can largely correspond to the time it takes for them to happen, although psychologically the tempo probably quickens at this point, since it is easier to follow events than discourse. Description of scenes and states of mind retard the tempo, while summary accelerates it. Commentary, finally, brings time to a complete standstill.

The following extract from Lion Feuchtwanger's historical novel *Jud Süß* illustrates some of the narrative techniques we have been discussing and raises one or two additional questions. Josef Süß Oppenheimer and Isaak Landauer are two successful Jewish financiers of the eighteenth century. But while Süß has been at great pains to become assimilated to West European customs (without, however, embracing the Christian faith), has become a courtier and chief financial adviser to Karl Alexander, Duke of Württemberg, Landauer has retained the outlook and costume of the traditional Jew.

Durch die prunkenden Säle des Süß schleifte Isaak Landauer seinen Kaftan, aufdringlich am Ärmel trug er das württembergische Juden-zeichen, das niemand von ihm verlangte, das S mit dem Horn. Die glänzenden Spiegel warfen zwischen Lapislazuli und Gold sein Bild zurück, den klugen, fleischlosen Kopf mit den Schläfenlöckchen, dem schütteren, rotblond verfärbten Bart. Der Finanzdirektor zeigte ihm sein Haus. Der Mann im Kaftan stand vor den Vasen, Gobelins, klingenden Pagoden, sah mit aufreizend spöttischem Lächeln hinauf zu dem Triumph des Merkur, klopfte mit der dürren, kalten Hand die Schimmelstute Assjadah, schritt durch die beiden Pagen, die Söhne des Domänenpräsidenten Lamprechts, die in Haltung am Eingang zu den Privatgemächern standen. Prüfte mit den Fingern die kostbaren Stoffe der Möbel, nannte mit stupender Sachkenntnis die Preise. Stand kopfschüttelnd vor den Büsten des Moses, Homer, Salomo, Aristoteles, äußerte: 'So hat Moses, unser Lehrer, sein Tage nicht ausgesehen.' Aber aus dem Bauer krächzte der Papagei Akiba: 'Wie geruhen Euer Durchlaucht geschlafen zu haben?'

[4] Arno Holz, *Das Werk* (Berlin, 1925), Volume 10, pp. 213–14.

Süß hatte Isaak Landauer lang erwartet. Er hatte für diesen Besuch sein Palais sorglicher vorbereitet als für den Besuch manches Fürsten. Er lauerte auf eine Bewegung der Überraschung, staunenden Anerkennens; dem Mann im Kaftan, gerade dem zu imponieren, verspürte er eine aufreizende, quälende Gier. Aber Isaak Landauer wiegte nur den Kopf, rieb die fröstelnden Hände, lächelte, sagte: 'Wozu, Reb Josef Süß?'

Durch das Kabinett ging neugierig die Sophie Fischerin, die Tochter des Kammerfiskals Fischer, die der Finanzdirektor seit zwei Wochen als seine erklärte Mätresse im Haus hielt, ein großes, stattliches Mädchen, weiß, üppig, rotblond, sehr schön, leicht ordinär. Als Süß sie wegen der Störung anfuhr, warf sie einen lässigen Vorwand hin, beschaute, die Lippen geschürzt, den Isaak Landauer, entfernte sich.

'Wozu, Reb Josef Süß?' wiederholte Isaak Landauer. 'Wozu gleich dreißig Diener? Könnt Ihr besser essen, besser schlafen, wenn Ihr habt dreißig Diener statt drei? Ich begreife, daß Ihr Euch die Schickse haltet, ich begreife, daß Ihr ein schönes Zimmer zum Essen wollt, ein gutes, breites Bett. Aber wozu den Papagei? Was braucht ein Jud einen Papagei?'

Süß schwieg, bis unters Haar erfüllt von zehrendem Ärger. Dies war nicht Einfältigkeit, dies war Hohn, klarer, offensichtlicher Hohn. Was kein Minister sich erkühnte, der Mensch im Kaftan tat es mit der schlichtesten Selbstverständlichkeit: machte sich ihm ins Gesicht hinein lustig über ihn. Und er war machtlos gegen ihn, er brauchte ihn, er konnte nur schweigen. Sicherlich wird er auch wieder von den altmodischen Geschichten anfangen, die für die Gegenwart ganz ohne Sinn und Bezug sind, dem Ravensburger Kindermordprozeß und solcher Narretei. Und er, Süß, mußte das alles anhören. Es war unmöglich, Geschäfte zu machen ohne Isaak Landauer. Ach wenn man diesen kompromittierenden Burschen beiseite drängen könnte! Aber man mußte froh sein, wenn er einen an sich heran ließ. Es gab vorläufig keinen Weg um ihn herum.

Man sprach von den Affären, die zu erledigen waren, belauerte sich, schacherte scharf. Eigentlich war Süß überall der Gebende; aber er mußte viel mehr sprechen als der andere und kam sich trotz allen Großgetues wie in der Verteidigung vor. Im Blick Isaak Landauers hielt keine noch so kunstvoll gepinselte Tünche stand, er drang sofort dahinter, alles Scheinwesen zerfiel vor ihm; mit kopfwackelndem Unglauben räumte er das schimmernde Beiwerk weg und nahm in seine fröstelnden Hände das Herz der Süßischen Dinge, die Ziffer. Je größer Süß sich spreizte, so leidiger füllte ihn Ärger und Unbehagen. Er gestand es sich nicht ein, aber der andere hatte ihn am Seil, der Mann im Kaftan ließ ihn tanzen.

Die Geschäfte beendet und signiert, kam Isaak Landauer diesmal nicht auf den Ravensburger Kindermord zu sprechen, sondern auf

c*

eine andere jüdische Historie aus den württembergischen Läuften.
Das war die Sache mit dem großen Judenkünstler Abraham Calorno
aus Italien — es mochte jetzt gut ein Jahrhundert her sein, unter
Herzog Friedrich I. — und seinem Generalkonsul Maggino Gabrieli.
Der Herzog hatte diese welschen Juden mit großen Versprechungen
ins Land gezogen. Er war von dem aimablen Wesen, der Gelehr-
samkeit, dem finanztechnischen Geschick des großen Judenkünstlers
wie verhext, er hatte grenzenloses Zutrauen zu ihm, wies alle Besch-
werden der Pfaffen und der Landschaft barsch und ungnädig zurück,
ja, er verbannte der Juden wegen den Oberpfaffen Osiander aus dem
Herzogtum, und Abraham Calorno und die Seinen saßen groß und
prächtig in Stuttgart. Aber schließlich endete die Geschichte doch
mit Graus und Schrecken, etliche wurden martervoll hingerichtet, der
Rest nackt und bloß aus dem Lande gejagt, Juden auf lange Zeit
nicht mehr ins Herzogtum gelassen. 'Nagende Würmer haben sie uns
geschimpft,' sagte Isaak Landauer. 'Nun ja, nagen sie selber etwa
nicht? Was lebt, nagt. Einer nagt am andern. Jetzt seid Ihr dran, Reb
Josef Süß. Nagt, nagt, solang sie Euch dalassen!' Und er lachte sein
kleines, gurgelndes Lachen.

(pp. 188–91)

Feuchtwanger, like Heinrich Mann, is fond of the dramatic
scene, and *Jud Süß* is composed of a large number of such scenes,
frequently brief, illustrating not only the various stages in the
career of Josef Süß, but also the historical background to the
times, and occasionally linked by passages of summary and
reflections on Jewish history and outlook. The effect of the novel
is frequently that of a series of tableaux. Clearly this has advantages for the historical novel; past events are thereby rendered
more plastic and colourful. Our extract is the beginning of one
such scene.

The stage is set in the first two paragraphs. The pluperfect
tenses of the second are particularly significant and a very common
feature of Feuchtwanger's scenic style. He could have related
events as a straightforward succession: Süß fitted out his palace in
a most sumptuous manner; he then waited impatiently for a visit
from Isaak Landauer; at last Isaak came. Instead he begins *in
medias res* with the arrival of Landauer and then explains that
Süß has been waiting for this visit for a long time, thus placing
everything in the perspective of the scene itself. Even the preterite
of the first paragraph might easily have been in the present tense,
for the impression created is that of the 'epic' stage setting at the
beginning of the plays of Gerhart Hauptmann or George Bernard

Shaw. Elsewhere Feuchtwanger makes frequent use of the 'historic present', an indication of his preoccupation with the dramatic.

The opening three paragraphs are descriptive, the first from the point of view of an external observer ('Der Finanzdirektor zeigte ...', 'Der Mann im Kaftan stand ...'), the second from the point of view of Süß, and the third from the point of view of the narrator once more, who explains who Sophie Fischerin is. But the description itself is dramatic; we are introduced to the pomp of Süß's house in relation to Isaak Landauer's passing through it, and the interruption of Sophie Fischerin leads on to Landauer's words in direct speech in paragraph four: it is not the immorality nor the luxury that he criticizes, but the non-Jewishness of it all. The fifth paragraph is an indirect interior monologue, *erlebte Rede* from the point of view of Süß, again the 'dramatic' way of making known Süß's unexpressed feelings; the form 'wird' rather than the expected 'würde' in the fifth sentence underlines this. Paragraph six consists of summary and commentary, mainly from the point of view of Süß. The final paragraph of our extract is a story within the story, basically Isaak Landauer's story, but told neither in direct speech—that would be too circumstantial— nor in reported speech—that would be too hypothetical—but by the narrator as historical fact. This suggests that the narrator himself is anxious to point out the parallel between this story and events of the novel, rather than have us put it down to superstitions on Isaak's part. The purpose of the story is to comment, but the commentary is dramatized in the form of a parable. The final words in direct speech point the moral via Landauer.

One striking feature of the extract is its lack of dialogue. In fact direct speech is used sparingly in the novel and for three main purposes: for historical atmosphere, for characterization (as in this extract) and to set the seal on a long passage of description or summary (again the extract provides an example). This comparative lack of dialogue seems the more surprising when one considers the dramatic, scenic tendencies we have discovered in it, and the fact that the novel started life as a play. Feuchtwanger much prefers to report conversations in indirect speech. One reason is perhaps related to the nature of the historical novel and its claims to historical truth: few lengthy dialogues have been handed down by history, so here the novelist would most obviously be seen to be inventing, and the problem of historical linguistics would be raised (should they speak in early eighteenth-century

German? Would it be readable over long stretches if they did?). Brief statements, on the other hand, coloured where appropriate with archaisms, have more the quality of quotations and are more easily accepted. Moreover, dialogue with its approximation to the tempo of real life necessarily slows down the tempo of the narrative; this could be a serious handicap in a novel which is based on the rapid succession of events. This in turn points to what is perhaps a basic weakness of *Jud Süß*. For this novel purports not merely to be a novel of events, but to show a clash of outlooks: assimilation versus traditionalism (Süß/Landauer), *vita activa* versus *vita contemplativa* (Süß/Rabbi Gabriel). But in this clash of ideas, Süß, the central character, who finds them conflicting even in himself, has remarkably little to say.

7   Imagery

For our purposes imagery means figures of speech, mainly simile and metaphor of all kinds, including metonomy, synecdoche and so on. Language as such, of course, is highly metaphorical. Our concern is with any figure which stands out from the established idioms or dead metaphors of the language. Compare for example: 'Sie glitt leise durch den Hof' and 'Niemand geht hier spazieren, und daß er nun selber hier spazieren geht, ist Joachim so unheimlich, als ob er irgendwo ins Gleiten geraten wäre.' (Broch, *Die Schlafwandler*, p. 25.) The first gliding is a dead metaphor, because although people do not literally glide unless on roller skates, it is a common term for a smooth gait. The second gliding is more striking. The 'als ob' draws the attention and the verbal noun is unusual. It is not a dead metaphor, for it is at once more literal than in the first sentence—it conjures up the disconcerting physical sensation of starting to slide on something slippery—and it evokes analogically a psychological experience of loss of control. The word 'Gleiten', then, stands out as a significant figure of speech.

The relationship between associative thought processes and the metaphorical structures of language is far beyond the scope of this study. Even as a workaday tool of literary criticism, the term imagery is rather unwieldy. Often it is sensible to use more specific terms, such as metonomy or personification and so on, and consider each case as it arises in a pragmatic way. Even a narrow term such as a simile conceals many kinds of comparison, and, of course, each instance is in the end unique in effect. For convenience, though, the blanket term is useful for tentative generalizations, intended only as signposts on the way to detailed study of individual works.

Imagery is less central to the novel than to poetry. This is because of the differences of scale and organization between the two modes. A line of poetry stands in an equivalent relation to the whole poem as perhaps a chapter to a whole novel. Even in a long poem, line divisions create a smaller local scale than paragraphs of prose. The single image in a poem is thus proportionately bigger in effect, its relation to the whole easier to see, than in a novel, where attention is focused on long-term effects. Nonetheless, imagery may play a crucial role in the art of the novelist. Imagery in novels falls into two categories: images of local, textural effect, and images of structural significance because of repetition or elaboration. Repetition need not mean word-for-word reproduction, but any sequence of related images. Elaboration of an image goes back to epic practice, notably the long epic similes of Homer, and analogous devices turn up in the twentieth-century novel. Such striking images or patterns need to stand out in relief. If there are too many of them, they will not come into focus sufficiently. A long work of large-scale architectural effects and intricacy of detail, demanding the kind of close reading appropriate to a poem, overstrains the reader's intellectual and aesthetic faculties. This is perhaps a valid criticism of Joyce's *Finnegans Wake*, for example, or of Broch's long, poetic evocation of the dying Virgil in *Der Tod des Vergil*, magnificent though it is in bits. The rest of the chapter will look first at some textural then at structural effects of imagery.

Most novels deal to some extent with the outer physical form of objects, places, people, with what can be experienced through the senses. Most novels deal also with inner experience, states of mind, psychology. And most novels have a tone or mixture of tones: they are pervaded by atmospheres, attitudes, feelings, which (if the novel works) guide the reader so that he at least sees how he is supposed to react, even if he does not do so (see *Tone*). Imagery may be a powerful means of communication in each of these spheres—which for convenience we shall call the physical, the experiential and the tonal. Generally, indeed, imagery is a connecting link between any two or all three of them. For example, an image may at once evoke an outer physical presence, suggest the inner nature of a character and indicate the author's attitude. This example of a series of images which work visually, tonally, and reveal the mentality of characters comes from Musil's *Der Mann ohne Eigenschaften*.

> Mit dem zuklappenden Buch klappte auch sein Gesicht zu, mit dem wortlos befehlenden Gesicht klappte auch der Sekretär zu einer ergebenen Verbeugung zusammen und nahm Fichte in Empfang, um ihn abzuservieren und nebenan in der Bibliothek zwischen allen anderen philosophischen Systemen der Welt wieder-

einzureihen; man kocht nicht selbst, sondern läßt das durch seine Leute besorgen. (Book I, Chapter 21, p. 87)

The comparison of a face with a book snapping shut very concisely evokes a sudden change of expression and the slight shock such suddenness would produce in any onlooker, just as the small but explosive sound of a book shutting would cause a start of surprise. The shutting suggests a forbiddingly grim or veiled expression, after the relaxed unselfconsciousness of someone reading. The nervous obsequiousness of the servant is conjured up through the comparison with a book, as if he too were a lifeless object to be snapped shut. The final effect is a vivid impression of a very quick succession of movements. The images conjure this up more concisely and effectively than a careful description could. Detailed description prevents rather than promotes visual impressions in the reader. We do not really see a clearer and clearer impression gradually materializing like the Cheshire cat, whisker by whisker. An image by its brevity helps us to 'see' instantaneously as we do in reality. In this example, concision is particularly important because of the split-second succession of events, brought out very nicely, too, by the construction of the sentence: the three fairly rapid repetitions of 'zuklappen', followed by the slower movement of the last section of the sentence as the secretary moves with dignity through to the library.

Besides physical impressions, the images help to uncover the personality of the characters, an insight it would otherwise take many words to convey. Most important of all they convey an attitude towards the characters. They cast the light in which the reader is invited to see them. The frozen social conventions of a world on the verge of apocalyptic disaster are shown in a comic, slightly grotesque light through the incongruous associations of human behaviour, the ungeometrical human body, the tiny fleeting changes in facial muscles with the automatic quality, the angularity, the suddenness of a book snapping shut. The comic effect is heightened as the passage continues. There is nothing odd about a secretary carrying off a book, but his action is made doubly ridiculous because the book is referred to by the name of its author, a kind of eponymous personification, as if Fichte himself were being carried out, carried out moreover like a vegetable dish when the appetite of the master is satisfied. The equation of metaphysicians and vegetable dishes deflates the former, perhaps, but more certainly it expresses Musil's amused, admiring horror at the attitude of Graf Leinsdorf towards products of the mind. Beyond that, it expresses his contempt for the ludicrous, finally macabre efforts of a section of the Viennese upper classes to choose some leading spiritual ideal for Austria just before the Great War—as if spiritual ideals were entries in a menu. One could think of no more concise and persuasive a way of conveying such criticism than this incongruous series of images. Imagery is a particularly useful means of persuasion in an anti-rhetorical age, and more generally in a genre which tries to show rather than tell. Musil contrives to be annihilating about mentalities without annihilating persons. The comic images make didactic or rhetorical condemnations unnecessary. He does not tell the reader what to think, but shocks him by the images into reacting in an appropriate way.

The Musil passage shows how images may serve multiple purposes, evoke sense impressions, reveal the mind of characters, and contribute to tone and atmosphere. To take up the first point, the physical or sensuous function of imagery: though images may evoke sense impressions, often this is not because one gets a clear impression of the image itself. The association of two unlike things, a book and a face, evokes, rather, the common denominator between them of sudden change producing a slight shock of surprise. The implied comparison is not so much between the two things as between their effects. There are, in fact, two sorts of comparison, one a factual statement of resemblance—that cloud is like a camel (has the shape of a camel)—and one more properly a figure of speech—my love is like a red rose (both have qualities of freshness and beauty affecting the observer emotionally and aesthetically). In the first case, the communication works if the reader has a clear visual impression of a camel-shaped cloud. In the second, a too vivid impression of a rose would be distracting, and a vivid impression of a rose-shaped face would probably be rather horrible! The following passage may illustrate this point. It shows a disconcerting mixture of factual comparison and associative comparison. In the end, what is evoked is a way of looking, not what is being looked at. It is an example of images suggesting a state of mind. It is taken from Broch's *Die Schlafwandler*:

> In ihrem Stuhl zurückgelehnt, blinzelte sie auf die herbstliche Landschaft, und das zurückgeworfene Gesicht, rechtwinklig fast

gegen den gespannten Hals abgebogen, war wie ein unebenes Dach auf diesen Hals aufgesetzt. Vielleicht mochte man auch sagen, daß es auf dem Kelch des Halses schwamm wie ein Blatt oder ihn abschloß wie ein flacher Deckel, denn eigentlich war es kein richtiges Gesicht mehr, sondern bloß ein Teil des Halses, sah aus dem Hals hervor, sehr entfernt an das Gesicht einer Schlange erinnernd. Joachim folgte der Linie des Halses; hügelartig sprang das Kinn vor und dahinter lag die Landschaft des Gesichtes. Weich lagen die Ränder des Mundkraters, dunkel die Höhle der Nase, geteilt durch eine weiße Säule. Wie ein kleiner Bart sproß der Hain der Augenbrauen und hinter der Lichtung der Stirne, die durch dünne Ackerfurchen geteilt war, war Waldesrand. (*Pasenow* III, p. 112)

Quite evidently this extraordinary series of images does not give a vivid visual impression of a girl's face. Rather it breaks up and analyses each element so that any coherent overall picture is lost. The comparisons hover between the factual and the associative, so that the impression of the things offered in comparison is sometimes *too* vivid. It is one thing to say that a girl has a face like a landscape, if you mean it is inexhaustibly varied in expression, yet calm and beautiful. It is quite another if what you mean is that her eyebrows look literally like bushes. Initially rather cubist (the angles, the contrasting planes of face and neck) the description continues in surrealist vein *literally* mixing leaves, vases, snakes, a face, culminating in a face-landscape. The face is robbed of its human qualities by the eye of the beholder, a young man called Joachim. A human face no longer produces in him the normal reactions of interpersonal relationships, but breaks up into its constituent parts, loses its humanity. Joachim is estranged, has lost his sense of his own and other people's identity. What is most vividly evoked is his manner of seeing, his state of mind, not the apparent object of the description.

This is a very extreme case of how an image may be more about a manner of seeing, an inner experience, than about what is seen. These images reflect the point of view of a character, just as tonal images reflect an authorial point of view. Indeed, imagery by its very nature implies a point of view. As soon as phrases such as 'like' or 'as if' or the striking associations of non-dead metaphor appear, it is clear that some filtering consciousness is at work. The camera with its purely physical 'point of view' may register a man bowing, but only a mind can tell us that he looked like a book snapping shut. Of course, in a sense we always know that a linguistic artefact is the product of a mind, but because we take our literate culture and the conventions of the novel form for granted, we may not always be especially aware of a filtering consciousness, even when it reveals itself through figures of speech. But where these figures are sufficiently striking they will tend to personalize the narration, to bring feelings and attitudes to the surface, and sometimes to remind us that we are reading a work of art. The following passage is an example of imagery that is almost wholly tonal in effect and exhorts the reader to share an attitude. It comes from Elisabeth Langgässer's novel *Das unauslöschliche Siegel*:

> In den tragischen ersten Septembertagen des Jahres 1914, als der Armeestab des Generals von Kluck in dem französischen Städtchen Senlis lag, und der Speer des Kriegsgottes, der nach Paris mit tödlicher Sicherheit zu zielen schien, plötzlich verhalten wurde; in dieser kurzen, glühenden Spanne, wo unsichtbare Gewichte des Schicksals unter nahem und fernerem Donner ihrer eingelassenen Zahlen ledig gesprochen wurden, so daß, was sie wirklich bedeutet hatten, später nicht mehr geprüft werden konnte, in einer Nachmittagsstunde, noch heiß wie der sonnenbeschienene Rainfern, in dem sich die Eidechsen tummelten — nahmen zwei Offiziere vom Stab den Weg zu der Kathedrale. (Book II, p. 263)

The image of the spear of Mars evokes a sense of war as an age-old disaster, while the interrupted movement suggests the pause before the catastrophe in classical tragedy and so a sense of some archetypal tragic pattern in human affairs. The same connotation is present in the image of the fate of Europe being weighed in some great balance, the deciding weights incomprehensible to human beings. In almost Homeric fashion, after this evocation of human catastrophe and mighty action in the sphere of the gods, comes a picture, by contrast full of pathos, of the innocent unchanging vitality of nature. The opening reference to 1914 and the closing one to the two officers recall particularities, now seen in a vast numinous context summoned up by the images. The passage is rhetorical, a chorus-like comment on the significance, the pathos of the situation, exhorting the reader to mourn over what is to come and to be fearful at the irony of man's ignorance of what fate has in store. The tone of pathos and mourning comes largely from the images.

So far the examples have shown some physical, experiential

and tonal effects images may have at any point of the texture of a novel. Through repetition, such effects can be emphasized and so take on a structural role. A sequence of related images may set up subliminally an atmosphere pervading the whole novel. *Das unauslöschliche Siegel*, for example, is pervaded by classical and biblical references, all tending to 'dehistoricize' the action, to put it into a timeless context. The landscape-face in the Broch excerpt, mixing the human and the botanical, points forward to ever more extreme forms of alienation, culminating in the figure of Hanna Wendling, a woman whose normal sense of identity crumbles away entirely so that she feels herself reduced, as Broch puts it, to the flora and fauna of her biological processes. The short excerpt quoted at the beginning of the chapter from *Die Schlafwandler:* 'Niemand geht hier spazieren, und daß er nun selber hier spazieren geht, ist Joachim so unheimlich, als ob er irgendwo ins Gleiten geraten wäre'—is only one instance of a whole series of gliding images, culminating in the title of the novel, since gliding is the movement associated with sleepwalkers.

The last example from Broch points to the connection between images, extended metaphors and symbolism. An extended metaphor, sleepwalking, underlies the whole novel, and particular images of gliding recall that metaphor and what it means, a peculiar kind of irrational experience which is the main theme of the novel. The gliding images thus take on symbolic significance. Thomas Mann uses a rather similar technique in *Der Zauberberg*. Some of his *leitmotivs* appear both as images and as what might be called symbolic properties, and tie in with an extended metaphor underlying the whole novel. For example, Hans Castorp first talks curiously in conversation about polar explorers. Later he uses polar exploration as a figure of speech to bring out the adventurous nature of his own activities. This gets tied up with smoking since he supposes that even polar explorers smoke sometimes, and so his own cigars, real objects in the novel, become what might be called symbolic properties, symbolic of inward-looking self-exploration induced by the narcotic effects of smoking. These objects and references, later shortened to metaphors or similes, reinforce the extended metaphor underlying the whole novel. The title of the novel renders explicit the metaphorical connection between the physical adventure of climbing a mountain and spiritual and intellectual exploration.

Perhaps the most striking examples of extended metaphor

in the whole of twentieth-century fiction are some of Kafka's stories. The metaphor in *Die Verwandlung*, for example, becomes explicit when the old charwoman addresses Gregor as 'Mistkäfer', recalling the common term of abuse 'Mistvieh', but in Gregor's case literally correct. The machine in *In der Strafkolonie* is so designed that its victims may 'etwas am eigenen Leibe spüren'. Perhaps most ingenious of all is *Ein Hungerkünstler*. The structure and every detail of this story depend on a logical working-out of the inherent contradictions in a literal 'art' of 'hungering', a circus metaphor for a particular kind of alienation and the attempt to turn this experience into an art. In his *Brief an den Vater*, Kafka writes of the terrible impression the violent metaphors of his father's language made on him as a child, metaphors such as: 'Ich zerreiße dich wie ein Fisch'.[1] It is a paradox of unfailing fascination that the 'literal metaphors' of Kafka terrify by the physical intensity they lend to his visions, yet are one of the main shaping, controlling devices of his art.

It could perhaps be argued that any novel is an extended metaphor for a meaning which could not be expressed in any other way, not a dead metaphor of the kind Kafka resurrects so disconcertingly, but a unique objective correlative for a unique combination of emotions, attitudes, mental experiences—those of the author—which should, if the metaphor works, be realized again in the reader. This is surely to over-extend the term, and the problems such an argument raises lead away from literary criticism into theory of criticism, philosophical aesthetics, psychology . . .

To close, here is an excerpt from Broch's *Die Schlafwandler* to illustrate the interaction of imagery, extended metaphor and symbolism. It comes from the second part of the trilogy, called *Esch oder die Anarchie*. The main character, Esch, is a book-keeper troubled by the injustice he sees all around him. He would like to 'balance society's books' by bringing more justice into the credit column to balance all the injustice on the debit side. The act of salvation he decides on is to save a girl called Ilona, a symbol to him of all oppressed humanity, from her life in the circus as target for a knife-thrower. To achieve this he too enters the world of vaudeville, and waiting in the office of a theatrical agent called Oppenheimer he sees a calendar on the wall with a

---

[1] *Hochzeitsvorbereitungen auf dem Lande und andere Prosa aus dem Nachlaß* (Frankfurt a.M., 1953), p. 177.

picture of an ocean-going liner. A few more paragraphs follow and then with no further introduction, Broch opens a new section of the narrative as follows:

Wenn ein braver Mann nach Amerika auswandert, dann stehen seine Verwandten und Freunde am Kai und winken dem Scheidenden mit ihren Taschentüchern. Die Schiffskapelle spielt 'Muß i denn, muß i denn zum Städtle hinaus', und mag man dies angesichts der Regelmäßigkeit der Ausfahrten auch als eine gewisse Scheinheiligkeit des Kapellmeisters betrachten, so greift es doch vielen ans Gemüt. Spannt sich dann das Seil zu dem kleinen Schlepper, schwimmt dann der Ozeanriese auf dem dunklen tragenden Spiegel, dann tönt über das Wasser spärlich und verloren noch immer das blecherne Zirpen lustigerer Weisen, mit denen der besorgte Kapellmeister die Scheidenden aufzuheitern sich bemüht. Dann wird manchem klar, wie schütter die Menschen über die Erd- und Wasseroberfläche verstreut sind und daß es zwischen ihnen nur ganz dünne Fäden gibt, die von dem einen zum anderen hinüberreichen. Wenn der Ozeanriese aus dem Hafen gleitet, das Wasser unter ihm farbloser wird und die Strömung des Flusses nicht mehr erkennbar ist und es gar aussieht, als hätte die Strömung sich gedreht und das Meer ströme in den Hafen hinein, dann schwimmt der Ozeanriese oft in einer großen Wolke unsichtbarer, dennoch gespannter Angst, so daß viele ihn zurückhalten wollen. An den Schiffen vorbei, die längs der rauchigen verwahrlosten Ufer liegen und ihre Krane rasselnd drehen lassen, unbestimmte Dinge zu unbestimmten Zwecken ein- und ausladen, vorbei an den verwahrlosten Ufern, die flußabwärts mit staubigem Grün sich bedecken und in einer kargen Ländlichkeit endigen, vorbei schließlich an den Dünen, wo man den Leuchtturm schon sieht, wird der Ozeanriese gezogen, gefesselt an seinen kleinen Wächter wie ein Ausgestoßener, und auf den Schiffen und an den Ufern stehen Menschen, die zusehen, wie dies geschieht, die Hand heben, als wollten sie ihn zurückhalten, es aber doch bloß zu einem schwächlichen und steif unbeholfenen Winken bringen. Schwimmt er dann weit draußen, verschwunden fast sein Rumpf in der Linie des Horizontes, kaum mehr seine drei Schlote sichtbar, so fragt sich mancher, der von der Küste aufs Meer hinausschaut, ob das Schiff dem Hafen zustrebt oder in eine Einsamkeit hinausgeht, die der Mensch am Ufer nie erfassen kann. Stellt man dann fest, daß es den Kurs zur Küste hält, dann ist ein jeder beruhigt, als trage ihm jenes Schiff ein Liebstes zu oder wenigstens einen Brief, auf den er lange gewartet hat, ohne es zu wissen. Manchmal treffen sich dort draußen in dem lichten Nebel der Grenze zwei Schiffe und man sieht, wie sie aneinander vorübergleiten. Da ist ein Augenblick, in dem die beiden zarten Silhouetten ineinander verschwimmen und eins werden, ein Augenblick von zarter Erhabenheit, bis sie sich sanft wieder voneinander lösen, so still und sanft wie der ferne Nebel, in dem dies geschieht, und jedes für sich wieder seine Bahn allein weitergleitet. Süße, nie erfüllte Hoffnung.

Doch der, der draußen auf dem Schiffe ist, weiß nicht, daß wir um ihn gebangt haben. Er sieht kaum den schwimmenden welligen Streifen der Küste und nur wenn er wie von ungefähr den gelblichen Strich des Leuchtturmes errät, weiß er, daß hier am Land noch welche sind, die um ihn bangen und an seine Gefahr denken. Er versteht nicht die Gefahr, in der er sich doch befindet, ist sich nicht bewußt, daß ein hoher Wasserberg ihn von dem Meeresgrunde trennt, der Erde ist. Nur wer Ziele hat, fürchtet die Gefahr, denn er fürchtet um das Ziel. Er aber geht über die glatten Schiffsplanken, die wie eine Radrennbahn im Kreise um das Deck herumführen und die ebener sind als alle Wege, die er bisher gegangen ist. Wer auf dem Meere ist, hat kein Ziel und vermag nicht sich zu vollenden; er ist abgeschlossen in sich. Was in ihm möglich ist, ruht. Wer ihn liebt, kann es bloß tun für das, was er verspricht, für das, was in ihm liegt, nicht für das, was er erreichen wird oder erreicht hat; er wird es nie erreichen. Darum weiß der Mensch auf dem Lande nicht, was Liebe ist und hält seine Angst für Liebe. Der Seereisende aber erkennt dies bald und die Fäden, die sich von ihm zu denen am Ufer hinübergespannt hatten, reißen ab, noch ehe die Küste versinkt. Fast ist es überflüssig, daß der Kapellmeister ihn durch seine Weisen aufheitere, denn dem Seereisenden genügt es, die Hand über die glatten braunpolierten Hölzer und die glänzenden Messingbeschläge gleiten zu lassen. Die blinkende See spannt sich vor ihm; er ist zufrieden. Mächtige Maschinen treiben ihn und ihr Dröhnen weist den Weg, der nirgendshin führt. Der Blick des Seereisenden ist anders geworden, es ist ein verwaister Blick, der uns nicht mehr kennt. Was einst Aufgabe war, der Seereisende hat es vergessen, er glaubt nicht mehr an die Richtigkeit der Addition von Kolonnen, und wenn ihn sein Weg bei der Kabine des Telegraphisten vorbeiführt und er hört das Ticken der Apparate, so bewundert er wohl die Mechanik, aber er kann nicht begreifen, daß jener damit Botschaft vom Lande empfängt, Botschaft zum Lande sendet, und wäre der Seereisende nicht ein nüchterner Mensch, er meinte, daß jener mit dem Weltall spreche. Er liebt die Walfische und die Delphine, die das Schiff umspielen, und er fürchtet nicht die Eisberge. Aber taucht eine ferne Küste auf, so will er sie nicht sehen und er verkriecht sich vielleicht im Bauche des Schiffes, bis jene wieder entschwunden ist, weiß er doch, daß ihn dort nicht Liebe erwartet, nicht Gelöstheit und Freiheit, sondern gespannte Angst und die Mauer des Zieles. Wer aber Liebe sucht, sucht das Meer: er spricht vielleicht noch von dem Lande, das jenseits des Meeres liegt, aber er meint es nicht, denn unermeßlich denkt er die Fahrt, Hoffnung der einsamen Seele, sich zu öffnen und aufzunehmen die andere, die im lichten Nebel auftaucht und einströmt in ihn, den Losgelösten, ihn erkennend als das Seiende, Ungeborene und Unsterbliche, das er ist.

So dachte Esch sicherlich nicht, wenn er auch von dem Gedanken besessen blieb, nach Amerika auszuwandern und die Buchhalter der Mittelrheinischen auf das Schiff mitzunehmen. Doch wenn er in das Büro des Herrn Oppenheimer kam, so betrachtete er lange und eindringlich die 'Kaiserin Augusta Victoria', wie sie die Wellen durchschneidet.

(Esch II, pp. 239–42)

This description of ships, by its length and its lack of connection with the immediate realistic context—a separation underlined by the last two sentences—stands out immediately as significant. It has the force of an extended epic simile, except that Broch omits the link phrase: 'So wie wenn ...' and does not immediately provide the second half of the equation: 'so ...'. The second half is in fact the action and characters of his novel. Just as the Homeric simile conjures up an unchanging universal order embracing and rendering coherent the apparent chaos of human struggle, so Broch's image of the ships conjures up a metaphysical truth underlying the empirical surface of events. This metaphysical truth is the ultimate isolation of man, his exposed existential condition. Man seeks to build harbours or havens of security, but like the ships, at certain times in history the half-realization of his ultimate exposure drives him out of all harbours, out of all traditional beliefs and systems. He may reach a new harbour—an 'America'—but it too can be only provisional. Human life is a lonely journey, even the union with another individual through love is a transitory condition, a 'süße nie erfüllte Hoffnung'. The inexorable silent gliding of the ships recalls the innumerable other images of gliding throughout the novel and the gliding motion of the sleepwalkers of the title, a metaphor comparable to the ships in our extract.

8   Tone

Tone is that quality or timbre of voice which reveals to the listener the feelings and attitude of a speaker, quite apart from what is actually said. In principle tone has three elements, though in practice these tend to merge into one another: the underlying feeling of a speaker about what he is saying; the attitude he wishes to project, which may be rather different; finally his assumptions about his audience, which may affect the manner and means he chooses to project an attitude. In practice it is difficult to distinguish between feeling and projected attitude. Since we have no direct access to another person's mind we are limited to a mixture of the two elements as mediated in words. Sometimes the attitude towards the listener may help. For example, if someone says something in a blustering tone there is an undertone of uncertainty about what he is saying, disguised by an overtone of dogmatic certainty which the speaker considers appropriate in addressing someone he is determined to impress. On the whole, however, the elements are so intertwined that it is sufficient to speak of simple or mixed tones. In the blustering tone, the un-uncertainty probably applies not only to what is being said, but also to whether the listener will be impressed, while the projected certainty has not come over as such. It has been affected by the underlying uncertainty. Each element modifies the other.

With no voice to help, establishing the tone of a piece of writing becomes a matter of teasing out from the written words emotional undercurrents and rhetorical elements. In other words, when it comes to written communication, the tone must be carried by the words themselves and is an integral part of the meaning. The intention of the writer as a historical person is not only difficult or even impossible to establish, it is largely irrelevant. What matters is not whether we can tell an author's true feelings and attitude from his tone, but in what way the tone modifies the meaning of the work. In practice the tone of a work probably often does reflect the feelings and intentions of its author, but even so these feelings and intentions have of necessity—and often as a deliberate dramatic device—become objectified, in the work, into a stance. It is sufficient to establish the stance of the work, as it emerges through its tone, and leave the *author* to biographers and psychologists.

Tone in writing has three elements corresponding to those of speech, elements equally difficult to keep separate. Corresponding to the feelings of a speaker is the emotional content of a passage of writing. This is as much a part of the meaning as factual or conceptual content. Corresponding to the projected attitude of a speaker are any rhetorical or persuasive elements which may emphasise or modify its emotional content and hence its total meaning. Finally a piece of writing may have a particular public 'in mind' corresponding to a listener, and this may affect the choice of rhetorical means, and even the quality of the emotional content.

Tone is an aspect of point of view. If a piece of writing is neutral in tone, this means that while we may know the physical angle of vision—a scientist describing an experiment for example —or the identity of the person or persons it purports to emanate from—for example post-office regulations—there is no point of view or attitude in the psychological sense. Neutrality of tone is rare in fiction, especially over a whole work, and often apparently neutral descriptive and informative passages have a subtle tonal flavour. This is because a writer, even if simply describing a location, is often trying to establish an atmosphere, or to make some kind of point, and so will guide his reader's reactions in an appropriate direction. Here is a fairly obvious example of a piece of description with emotional undertones and projected attitude with a specific audience in mind. It comes from near the beginning of Heimito von Doderer's long novel *Die Strudlhofstiege*:

Mary war beim Teetisch gesessen, den Blick draußen in der kaum beginnenden Dämmerung eines Nachsommer-Abends. Man sah hier eine Gasse entlang und dann über den Donau-Kanal (der kein Kanal ist, sondern ein erheblicher, breiter und tiefer, rasch fließender Teil des Stromes) hinüber ans andere Ufer. Von der Straße kam das Rufen der Buben beim Spiel bis hier herauf in den dritten Stock, ein allabendliches Geräusch, das durch den ganzen Sommer geleitete, soweit man ihn nicht in Pörtschach oder Millstatt verbracht hatte, ein Geräusch, das am Abend nach der Rückkehr vom Lande einen begrüßte als ein verläßlich dagebliebenes, zur Jahreszeit gehöriges, und das jetzt noch durch Wochen anhielt, denn es blieb warm, wenn auch gemäßigter: das beste Tenniswetter, wie Oskar sagte, der 'Indianersommer'. Oskar wird in einer halben Stunde kommen. (Part I, p. 12)

From its tone one could make a guess about the kind of work this passage comes from. The tone is that of someone setting the scene of a drama about to commence, suggested by the shift to the future tense in the last sentence. The tone invites intimacy. We are on first-name terms with the characters—we never hear Oskar's surname—while the reference to Pörtschach and Millstatt, with no further explanation, suggests that the narrator, the characters, and no doubt the reader, come from that circle of people who spend the summer out of the city and who know all about these places, a circle of tennis-playing people who drink tea of an afternoon. The novel is probably a human drama, probably social comedy for one does not associate tea and tennis with tragedy. Or is it perhaps a tragi-comedy? There is a trace of autumnal melancholy in the qualification 'kaum beginnend' and the hyphenating of 'Nachsommer' and 'Abend': a beautiful hovering moment between winter and night. There is too an undertone of loving celebration of a city in the insistence that the Donau-Kanal is no mere canal, a loving pleasure taken in the city-sounds of children at play, suggested by the colloquial word 'Buben'. The city too has its seasonal round of sounds no less beautiful than the bird-song of the country. This faint lyrical and celebratory undertone then modulates into one of perhaps indulgent amusement at Oskar, who takes such a hearty unlyrical attitude to the city summer, who thinks in terms of tennis.

The passage is, in fact, typical of *Die Strudlhofstiege*, a tragi-comedy of Viennese life and a celebration of the city of Vienna, told by a narrator who is obviously part of that society to a reader who will understand, who even knows some of the fringe characters personally, though he is not acquainted with the main actors. The faint hint of a producer setting a scene is typical, for there is a baroque theatricality in this elaborate comedy of errors with some tragic consequences. Descriptions of location often carry a suggestion of stage scenery, notably the Strudlhofstiege itself, a little staircase connecting different street levels. It is the point where all the threads cross and the characters meet in shifting groups or ensembles to 'sing', as it were, against a charming backcloth of steps and lamplight shining through trees. At such points the narrator's tone adds to the theatrical effect, takes on a heightened celebratory note of one who both loves and enjoys his creatures.

As this passage shows, tone derives from all the minutiæ of style, from this adjective, that unexpected metaphor, from the register of the language and from the context within the work as a whole. Generally the reader is aware intuitively of a tone, without need of close analysis to see how this or that effect is achieved. But often it is necessary to see a particular passage within the context of the whole work before deciding finally on the quality of the tone. *Die Blendung* by Elias Canetti is a case in point. Unlike Doderer's novel, which is constantly suffused with emotional undercurrents, Canetti's work is at first sight virtually toneless. It seems cold, inhuman, at any rate disconcerting.

Die Blendung tells the story of a great scholar of Chinese civilization called Kien. He has devoted his whole life to things of the mind. The pattern of his life is shattered when in middle age he makes the terrible mistake of marrying his housekeeper, a rapacious female whose rage knows no bounds when the marriage turns out disappointing both sexually and financially. Kien decides to freeze her out of his life again—quite literally—by 'petrifying' himself. He will remain motionless, silent, unmoved like a stone. But when his wife Therese decides at last to take his bankbook by force and in searching his desk disturbs his precious manuscripts, his resolve breaks down:

Plötzlich erhebt sich Kien und fällt mit Wucht auf Therese. Er bleibt ganz stumm, die Lippen zwickt er sich mit den Zähnen, einer Zange, zu; spricht er, ist er kein Stein, die Zähne beißen tief in die Zunge hinein. 'Wo ist das Bankbuch?' schreit gellend Therese, bevor sie zerbricht. 'Wo ist das Bankbuch? Säufer — Verbrecher — Dieb!' Das Bankbuch hat sie gesucht. Er lächelt über ihre letzten Worte.

Es sind aber nicht die letzten. Sie greift nach seinem Kopf und stößt ihn gegen den Schreibtisch. Sie schlägt ihre Ellbogen zwischen seine Rippen. Sie schreit: 'Hinaus aus meiner Wohnung!' Sie speit, sie speit in sein Gesicht. Er spürt alles. Es tut weh. Er ist kein Stein. Da sie nicht zerbricht, zerbricht seine Kunst. Alles ist Lüge, es gibt keinen Glauben. Es gibt keinen Gott. Er weicht aus. Er wehrt sich. Er schlägt zurück. Er trifft sie, er hat spitze Knochen ... (*Die Erstarrung*, p. 146)

In the end Therese wins, throws him out, throws out his coat, hat and briefcase. But he has the bankbook in his pocket.

The whole novel maintains this style of short jerky sentences, most untypical of literary German. There are no clues to the narrator's attitude, no undercurrent of feeling is perceptible. Except for factual information—'sie greift nach seinem Kopf'—everything reflects the point of view of Kien. And this point of view is scarcely presented in a very involving way. The short sentences, the abrupt transitions rob the presentation of Kien's reactions of any emotional or persuasive qualities. The reader bounces breathlessly from sentence to sentence. It is more like a boxing commentary than an insight into the mysteries of the human mind. This effect comes, of course, not just from the syntax but from the meaning of the passage. It is clear that Kien expects Therese to shatter when he first attacks her: ' "Wo ist das Bankbuch?" schreit gellend Therese, bevor sie zerbricht.' Therese wears very stiffly starched skirts, so stiff they appear brittle. Kien takes her to be brittle all through because of her surface appearance, as if she were a vase perhaps, not a human being. His strategy of freezing her out of his life is not calculated to arouse natural understanding and sympathy in the reader. We may harden ourselves against an enemy, but we do not generally harden to the point of trying to turn literally to stone. And so the terrible discovery: 'Er ist kein Stein', arouses laughter not sympathy.

Kien and Therese are each in their way monstrous, scarcely human at all. The neutral tone of the narration actively dehumanizes them so that we are prevented from an emotional involvement. If Doderer's *Strudlhofstiege* is social comedy with an operatic element, Canetti's *Die Blendung* is satire with an element of savage farce. Is not this description of two people banging each other about reminiscent of slapstick? The short galvanic sentences are the verbal equivalent of the frenetic movements of farce. Are not the grotesque suggestions of a brittle woman and a stone-hard man reminiscent of cinema cartoons or horror comics? The reader feels as little concern about the possible shattering of Therese by a stone-hard Kien, as he would for, say, a flattened, immediately reconstituted cat in a *Tom and Jerry* cartoon. Farce is uncaring, amoral, sometimes savage, a descent into the world of the *id*, an irresponsible holiday from civilized restraints, where violence has no real consequences because its objects are not really human. *Die Blendung* is so disconcerting because it is *not* in the end amoral and uncaring, because the farce has a point. It is a means of satire, satire of a society in which 'farce' threatens to obtrude into reality, in which an all too real violence is about to erupt because the forces of 'civilized restraint' are bankrupt. The grotesque marriage of Kien and Therese symbolizes a diseased civilization marked by total dissociation between an atrophied 'higher' culture and the brute realities of human frustration, violence and acquisitiveness.

Die Blendung, then, is not neutral in tone in the same way as a scientific paper. Its apparent tonelessness is rather a means of satire, and while at any point in the texture the tone can be called neutral, the cumulative effect is quite the opposite. To put it paradoxically, Canetti uses a rhetoric of anti-rhetoric. His seeming neutrality is a battle cry against the forces of destruction.

At the opposite extreme from such indirectness is the obtrusive tone of overt rhetoric. Take the following passage:

> Furchtbare Stunde des Todes und der Zeugung! furchtbare Stunde des Absoluten, getragen und ertragen von einem Geschlecht, das sich ausgelöscht hat, das nichts von der Unendlichkeit weiß, in die es durch seine eigene Logik getrieben wird — unbelehrt, hilflos, sinnlos sind sie dem Orkan des Eisigen preisgegeben, sie müssen vergessen, um leben zu können, und sie wissen nicht, warum sie sterben. Ihr Weg ist der Weg Ahasvers, ihre Pflicht ist Ahasvers Pflicht, ihre Freiheit ist die Freiheit des Gehetzten und ihr Ziel ist das Vergessen. Verlorenes Geschlecht! (*Huguenau*, 88, p. 684)

Whatever it may mean, there is no mistaking the tone of high pathos produced by the rhythmic prose, the repetitions, the crescendo of adjectives: 'unbelehrt, hilflos, sinnlos', the punctuation of exclamation marks. Here is no emotional undercurrent but a raging torrent, no subtly projected attitude but keening lament. Faced by this in a 'Place the Quotation' competition one might be tempted to turn it into an ode by dividing it into lines. It is certainly a tone more suggestive of lyric poetry than of narrative prose, but this tone is an essential element in the art of Hermann Broch and the passage comes from the end of *Die Schlafwandler*. Broch is saying something not so very different from Canetti about a world on the verge of apocalyptic disaster, but saying it in a very different way.

Rather like Wagner, Broch aspires to a kind of *Gesamtkunstwerk*. He tries to combine in one work the epic, lyric and dramatic modes, and to cover the gamut of tone from scientific neutrality, to objective dramatization of the feelings and attitudes of his characters, to the naked expression of emotion. Sharp tonal contrast is a striking element in the structure of his novel. *Die Strudlhofstiege* and *Die Blendung*, on the other hand, are fairly uniform in tone, though particularly in *Die Strudlhofstiege*, this dominant tone is itself very complex. It is a blend of subtle, constantly changing shades of emotion and mixed attitudes, shot-silk to Broch's more violent primary contrasts.

Tone is a very general term. It denotes the combined effect of many aspects of writing, which cannot finally be separated from each other, the effect of the whole manner of narration including handling of register, point of view, details of style and presentation. The examples quoted above show how the tone of a novel is crucial in determining its final impact. To call Doderer's *Strudlhofstiege* a tragi-comedy, for example, is largely to generalize about its overall tone. The multiple tones of Broch's *Die Schlafwandler* are less easy to summarize. His is a work which does not fit into any traditional category. It moves through the modes from didactic comedy to metaphysical tragedy, to lament. But perhaps the tone that finally dominates, that reverberates longest though it is most sparingly employed, is the lyric tone of lament. In such passages the tonal elements of feeling and attitude are most emancipated from the task of narrating, or informing. Pure expression is all.

To close, here is a passage from Kafka's story *Bericht für eine Akademie*. It may seem an odd choice since it comes not from a novel but from a dramatic monologue delivered to a specific audience. But, because of this, it illustrates particularly clearly the three basic ingredients of tone: underlying emotion, projected attitude, and the effect on these of having a specific audience in mind. The *Bericht* in question is the report of an ape who has adapted himself to human life in order to escape from imprisonment in a cage after he has been captured from the jungle by sailors. The *Akademie* is presumably a body of learned scientists who are expecting to hear about the ape's former existence in the jungle. But the ape tells them he has already forgotten his past life and describes instead the process of his transformation into a being fit for human society. On the ship he learns to imitate human beings, to shake hands, to spit, to drink brandy and to 'ape' human pleasure in alcohol by rubbing his belly and grinning even though he dislikes its taste. He even manages to say 'Hello'—his first venture into speech. He does not like human ways, but it is the only way out of the cage. Then the ship berths in Hamburg:

Als ich in Hamburg dem ersten Dresseur übergeben wurde, erkannte ich bald die zwei Möglichkeiten, die mir offenstanden: Zoologischer Garten oder Varieté. Ich zögerte nicht. Ich sagte mir: setze alle Kraft an, um ins Varieté zu kommen; das ist der Ausweg; Zoologischer Garten ist nur ein neuer Gitterkäfig; kommst du in ihn, bist du verloren.

Und ich lernte, meine Herren. Ach, man lernt, wenn man muß; man lernt, wenn man einen Ausweg will; man lernt rücksichtslos. Man beaufsichtigt sich selbst mit der Peitsche; man zerfleischt sich beim geringsten Widerstand. Die Affennatur raste, sich überkugelnd, aus mir hinaus und weg, so daß mein erster Lehrer selbst davon fast äffisch wurde, bald den Unterricht aufgeben und in eine Heilanstalt gebracht werden mußte. Glücklicherweise kam er wieder bald hervor.

Aber ich verbrauchte viele Lehrer, ja sogar einige Lehrer gleichzeitig. Als ich meiner Fähigkeiten schon sicherer geworden war, die Öffentlichkeit meinen Fortschritten folgte, meine Zukunft zu leuchten begann, nahm ich selbst Lehrer auf, ließ sie in fünf aufeinanderfolgenden Zimmern niedersetzen und lernte bei allen zugleich, indem ich ununterbrochen aus einem Zimmer ins andere sprang.

Diese Fortschritte! Dieses Eindringen der Wissensstrahlen von allen Seiten ins erwachende Hirn! Ich leugne nicht: es beglückte mich. Ich gestehe aber auch ein: ich überschätzte es nicht, schon damals nicht, wieviel weniger heute. Durch eine Anstrengung, die sich bisher auf der Erde nicht wiederholt hat, habe ich die Durchschnittsbildung eines Europäers erreicht. Das wäre an sich vielleicht gar nichts, ist aber insofern doch etwas, als es mir aus dem Käfig half und mir diesen besonderen Ausweg, diesen Menschenausweg verschaffte. Es gibt eine ausgezeichnete deutsche Redensart: sich in die Büsche schlagen; das habe ich getan, ich habe mich in die Büsche geschlagen. Ich hatte keinen anderen Weg, immer vorausgesetzt, daß nicht die Freiheit zu wählen war.

Überblicke ich meine Entwicklung und ihr bisheriges Ziel, so klage ich weder, noch bin ich zufrieden. Die Hände in den Hosentaschen, die Weinflasche auf dem Tisch, liege ich halb, halb sitze ich im Schaukelstuhl und schaue aus dem Fenster. Kommt Besuch, empfange ich ihn, wie es sich gebührt. Mein Impresario sitzt im Vorzimmer; läute ich, kommt er und hört, was ich zu sagen habe. Am Abend ist fast immer Vorstellung, und ich habe wohl kaum mehr zu steigernde Erfolge. Komme ich spät nachts von Banketten, aus wissenschaftlichen Gesellschaften, aus gemütlichem Beisammensein nach Hause, erwartet mich eine kleine halbdressierte Schimpansin und ich lasse es mir nach Affenart bei ihr wohlgehen. Bei Tag will ich sie nicht sehen; sie hat nämlich den Irrsinn des verwirrten dressierten Tieres im Blick; das erkenne nur ich und ich kann es nicht ertragen.

Im Ganzen habe ich jedenfalls erreicht, was ich erreichen wollte. Man sage nicht, es wäre der Mühe nicht wert gewesen. Im übrigen will ich keines Menschen Urteil, ich will nur Kenntnisse verbreiten, ich berichte nur, auch Ihnen, hohe Herren von der Akademie, habe ich nur berichtet.

(Erzählungen, pp. 162–4)

The situation—a gifted, self-educated speaker addressing a learned congress—determines the dominant register. The style is a mixture of the colloquial with occasional more elevated turns of phrase, such as 'Dieses Eindringen der Wissensstrahlen'. The speaker is not himself an expert, but speaks with the ease and fluency of one who knows that he is providing unique material for experts. He wishes to give them the benefit of his inside knowledge and so combines colloquial presentation of his inner reactions with a summarizing account of his progress in more impersonal terms.

What is his attitude towards his audience and how does he project his own personality in addressing them? At first sight he seems to be trying, in a man-to-man way, to convey to them his strange experience. He apparently assumes their sympathetic understanding. 'Und ich lernte, meine Herren. Ach, man lernt, wenn man muß'. The tone here is of someone who knows his listeners will appreciate what he has gone through. Although he faces a prestigious audience he places himself on an equal footing with them—indeed on a more than equal footing. Far from being abashed, a note of arrogance creeps in at times. He has achieved something none of his audience ever could for all their expertise. And yet he does not rate this achievement very highly. For him, to be a human being, even an educated human being, is only a second best, a way out of an intolerable situation. The undertone of contempt for his achievement surely applies also to his audience —they too mere educated human beings. By the end of the story a sardonic note of false humility is present as he addresses these 'Hohe Herren', for they can never understand his experience, still less presume to judge him.

What are the underlying feelings of the speaker towards what he is recounting? The note of pride in his success story is false, there only for the benefit of his audience. A much stronger undertone is contempt of his way of life, of his great achievement, of himself. The ape who swung, magnificent and free, through the jungle now sits in a rocking-chair and follows a routine. A strong but controlled undertone of pain and suffering is evident.

The violent metaphors: 'Man beaufsichtigt sich mit der Peitsche; man zerfleischt sich beim geringsten Widerstand' imply a suffering beyond description, all the more so since the ape has trained for a music-hall act so that the metaphors have a shade of literal meaning recalling the cruelty of animal training. This suffering is controlled by resignation, a subterranean sense of humour and a reluctant pleasure in some human characteristics. The ambivalence of his attitude comes out particularly clearly when he says: 'Durch eine Anstrengung, die sich bisher auf der Erde nicht wiederholt hat, habe ich die Durchschnittsbildung eines Europäers erreicht. Das wäre an sich vielleicht gar nichts, ist aber insofern doch etwas, als es mir aus dem Käfig half, diesen besonderen Ausweg, diesen Menschenausweg verschaffte.' His sense of humour, of self-irony, comes out in the admission that his immense effort has led only to an *average* standard of education. Yet his contempt is modified by his recognition that this despised way of life is at least tolerable and even has its intellectual pleasures. The emotional undertones of the passage are, then, a disturbing mixture of pain, resignation, contempt, ironic self-mockery. If his attitude towards the audience is ironic flattery concealing contempt, the emotions aroused in him by his own history are more complex, the irony concealing an ambivalent confusion of feelings.

But, of course, the reader of Kafka's story is not quite in the same position as the 'hohe Herren der Akademie' faced by the man-ape. So far we have accepted the situation at its face value. But the most disturbing aspect of the tone comes from the circumstance that this self-educated fluent speaker is an ape. Is Kafka writing science fiction? Surely not. When the ape says: 'Es gibt eine ausgezeichnete deutsche Redensart: sich in die Büsche schlagen; das habe ich getan, mich in die Büsche geschlagen', the reader is struck by the oddity of this. Generally animals escape into bushes *away from* human beings. Here is an animal who has emerged from bushes and escapes *into* the society of human beings. This paradoxical twist to a common turn of phrase may remind the reader of another common metaphor underlying the whole story: the expression 'nachäffen'. Kafka conveys with peculiar vividness the experience of imitating an unnatural, totally alien mode of life in order to survive. He does so by a sustained metaphor: an ape so brilliant at 'aping' that he becomes virtually human.

Apart from the surface tone of the ape, is there any tonal

D

indication, however submerged, of the author's attitude towards someone, embodied here as an ape, who must go through such contortions to find a *modus vivendi*? The main additional quality in the tone, indicating the author's attitude, is surely an intensification of the elements already noted in the ape's tone: self-contempt, self-irony, intense but controlled suffering, grim humour, a defensive refusal to be judged or pitied.

The author's attitude towards someone who conforms with ordinary human behaviour against all the demands of his nature clearly has an element of contempt. He has chosen an ape to embody such a person, an animal whose physical appearance is a grotesque caricature of the human form, whose semi-human behaviour evokes laughter in zoos. It is an immense achievement for an ape to acquire 'die Durchschnittsbildung eines Europäers'. But if we take the *ape* as a metaphor, there is something ludicrous about a *person* for whom such 'average' achievement demands such unaverage effort. The attitude towards the sexual behaviour of the ape takes on an extra note of contempt if the word 'Affenart' is applied, not literally to an ape, but metaphorically to 'bestial' human behaviour.

But if the author is contemptuous of the ape, surely he also identifies with the ape's suffering. The note of suffering in the story is intensified if its metaphorical quality is appreciated. The very extreme transition from animal to man brings out with shocking vividness the horror of life for someone to whom the normal modes of human behaviour are unnatural and alien. It brings out the horror of a choice between total isolation or constant pretence demanding inconceivable 'inhuman' effort. The tone of the story, then, despite the grotesque humour, the ironic mockery of the ape-man, remains finally ambivalent, so strong is the identification with the ape's suffering. Indeed, the greater the mockery, the greater the suffering, for what could be more bitter than to appear ludicrous because of the very contortions of pain. The mockery is held in balance by the suffering of the man within the ape, by the dignity of his refusal of either pity or condemnation.

Kafka's story is an example of a work where tone is all-important. It shows too how no amount of generalizing can cover all the subtleties of particular works. It is a story which shifts disconcertingly, from satire, to tragedy, to farce, to savage comedy. It is at once deeply moving, horribly comic and perfectly controlled.

9   Character

Theorists of the novel from Cicero onwards concentrated on two categories: plot and character. The most famous aspects of E. M. Forster's book are his distinction on the one hand between 'story' and 'plot' and on the other between 'flat' and 'round' characters; Edwin Muir spoke of 'Novels of Action' and 'Novels of Character', Wolfgang Kayser of 'Geschehnisromane' and 'Figurenromane' (according to the dominating element). In this approach one must probably see the influence of drama theories, for the drama was, especially in Germany and right into the twentieth century, a much more respectable genre than the novel: in 1889 Gottfried Keller castigated the decadence of an age which was preparing to celebrate his seventieth birthday although he had never in his life managed to write a drama, and even Thomas Mann reports the mistrust with which a mere novelist was viewed by the academic critics of his early days. Since today the emphasis is if anything on the other side, features such as point of view and tempo, which are more specific to the novel, now receive greater attention. But the demotion of plot and character has another reason: the scepticism with which the modern novelist himself views these categories. And since plot—actions and events—depends on people, characters, the oft-heard lament of the modern reader, 'why can't they write any good stories nowadays?', is perhaps best answered in the words of Gottfried Benn:

> Warum Gedanken in jemanden hineinkneten, in eine Figur, in Gestalten, wenn es Gestalten nicht mehr gibt? Personen, Namen, Beziehungen erfinden, wenn sie gerade unerheblich werden? (*Roman des Phänotyp, Der Stundengott*, p. 154)

The novel was born in the great age of the individual—in many ways it is the middle-class genre, the product of the 'liberal imagination'. Traditionally it was expected to present model figures—the German *Bildungsroman* is the clearest example of this. The twentieth century, on the other hand, is the age of mass industrial society, standardization and great collective movements, the age of the debunking of historical heroes. Against Benn's statement, however, must be set Hermann Hesse's declaration that the art of 'übermorgen' will no longer be 'eine Darstellung von Geschehnissen und Beziehungen zwischen handelnden Menschen ... , sondern nur die Offenbarung des inneren Seelenraumes eines einzelnen, einsamen Menschen',[1] and his description of his own works as 'eine Verteidigung (zuweilen auch als Notschrei) der Persönlichkeit, des Individuums'.[2] These two positions may be taken as symptomatic of the age; both Benn and Hesse point to the problematic position of individual character, although they draw the opposite conclusions. In practice, characters or at least human beings are indispensable to the novel. Benn's own *Roman des Phänotyp* has indeed no plot nor story, no progression of events in time, but it does have a character, the 'Phänotyp' of the title, Benn himself or a projection of him, whose consciousness is reflected in the meditations and recollections of the novel. What is, therefore, interesting about this aspect of the modern novel is the peculiar twentieth-century conception of character—personality, individuality—and the way in which it becomes itself a theme of the novel.

One must always be sceptical about theories of the influence of scientific thinking on writers and artists. In general, art and science run parallel; often writers anticipate scientific thinking in their books. Nevertheless, the development of two new sciences about the beginning of the century does help us to understand the changes in the writer's conception of character. These were sociology and depth psychology. The former reduces the individual to a mere statistical item, meaningless in itself. Reality consists of collective processes; history is not made by a succession of great individuals, but is determined by the price of butter or the discovery of new means of production. In a sense, therefore, sociology puts into practice Marx's sixth Thesis on Feuerbach, in which he describes 'das menschliche Wesen' as 'das Ensemble der gesellschaftlichen Verhältnisse'; and since the novel has always been concerned with portraying society, the most important single aspect of character in the novel is man's relation to society. This will be examined in the chapter which follows. Nevertheless,

[1] Quoted by Fritz Strich, 'Dank an Hermann Hesse', in *Der Dichter und die Zeit. Eine Sammlung von Reden und Vorträgen* (Berne, 1947), p. 382.
[2] Letter of March 1954, in *Briefe*, neue, erweiterte Ausgabe (Frankfurt a.M., 1959) p. 446.

few novels succeed in presenting purely collective processes. Döblin's *Berge Meere und Giganten* perhaps comes closest to it, but even here we find a number of individually defined characters who are caught up in the futuristic upheavals which this novel relates. Where sociological attitudes are reflected in the twentieth-century novel is rather in the shift of attention from the outstanding individual to the minor figure. This is more pronounced in the field of drama, for the novel has always been concerned with 'ordinary people'. However, figures like Franz Biberkopf, a petty criminal, dominated by instinct, barely articulate, or Esch, the book-keeper hero of part of the *Schlafwandler* trilogy, would scarcely have become the centres of traditional novels. Important too is the typical passivity of the hero; talk rather than action is the keynote, a reflection perhaps of a general scepticism about the individual's ability to change his own environment. Many twentieth-century novels might be called, like Benn's *Roman des Phänotyp*, 'ein Roman im Sitzen' (*Bordeaux*, p. 182); the 'horizontale Lebenslage' of the characters in *Der Zauberberg* seems to take this one step further!

'Psychology' in literature is, of course, a very ancient concept. Friedrich von Blankenburg's *Versuch über den Roman* of 1774 included the demand that every detail of any novel should be psychologically motivated; such emphasis on the inner workings of the soul marks the development of the German *Bildungsroman* over the following century. The nineteenth century saw an ever-increasing refinement of the presentation of psychological subtleties, culminating in the early stories of Thomas Mann and Musil's *Die Verwirrungen des Zöglings Törleß*. A reaction against 'Seelenanalyse' set in about the time of Expressionism, however. Kafka's exclamation in his notes: 'Zum letzten Mal Psychologie!'[3] bears witness to this, as does the following passage from Döblin's Berlin programme 'An Romanautoren und ihre Kritiker':

> Immer war der Rationalismus der Tod der Kunst; der zudringlichste, meist gehätschelte Rationalismus heißt jetzt Psychologie. Viele als 'fein' verschrieene Romane, Novellen — vom Drama gilt dasselbe — bestehen fast nur aus Analyse von Gedankengängen der Akteure; es entstehen Konflikte innerhalb dieser Gedankenreihen, es kommt zu dürftigen oder hingepatzten 'Handlungen'. Solche Gedankengänge gibt es vielleicht, aber nicht so isoliert; sie besagen an sich nichts, sie sind nicht darstellbar, ein amputierter Arm; Atem ohne

---

[3] *Hochzeitsvorbereitungen*, p. 51.

den Menschen, der atmet; Blicke ohne Augen. Die wirklichen Motive kommen ganz anderswoher; dieses da, der lebendigen Totalität ermangelnd, ist Schaumschlägerei, ästhetisches Gequirle, Geschwafel eines doktinären, gelangweilten Autors, dem nichts einfällt, zu Gebildeten, die sich belehren lassen wollen.

Man lerne von der Psychiatrie, der einzigen Wissenschaft, die sich mit dem seelischen ganzen Menschen befaßt ... [4]

Döblin approved of 'psychiatry' because he believed it was not interested in why and how but contented itself with noting the facts. Depth psychology, as distinct from the traditional psychology which Döblin rejected, is reflected in modern novels in two main ways. The recognition that the decisive events in a man's life may be beneath the surface of his consciousness is seen in the first place in the frequency of irrational non-willed outbursts of activity in the novels and stories of Kafka, Hofmannsthal and Döblin, and especially in the domination of sexuality as opposed to 'love' in the modern novel in general, and in the second place in the direct presentation of subconscious processes in the various types of interior monologues and stream of consciousness narratives. Of course the works of Kafka cannot be *explained* by the theories of Freud, nor can the stream of consciousness narrative be explained by reference to William James; in both cases the forming, conscious will of the author has to be remembered. Nevertheless, both trends point to a new conception of character, one different from that of the nineteenth century and earlier, which emphasized rather the conscious will. Goethe's insistence on the exact correlation of 'Denken' and 'Tun' [5] expresses in a nutshell the classical harmony of body and mind, the inner and outer worlds. This harmony, as David Daiches has suggested, is reflected in the importance of external events for the traditional novel, the journey, marriage, the acquisition of property, all of which correspond to the inner action of the novel. [6] Hugo von Hofmannsthal's note: 'Das Tun setzt den Übergang aus dem Bewußten zum Unbewußten voraus', [7] suggests that this harmony has been lost. Accordingly, many modern novels show little external action at all.

A more general, 'philosophical' scepticism concerning character underlines the findings of sociology and psycho-analysis. The

[4] *Aufsätze zur Literatur*, ed. Walter Muschg (Olten/Freiburg i. Br., 1963), p. 16.
[5] E.g. *Wilhelm Meisters Wanderjahre*, Book II, Chapter 9.
[6] *The Present Age. After 1920* (London, 1958), p. 92.
[7] *Aufzeichnungen*, ed. Herbert Steiner (Frankfurt a.M., 1959), p. 226.

influence of Ernst Mach's philosophy, for example, may be seen in Hofmannsthal's dissolution of the individual character into the surrounding world:

> Wollen wir uns finden, so dürfen wir nicht in unser Inneres hinab-steigen: draußen sind wir zu finden, draußen. Wie der wesenlose Regenbogen spannt sich unsere Seele über den unaufhaltsamen Sturz des Daseins. Wir besitzen unser Selbst nicht: von außen weht es uns an, es flieht uns für lange und kehrt uns in einem Hauch zurück. Zwar — unser 'Selbst'! Das Wort ist solch eine Metapher. Regungen kehren zurück, die schon einmal früher hier genistet haben. Und sind sies auch wirklich selber wieder? Ist es nicht vielmehr nur ihre Brut, die von einem dunklen Heimatgefühl hierher zurückgetrieben wird? Genug, etwas kehrt wieder. Und etwas begegnet sich in uns mit anderem. Wir sind nicht mehr als ein Taubenschlag.[8]

Hofmannsthal concludes that under these premises it is infinitely difficult to write a drama or to sit in judgment on a murderer, since both of these activities imply acceptance of a conception of character as something stable, determinable and determining. Drama is clearly more limited in scope than the novel in analysing character. And the question of responsibility for one's actions, especially criminal actions, is one of the major themes of the unfinished novel *Der Mann ohne Eigenschaften* by Robert Musil, one of Hofmannsthal's fellow-countrymen, who wrote a dissertation on Mach. In this novel it forms part of an exhaustive discussion of character. The hero, Ulrich, is a 'Möglichkeitsmensch', more concerned with potentiality than reality; at one point he—only half-jokingly—describes his ambition as to 'abolish reality' altogether (Book I, 69, p. 296). He takes a year's 'Urlaub von seinem Leben' (Book I, 14, p. 48), abandons what gives the majority of people their social reality, his profession, and later embarks on an incestuous relationship—again socially 'unreal'—with his sister Agathe. He demands 'daß man Geschichte erfinden müßte, daß man Ideen-, statt Weltgeschichte leben sollte, daß man sich dessen, was sich nie ganz verwirklichen läßt, zu bemächtigen und am Ende vielleicht so zu leben hätte, als wäre man kein Mensch, sondern bloß eine Gestalt in einem Buch, von der alles Unwesentliche fortgelassen ist, damit sich das übrige magisch zusammenschließe ...' (Book I, 116, pp. 605–6). One

[8] 'Das Gespräch über Gedichte', in *Prosa II*, ed. Herbert Steiner (Frankfurt a.M., 1951), pp. 82–3.

of his counterparts is Arnheim, the Prussian industrialist and writer, a man who appears to reconcile within himself all the spheres of twentieth-century life: politics, industry, literature, science. Arnheim models himself on Goethe, the 'Universalgenie' of an earlier age, and takes as his motto a paraphrase of Goethe's words: 'Denken, um zu tun; tun, um zu denken' (Book I, 112, p. 554). But in fact, Musil shows, this attempt to transpose the idyllic conditions of tiny, pre-capitalist Weimar into modern industrial society with its mammoth concerns and concealed interests is only a sham. Arnheim's writings are popular but superficial and an attempt to cover up the ruthlessness of the capitalist businessman with the sentimental veneer of another epoch. For Arnheim 'Tun' remains basic, his wealth is the prerequisite to his literature; his presence in Austria relates not to the Utopian ideals of the 'Parallelaktion' but to the oil concessions which he hopes to obtain. Ulrich is an intellectual; but it is not merely that he is interested in ideas, he is almost indifferent to the realization of his ideas. For this reason he is a 'man without qualities', since individual character is normally expressed in terms of what one *does* rather than what one believes, ideas being abstract and non-individual. At the same time he thereby moves into mystical proximity with the psychopath criminal Moosbrugger; the latter is barely responsible for his murders, Ulrich is indifferent to the catastrophes which may proceed from his ideas.

Musil's novel is in some ways the most radical example of what he calls the 'Auflösung des anthropozentrischen Verhaltens' (Book I, 39, p. 154). Essayistics, theory, the play of ideas form the basis of the novel rather than any development in terms of plot or individual character. Many other examples might be cited. The dialectic of the intellectual and the instinctual seen in the Ulrich-Moosbrugger constellation is, for example, a theme of Thomas Mann's *Doktor Faustus*: the extreme abstraction and intellectualism of Leverkühn's music is linked by implication with the barbarities of the Nazis and the Second World War. This theme recurs in Hermann Hesse's *Der Steppenwolf*. In Kafka's novels the hero's passivity, the endless deliberations on possible interpretations of the situation, are interrupted only by sudden outbursts of sordid sexuality. The important role of adolescents from *Törleß* to *Katz und Maus* can be explained in these terms too. Max Frisch (*Mein Name sei Gantenbein*) and Martin Walser

(*Halbzeit*) resolve the problem of the reality or unreality of individual character by the theory of 'Rollen'; we are what we decide we wish to be or what other people think we are; in this way the problem is transferred to a higher, self-conscious level: we are aware that individuality is a facade, nevertheless we do what is expected of us and pretend that it is not. Jakob Abs, the central character of Uwe Johnson's first novel, is the subject of 'Mutmaßungen'; the individual is ultimately unknowable. In *Die Blechtrommel* Günter Grass makes use of a kind of 'alienation effect'. The device of choosing as hero a dwarf, the inmate of a lunatic asylum, who claims to be possessed of various supernatural qualities, suggests that individuality itself is 'unreal', and yet allows the author to introduce the idiosyncrasies of an eccentric individual, the basis of so many traditional novels, as it were through the back door.

The following extract from Heinrich Böll's novel *Billard um halbzehn* illustrates some typical features of the portrayal of character in the twentieth century. *Billard um halbzehn* is told from five different points of view; in general, however, there is unity of perspective within each chapter. This feature, as suggested earlier, in itself points at an important aspect of character presentation— namely, isolation and lack of communication with others, with a consequent retreat into the self and its memories. The first chapter is told from the point of view of Leonore, Robert Fähmel's secretary, the second from that of the porter at the Hotel Prinz Heinrich, where he plays billiards every morning between half past nine and eleven o'clock. Our extract consists of the beginning of the third chapter, in which we meet Robert Fähmel himself.

Er spielte schon lange nicht mehr nach Regeln, wollte nicht Serien spielen, Points sammeln; er stieß eine Kugel an, manchmal sanft, manchmal hart, scheinbar sinnlos und zwecklos, sie hob, indem sie die beiden anderen berührte, für ihn jedesmal eine neue geometrische Figur aus dem grünen Nichts; Sternenhimmel, in dem nur wenige Punkte beweglich waren; Kometenbahnen; weiß über grün, rot über grün geschlagen, Spuren leuchteten auf, die sofort wieder ausgelöscht wurden; zarte Geräusche deuteten den Rhythmus der gebildeten Figur an: fünfmal, sechsmal, wenn die angestoßene Kugel die Bande oder die anderen Kugeln berührte; nur wenige Töne hoben sich aus der Monotonie heraus, hell oder dunkel; die wirbelnden Linien waren alle an Winkel gebunden, unterlagen geometrischen Gesetzen und der Physik; die Energie des Stoßes, die er durch die Queue dem Ball

D*

mitteilte und ein wenig Reibungsenergie; alles nur Maß; es prägte
sich dem Gehirn ein; Impulse, die sich zu Figuren umprägen ließen;
keine Gestalt und nichts Bleibendes, nur Flüchtiges, löschte sich im
Rollen der Kugel wieder aus; oft spielte er halbe Stunden lang nur
mit einem einzigen Ball: weiß über grün gestoßen, nur ein einziger
Stern am Himmel; leicht, leise, Musik ohne Melodie, Malerei ohne
Bild; kaum Farbe, nur Formel.

Der blasse Junge bewachte die Tür, lehnte gegen das weißlackierte
Holz, die Hände auf dem Rücken, die Beine gekreuzt, in der violetten
Uniform des Prinz Heinrich.

'Sie erzählen mir heute nichts, Herr Doktor?'

Er blickte auf, stellte den Stock ab, nahm eine Zigarette, zündete
sie an, blickte zur Straße hin, die im Schatten von Sankt Severin lag.
Lehrjungen, Lastwagen, Nonnen: Leben auf der Straße; graues
Herbstlicht fiel von dem violetten Samtvorhang fast silbern zurück;
von Velourvorhängen eingerahmt, frühstückten verspätete Gäste;
selbst die weichgekochten Eier sahen in dieser Beleuchtung lasterhaft
aus, biedere Hausfrauengesichter wirkten in diesem Licht verworfen;
Kellner, befrackt, mit einverstandenen Augen, sahen aus wie Beelze-
bubs, Asmodis unmittelbare Abgesandte; und waren doch nur
harmlose Gewerkschaftsmitglieder, die nach Feierabend beflissen die
Leitartikel ihres Verbandsblättchens lasen; sie schienen hier ihre
Pferdefüße unter geschickten orthopädischen Konstruktionen zu
verbergen; wuchsen nicht elegante kleine Hörner aus ihren weißen,
roten und gelben Stirnen? Der Zucker in den vergoldeten Dosen
schien nicht Zucker zu sein; Verwandlungen fanden hier statt, Wein
war nicht Wein, Brot nicht Brot, alles wurde zum Ingredienz geheim-
nisvoller Laster ausgeleuchtet; hier wurde zelebriert; und der Name
der Gottheit durfte nicht genannt, nur gedacht werden.

'Erzählen, Junge, was?'

Seine Erinnerung hatte sich nie an Worte und Bilder gehalten, nur
an Bewegungen. Vater, das war sein Gang, die kokette Kurve, die
das rechte Hosenbein mit jedem Schritt beschrieb, rasch, so daß das
dunkle blaue Stoßband nur für einen Augenblick sichtbar wurde,
wenn er morgens an Gretzens Laden vorüber ins Café Kroner ging,
um dort zu frühstücken; Mutter, das war die kompliziert-demütige
Figur, die ihre Hände beschrieben, wenn sie sie auf der Brust faltete,
immer kurz bevor sie eine Torheit aussprach: wie schlecht die Welt
sei, wie wenig reine Herzen es gebe; ihre Hände schrieben es in die
Luft, bevor sie es aussprach; Otto, das waren seine marschierenden
Beine, wenn er durch den Hausflur ging, in Stiefeln, die Straße
hinunter; Feindschaft, Feindschaft, schlug der Takt auf die Fliesen,
schlugen diese Füße, die in den Jahren davor einen anderen Takt
geschlagen hatten; Bruder, Bruder. Großmutter: die Bewegung, die
sie siebzig Jahre lang gemacht hatte, und die er viele Male am Tag

von seiner Tochter ausgeführt sah; jahrhundertalte Bewegung, die sich vererbte und ihn jedesmal erschrecken ließ; seine Tochter Ruth hatte ihre Urgroßmutter nie gesehen; woher hatte sie diese Bewegung? Ahungslos strich sie sich das Haar aus der Stirn, wie ihre Urgroßmutter es getan hatte.

Und er sah sich selbst, wie er sich nach den Schlaghölzern bückte, um seins herauszusuchen; wie er den Ball in der linken Hand hin und her rollte, her und hin, bis er ihn griffig genug hatte, ihn im entscheidenden Augenblick genau dorthin zu werfen, wo er ihn haben wollte; so hoch, daß die Fallzeit des Balles genau der Zeit entsprach, die er brauchte, um umzugreifen, auch die linke Hand ums Holz zu legen, auszuholen und den Ball zu treffen, mit gesammelter Kraft, so daß er weit fliegen würde, bis hinters Mal.

Er sah sich auf den Uferwiesen stehen, im Park, im Garten, gebückt, richtete sich auf, schlug zu. Es war alles nur Maß; sie waren Dummköpfe, wußten nicht, daß man die Fallzeit errechnen konnte, daß man mit denselben Stoppuhren auch erproben konnte, wie lange man braucht, den Griff zu wechseln; und daß alles weitere nur eine Frage der Koordinierung und der Übung war; ganze Nachmittage lang, auf den Wiesen, im Park, im Garten geübt; sie wußten nicht, daß es Formeln gab, die man anwenden, Waagen, auf denen man Bälle wiegen konnte. Nur ein bißchen Physik, ein bißchen Mathematik und Übung; aber sie verachteten ja die beiden Fächer, auf die es ankam; verachteten Training, mogelten sich durch, turnten wochenlang auf knochenweichen Sentenzen umher, fuhren Kahn auf nebulosem Dreck, fuhren Kahn sogar auf Hölderlin; sogar ein Wort wie Lot wurde, wenn sie es aussprachen, zu breiigem Unsinn; Lot, so etwas Klares; eine Schnur, ein Stück Blei, man warf es ins Wasser, spürte, wenn das Blei den Boden erreichte, zog die Schnur heraus und maß an ihr die Tiefe des Wassers ab; doch wenn sie loten sagten, klang es wie schlechtes Orgelspiel; sie konnten weder Schlagballspielen noch Hölderlin lesen. *Mitleidend bleibt das ewige Herz doch fest.*

(pp. 40–43)

Dr. Robert Fähmel is a 'Statiker' by profession, a statics consultant, a mathematician who works closely with firms of architects in calculating stresses and dynamics in large building projects. This profession, which at once associates him with characters of other modern German novels—Ulrich, the mathematician hero of *Der Mann ohne Eigenschaften*, Walter Faber, the technologist of Max Frisch's *Homo Faber*—clearly reflects some of his personal characteristics: the precision with which he invariably calculates the movements of the billiard balls or the relation between bat and ball in the game of 'Schlagball', and his pedantic exactness in everything he does, whether it is the extreme politeness with which he treats his secretary or the rigid timetable into which he divides his day. One may also see in the implied association of the word 'Statiker' with 'statisch' another feature of Fähmel's character, his passivity, his preoccupation with the past, his failure to progress.

The mechanical repetition of a trivial action or phrase frequently gives rise to laughter and is a common feature of traditional comedy—one thinks of Mrs. Micawber's standard declaration 'I never will desert Mr. Micawber'. There would indeed be something comical about Robert Fähmel's habit of playing billiards every morning of the working year in the same place and at the same time, accompanied by the same hotel boy, were it not for the serious *tone* of the context, which makes it grotesque rather than simply comical. For Leonore, his habits are 'unheimlich'. Robert's father, Heinrich Fähmel, has the similarly grotesque custom, which he has observed for the past fifty-one years, of breakfasting on 'Paprikakäse' at nine o'clock every morning in the Café Kroner. Heinrich's habit was the deliberate creation of a 'myth'; it gave his individual life meaning within the natural context of the recurrence of events in time, sunrise, sunset and the seasons; it was then indicative of the stability of the historical traditions in which he grew up. Since the National Socialist destruction of all German traditions, however, this gesture has become meaningless; at the close of the novel Heinrich at last recognizes this and cancels his breakfast. In Robert's case the daily routine has a slightly different import; it is, and always has been, an escapist gesture, an attempt to bring order into the chaos created by the National Socialists and their war by shutting out reality and devoting himself to the abstract, exactly calculable motions of the billiard balls. In the course of the novel he too recognizes the irresponsibility of this life, and breaks out of the mechanical routine by adopting Hugo, the hotel boy with whom he had shared his memories during the sessions at the billiard table.

The irresponsibility of habit is reflected in the abstractness of the game which Fähmel plays—without an opponent, without even the attempt to score points. This in turn recalls Fähmel's profession: statics consultant rather than architect, he himself is not constructive, but merely provides data on which others can build—indeed he assisted at the wartime demolition of the abbey which had been his father's masterpiece. And the abstract patterns of the game further reflect the constellations of characters in the novel. Just as a stroke from Robert's cue will alter the positions of all the balls on the table, so the arrival of two figures from the past, Nettlinger and later Schrella, alters the pattern of people in the novel, and ultimately breaks the Fähmel routine. The analogy betrays in a striking way an attitude to character: people appear as the will-less objects of higher powers, thrown helplessly hither and thither from one moment to the next. And yet their movements are determined according to certain mathematical laws.

Another important feature of Böll's presentation of character is illustrated in our extract, the role played by reflection and memory. For most of Böll's characters the past is more important than the present; most of Böll's novels are taken up with memories of past events. Two effects result. In the first place it emphasizes the abstractness of Böll's presentation; life is experienced not directly but through the medium of someone's mind. This is perhaps especially true of Fähmel, who remembers not words or images, but 'Bewegungen'. There is something schematic about this reduction of his father to the movements of his trouser leg or of his mother to the gesture of folding her arms, and this is a tendency of *Billard um halbzehn* in general. In the second place we find that Böll's characters are typically passive: they do not act, they react—like the billiard balls; playing billiards every morning is hardly the stuff of which the traditional novel constructed its plot! It is true that Robert Fähmel is critical of society, as we see in the third paragraph quoted. But he views society as an outsider, through the window of the billiards room, and fails—up to the end of the novel—to interfere in its workings and try to change it.

Abstraction, however, is only one pole of *Billard um halbzehn*. Its opposite, feeling or perhaps better 'Seele', is a keynote of Böll's demands on personality, and the Hölderlin quotation with which our extract closes is an important *leitmotiv* of the novel. Anger, the refusal to be reconciled with evil, is one aspect; love, 'sympathy' with the oppressed, is another. These are the attributes of the 'Lämmer' of *Billard um halbzehn*. It must be emphasized that the message is no vague, sentimental one of universal love. Johanna Fähmel, Robert's mother, tries at the end of the novel to shoot a prominent ex-Nazi. Ferdi Prokulske, another of the 'Lämmer', was executed by the Nazis for a similar assassination attempt. Robert expresses nothing but scorn for the 'knochen-weichen Sentenzen' of his fellow-pupils, whose Nazi maxims are woolly and who lack the courage of their convictions. In the Hölderlin quotation both the first and last words are important: firmness of purpose must accompany love. And in this association of mathematical precision with emotion *Billard um halbzehn* can be related to two of the most prominent German novels of the twentieth century, *Der Mann ohne Eigenschaften* and *Doktor Faustus*. In the former, Ulrich, the mathematician, evolves an 'Utopie des exakten Lebens' (Book I, 61). Twentieth-century developments have divorced feeling and precision: technology has put the coldly rational on a pedestal regardless of human considerations; and the corresponding relegation of feeling into the province of the uncontrolled and irrational makes possible, for example, the disastrous outbreaks of nationalism and lust for power manifested in the First World War. Ulrich, therefore, proposes the setting up of a 'Generalsekretariat der Genauigkeit und Seele' (Book I, 116, p. 610); much of his own activity is devoted to the attempt to define feeling, to make it possible for people to feel emotions in a more exact manner. And in *Doktor Faustus* this theme is struck in the music of Adrian Leverkühn: the liberation of music from its formal restraints has resulted in uncontrolled emotionalism; the stricter and more abstract the form in which Leverkühn clothes his music, the more possible the expression of emotion becomes once more. In *Billard um halbzehn* Böll is attempting something similar. What makes the emotionality of this novel so much more acceptable than that of, say, *Ansichten eines Clowns*, is its greater degree of organization through *leitmotiv* and perspective patterns, the abstractness of its form.

10 Man and Society

The kings and queens of classical tragedy lack social reality. Their high birth does not serve to place them within the class system but rather to set them on a pinnacle on which absolute conflicts may be fought out—duty versus inclination, self-assertion versus the will of the gods. Only much later did class distinctions (Schiller's *Kabale und Liebe*) or professional or financial considerations (Ibsen's *A Doll's House*) come to play a leading part in the tragic conflict. Lyric poetry too has tended to express the subjective feelings or beliefs of an individual rather than of the representative of a class or group. The novel, however, in this akin rather to comedy, has always seen man as a social being, belonging to a historically defined group of other people, limited according to group attitudes and conventions. And if the novel shows that the individual, despite his egoism and aspirations, is merely relative, irony may be expected, since irony is a device which reveals the relativity of things. Irony, as we shall see, is indeed one of the keys to the novel.

That man is the ensemble of his social connections is thus most obviously applicable to the world of the novel. A sociological approach seems appropriate in this field at least. How does a particular novel reflect the society of the age in which it is written? What relevance does it have for the age in which it is being read? One reason for the peculiar qualities of the older German novel, qualities which distinguish it from the English or French novel of its age, is the absence, into the nineteenth century, of a strongly profiled German society with long-standing traditions, a clearly defined structure and a generally accepted system of social values. Up to 1870 Germany consisted of a number of mainly rural, independent states of still fundamentally feudal constitution. Goethe's novels may be taken as symptomatic: *Die Leiden des jungen Werther* is a novel in letters written by a highly subjective, lonely, lyrical hero; *Wilhelm Meisters Lehrjahre* concerns partly a troupe of travelling actors, partly the secret, pseudo-masonic 'Society of the Tower', neither of which has a specifically social

position; and *Die Wahlverwandtschaften* restricts itself to the relations between four people who live in some isolation from the
rest of the world. However, from 1870-1 onwards Germany was
very rapidly transformed into a modern, industrialized, urban
state, outwardly resembling the longer-established democracies of
Europe, although the speed of the transformation caused many
inner conflicts which expressed themselves in various ways and
which form the material for many of the novels of the period.
The German novel, at least since 1900, has become more accessible
to the European reader, partly because it now reflects a social
system more recognizable to the English and French reader.
Thomas Mann, for example, is a European name; *Buddenbrooks*
is remarkably similar in many respects to Galsworthy's *Forsyte
Saga*. Features peculiar to the German novel of the period shed
an interesting light on social conditions in Germany. For example,
the important place allotted to politics—and the historical novels
which, somewhat surprisingly, stand out in German writing of
this time almost invariably reflect contemporary political issues
—clearly springs from the unstable political situation in Germany.
The extraordinary readiness to experiment manifested by German
writers up to 1933 and again since 1945 may be taken to reflect a
lack of historical traditions such as those which form the background for the more conservative English novelist.

As was suggested in the previous chapter, the novel has tended
to be a middle class product, written by, about and for middle
class people, a product of the—generally liberal—middle class
outlook. Cervantes's *Don Quixote* is, on one level, about the
difficulties a romantic dreamer experiences in a down-to-earth
bourgeois society; the dominance of the novel since the eighteenth
century can be explained by the dominance of the middle classes
since that time. The German novel of the eighteenth and nineteenth centuries, however, abounds in *Barone* and *Baroninnen*.
Gustav Freytag's *Soll und Haben* is one of the earliest German
novels to dip into the commercial middle class milieu familiar to
the readers of Dickens; that it refuses to satirize as *Buddenbrooks*
and *Der Untertan* do later the mentality of this milieu is, like the
predominance of the minor nobility elsewhere, a sign of the social
ideology of the time. The twentieth-century German novelist is
similarly selective in his choice of social classes. Middle class
professional people are numerous, industrial workers almost non-
existent. Where the proletariat does appear, it is usually as the

better educated section—Esch of *Die Schlafwandler,* Jakob Abs of *Mutmaßungen über Jakob*—or as the slightly picturesque semi-criminal type represented by Franz Biberkopf in *Berlin Alexander-platz.* This selectivity is significant: the descent in the social order is, for example, not merely a sign of changing social conditions but also indicates the author's conception of character; lack of financial or social freedom is often accompanied by lack of intellectual freedom. Ideological possibilities are illustrated by the peasant farmer motif of Nazi *Blut- und Bodenliteratur* and the boy-meets-tractor literature of East Germany; elsewhere agrarian society is almost totally replaced by city life.

One very important group of figures, however, appears to belong to no social class at all. These are the artists, writers and musicians who have always been prominent in German literature and continue to populate the novels of Thomas Mann, Hermann Hesse, even Günter Grass (Eduard Amsel in *Hundejahre*). This brings us to a more general phenomenon, the outsider motif, which takes us rather more deeply into the way in which society can be reflected in the novel. There is a very long tradition of 'Sonderlinge' in German literature—non-conformists, people who in some way stand outside society or the recognized conventions. Herman Meyer has shown that whereas earlier these were the object of ridicule, about the middle of the nineteenth century they began to take on more positive features, to become indeed the repositories of true humanity in a sterile, conventional and standardized society.[1] The best examples of such figures are to be found in the later novels of Wilhelm Raabe. This process may be said to have been accelerated in the twentieth-century novel, where the outsider, bohemian or criminal is the rule rather than the exception: Felix Krull, Harry Haller, Ulrich, the man without qualities, Karl Roßmann of *Amerika*, K. of *Das Schloß*, Biberkopf and the criminals of *Berlin Alexanderplatz,* down to Oskar Matzerath and the narrator of *Mein Name sei Gantenbein,* who, whoever he is, is looking for but not finding his role in society. Clearly the attitude towards 'non-integration' varies from work to work. Nevertheless, it generally implies criticism of modern society. Individuality, as discussed in the previous chapter, can no longer be developed within but only against society.

Professions and occupations are another social aspect of character worth examining. These tend to go further than merely

[1] *Der Sonderling in der deutschen Dichtung,* (2nd edn., Munich, 1963).

identifying a person's social status and have symbolic significance. Kafka's country doctor, for example, reflects that in former times people would have consulted a priest, but now in a more materialist age they come to him. The 'Landvermesser' of *Das Schloß* is by implication concerned with surveying not merely in the physical but also in the social or even metaphysical sense, mapping out the possibilities and limitations of Man. The profession of Robert Fähmel in *Billard um halbzehn*, is, as we have seen, indicative of his character and suggestive of his social failings. Walter Faber too, as the title of Max Frisch's novel suggests, is not merely a technologist but representative of man in the technological age. Military people play an important role in the novels of our period: Leutnant Gustl, Hans Castorp's cousin Joachim, General Stumm von Bordwehr in *Der Mann ohne Eigenschaften*, Pasenow in *Die Schlafwandler*. Here it is more clearly the set of values, the system, which is the novelist's interest. The army is a society in miniature, in which the relationships between people are determined not on a personal level but according to the position they hold within the community; it is also a society with a very strictly defined system of values (discipline, loyalty, honour etc.). Either, therefore, the military world is regarded as a contrast to the more loosely organized society at large, or else it is viewed as a microcosm of society itself, illustrating the latent tendencies within society. In both cases the military will usually find themselves the target of criticism: the novelist's values—liberal in the main— are rather those of tolerance, approval of the 'open' society, distrust of traditional forms carried over unthinkingly.

Other values besides the military ones professed by characters in novels, can be identified with particular sections of the community and may again be clues to the novelist's critical intention. Both Pasenow, the lieutenant of the first part of the *Schlafwandler* trilogy, and Esch, the bookkeeper hero of the second, are looking for order in the anarchic universe in which they live. They find this 'Ordnung' in their respective professions, and there is in this the implication of escapism. 'Ordnung', as Brecht remarks in his *Flüchtlingsgespräche*, is in itself a sterile virtue: 'Wo nichts am rechten Platz liegt, da ist Unordnung. Wo am rechten Platz nichts liegt, da ist Ordnung.'[2] 'Ordnung' can be political, social or personal; it can even imply the aesthetic form of the novel; but where it is imposed from above it will always run counter to the

[2] *Gesammelte Werke* (Frankfurt a.M., 1967), Volume 14, p. 1390.

liberal outlook. Another social virtue, one which plays an important part in such novels as *Die Schlafwandler, Berlin Alexanderplatz* and *Billard um halbzehn*, is 'Anständigkeit'; again it is a negative kind of virtue, consisting in omitting to do certain things, rather than doing certain other things. Both 'Ordnung' and 'Anständigkeit' can be identified with the petty bourgeois milieu. But the most important social grouping as far as the novel is concerned is the family. Like the army, the family is most frequently a synecdochal device to represent the state itself. Thus the authoritarian father of *Der Untertan* implies the anti-democratic monarch; the decline of a family (*Buddenbrooks*) suggests the disintegration of the rigid hierarchical order in society.

The changing relationship between man and society may, however, be reflected in a still more subtle way. As suggested in the chapter on *Point of View*, the lack of an 'omniscient' narrator may well imply social and ideological disorientation. The lack of a clearly defined social structure on which order is imposed from above is seen in the absence of any overall point of view from which the whole can be surveyed and understood. Kafka's K. is forced to surmise, dependent on hearsay; so too the reader. The interior monologue reflects the social isolation of the individual. Similarly the 'fugal' novel discussed in the chapter on *Time* may have social implications. The linear novel of traditional literature reflected a degree of confidence in historical continuity and the validity of organic progression which is not shared by the twentieth-century writer. This can be seen in *Doktor Faustus* and is most explicit in the novels of Heinrich Böll, whose time-structures imply that the National Socialists and the Second World War have cut off postwar Germany completely from earlier traditions.

The previous chapter was concerned with one of the traditional categories of the novel, character; in speaking of the relationship between the individual and society we are touching on the other, plot. For plot can perhaps best be described in terms of a conflict or tension and its resolution, and the conflict or tension between the individual and society forms the basis of the majority of novels. Georg Lukács, in his *Theorie des Romans*, detected three main structures in the novel, which are constituted by the relationship between the individual and what he called 'Welt'. The first, exemplified by *Don Quixote*, shows the man who tries to confine the world into the straitjacket of his idea of it; the individual is limited, the world too manifold for him to comprehend. The second type (Flaubert's *L'Education sentimentale*) shows the opposite: here the nobility of the hero is not matched by the world in which he finds himself, which is narrow and petty. The third attempts a synthesis: *Wilhelm Meisters Lehrjahre* shows not merely the individual learning to submit to the world, but also the world profiting from the individual.

When trying to fit a particular novel into any one pigeonhole it is easy to forget that not the system but the individual example is important; moreover, there will often be room for disagreement on the interpretation of any given novel. Nevertheless, Lukács's categories may usefully be modified in terms of the individual's relationship with society and provide a useful framework for discussion of each case. Three possibilities can be imagined. In the first, the individual eventually submits and is integrated into society; society, the collective, is the standpoint from which events have to be judged. This type tends to be didactic, like the older *Erziehungsroman* and a number of contemporary East German novels, such as Erik Neutsch's *Spur der Steine*. *Berlin Alexanderplatz* to some extent follows this pattern: Biberkopf has to learn to submit, to desire no longer to be individually strong; at the same time, however, he has to retain his individual 'Vernunft' so that he does not identify himself with the false collective. The second type is much more common, embracing many of the novels mentioned in connection with the 'Sonderling' or outsider theme. Hesse's novels all vindicate the individual in his struggle against conformity in society, all show a movement away from the collective herd. Even Josef Knecht in *Das Glasperlenspiel* abandons the position of a fully integrated member of the Castalian community when he realizes that the order has become too rigid. Again, however, the resolution of the conflict is not always unambiguous. Is Oskar Matzerath to be taken seriously? Is it ultimately possible to avoid being contaminated by society? The third group is therefore the largest. In this type both individual and society are to some extent justified; where the individual appears to triumph his victory is ironic; where society dominates, this too is less than clear. The ironic stance is indeed the keynote of this type. Thomas Mann's novels show the balance of artist and bourgeois, outsider and citizen. The hero of *Der Mann ohne Eigenschaften* always remains part of society, even to the extent of becoming honorary secretary of a patriotic committee; Ulrich and Agathe's attempts to 'abolish reality', to ignore society, fail; and while Austrian society is in no way vindicated, ultimately Ulrich too cuts a much less attractive figure than one might have expected. Kafka's three novels taken together present an interesting constellation: the hero of *Amerika*, Karl Roßmann, remains outside American society in its various manifestations; K. of *Das Schloß* likewise fails to be accepted by the village community; between them, however, lies *Der Prozeß*, the novel of a superior bank clerk, one who *has* a secure position in society and who is throughout the novel beset with the guilty feeling that he is neglecting his job. Integration appears positive only to those who are not already integrated, and Josef K. has his counterparts elsewhere in Walter Faber of *Homo Faber* and Diederich Heßling of Heinrich Mann's *Der Untertan*.

The following extract from *Der Untertan* illustrates some of the ways in which society and the relationship between it and the individual hero can be presented. Diederich Heßling is the son of a provincial paper manufacturer. His father is authoritarian, his mother weak and sentimental. From his earliest days Diederich is terrified by authority in all its forms, but secretly admires it and longs to prostrate himself before it. After an undistinguished school career he comes to Berlin to study chemistry. Torn from his accustomed surroundings he is at first completely bewildered; visits to the home of Herr Göppel, a business connection of his father, where he meets Agnes Göppel and Mahlmann, a student admirer of Agnes, disconcert him still further. After a term Diederich flees, taking lodgings in a distant part of Berlin, but he is eventually persuaded by a former schoolmate to visit a student fraternity, the Neuteutonen, where he drinks himself under the table.

Als er ausgeschlafen hatte, holten sie ihn zum Frühschoppen; Diederich war Konkneipant geworden.

Und für diesen Posten fühlte er sich bestimmt. Er sah sich in einen großen Kreis von Menschen versetzt, deren keiner ihm etwas tat oder etwas anderes von ihm verlangte, als daß er trinke. Voll Dankbarkeit und Wohlwollen erhob er gegen jeden, der ihn dazu anregte, sein Glas. Das Trinken und Nichttrinken, das Sitzen, Stehen, Sprechen oder Singen hing meistens nicht von ihm selbst ab. Alles ward laut kommandiert, und wenn man es richtig befolgte, lebte man mit sich und der Welt in Frieden. Als Diederich beim Salamander zum ersten Male nicht nachklappte, lächelte er in die Runde, beinahe verschämt durch die eigene Vollkommenheit!

Und das war noch nichts gegen seine Sicherheit im Gesang! Diederich hatte in der Schule zu den besten Sängern gehört und schon in seinem ersten Liederheft die Seitenzahlen auswendig gewußt, wo jedes Lied zu finden war. Jetzt brauchte er in das Kommersbuch, das auf großen Nägeln in der Lache von Bier lag, nur den Finger zu schieben und traf vor allen anderen die Nummer, die gesungen werden sollte. Oft hing er den ganzen Abend mit Ehrerbietung am Munde des Präses: ob vielleicht sein Lieblingsstück darankäme. Dann dröhnte er tapfer: 'Sie wissen den Teufel, was Freiheit heißt', hörte neben sich den dicken Delitzsch brummen und fühlte sich wohlig geborgen in dem Halbdunkel des niedrigen altdeutschen Lokals, mit den Mützen an der Wand, angesichts des Kranzes geöffneter Münder, die alle dasselbe tranken und sangen, bei dem Geruch des Bieres und der Körper, die es in der Wärme wieder ausschwitzten. Ihm war, wenn es spät ward, als schwitze er mit ihnen allen aus demselben Körper. Er war untergegangen in der Korporation, die für ihn dachte und wollte. Und er war ein Mann, durfte sich selbst hochachten und hatte eine Ehre, weil er dazu gehörte! Ihn herausreißen, ihm einzeln etwas anhaben, das konnte keiner! Mahlmann hätte sich einmal herwagen und es versuchen sollen: zwanzig Mann wären statt Diederichs gegen ihn aufgestanden! Diederich wünschte ihn geradezu herbei, so furchtlos war er. Womöglich sollte er mit Göppel kommen, dann mochten sie sehen, was aus Diederich geworden war, dann war er gerächt!

Gleichwohl gab ihm die meiste Sympathie der Harmloseste von allen ein, sein Nachbar, der dicke Delitzsch. Etwas tief Beruhigendes, Vertrauengestattendes wohnte in dieser glatten, weißen und humorvollen Speckmasse, die unten breit über die Stuhlränder quoll, in mehreren Wülsten die Tischhöhe erreichte und dort, als sei nun das Äußerste getan, aufgestützt blieb, ohne eine andere Bewegung als das Heben und Hinstellen des Bierglases. Delitzsch war, wie niemand sonst, an seinem Platz; wer ihn dasitzen sah, vergaß, daß er ihn je auf den Beinen erblickt hatte. Er war ausschließlich zum Sitzen am Biertisch eingerichtet. Sein Hosenboden, der in jedem anderen Zustand tief und melancholisch herabhing, fand nun seine wahre Gestalt und blähte sich machtvoll. Erst mit Delitzschs hinterem Gesicht blühte auch sein vorderes auf. Lebensfreude überglänzte es, und er ward witzig.

Ein Drama entstand, wenn ein junger Fuchs sich den Scherz machte, ihm das Bierglas wegzunehmen. Delitzsch rührte kein Glied, aber seine Miene, die dem geraubten Glase überallhin folgte, enthielt plötzlich den ganzen, stürmisch bewegten Ernst des Daseins, und er rief in sächsischem Schreitenor: 'Junge, daß du mir nischt verschüttest! Was entziehst de mir überhaupt mein' Läbensunterhalt! Das ist 'ne ganz gemeine, böswillige Existenzschädichung, und ich kann dich glatt verklaachen!'

Dauerte der Spaß zu lange, senkten sich Delitzschs weiße Fettwangen, und er bat, er machte sich klein. Sobald er aber das Bier zurück hatte: welche allumfassende Aussöhnung in seinem Lächeln, welche Verklärung! Er sagte: 'Du bist doch ä gutes Luder, du sollst läm, prost!' — trank aus und klopfte mit dem Deckel nach dem Korpsdiener: 'Herr Oberkörper!'

Nach einigen Stunden geschah es wohl, daß sein Stuhl sich mit ihm umdrehte und Delitzsch den Kopf über das Becken der Wasserleituͬg hielt. Das Wasser plätscherte, Delitzsch gurgelte erstickt, und ein paar andere stürzten, durch seine Laute angeregt, in die Toilette. Noch ein wenig sauer von Gesicht, aber schon mit frischer Schelmerei, rückte Delitzsch an den Tisch zurück.

'Na, nu geht's ja wieder', sagte er; und: 'Wovon habt 'r denn geredt, während ich anderweitig beschäftigt war? Wißt ihr denn egal nischt wie Weibergeschichten? Was koof ich mir für die Weiber?' Immer lauter: 'Nich mal ä sauern Schoppen kann 'ch mir dafür koofen. Sie, Herr Oberkörper!'

Diederich gab ihm recht. Er hatte die Weiber kennengelernt, er war mit ihnen fertig. Unvergleichlich idealere Werte enthielt das Bier. Das Bier! Der Alkohol! Da saß man und konnte immer noch mehr davon haben, das Bier war nicht wie kokette Weiber, sondern treu und gemütlich. Beim Bier brauchte man nicht zu handeln, nichts zu wollen und zu erreichen, wie bei den Weibern. Alles kam von selbst. Man schluckte: und da hatte man es schon zu etwas gebracht, fühlte sich auf die Höhen des Lebens befördert und war ein freier Mann, innerlich frei. Das Lokal hätte von Polizisten umstellt sein dürfen: das Bier, das man schluckte, verwandelte sich in innere Freiheit. Und man hatte sein Examen so gut wie bestanden. Man war 'fertig', war Doktor! Man füllte im bürgerlichen Leben eine Stellung aus, war reich und von Wichtigkeit: Chef einer mächtigen Fabrik von Ansichtskarten oder Toilettenpapier. Was man mit seiner Lebensarbeit schuf, war in tausend Händen. Man breitete sich, vom Biertisch her, über die Welt aus, ahnte große Zusammenhänge, ward eins mit dem Weltgeist. Ja, das Bier erhob einen so sehr über das Selbst, daß man Gott fand!

Gern hätte er es jahrelang so weitergetrieben. Aber die Neuteutonen ließen ihn nicht. Fast vom ersten Tage an hatten sie ihm den moralischen und materiellen Wert einer völligen Zugehörigkeit zur Verbindung geschildert; allmählich aber gingen sie immer unverblümter darauf aus, ihn zu keilen. Vergebens berief sich Diederich auf seine anerkannte Stellung als Konkneipant, in die er sich eingelebt habe und die ihn befriedige. Sie entgegneten, daß der Zweck des studentischen Zusammenschlusses, nämlich die Erziehung zur Mannhaftigkeit und zum Idealismus, durch das Kneipen allein, soviel es auch beitrage, noch nicht ganz erfüllt werde. Diederich zitterte; nur zu gut erkannte er, worauf dieses hinauslief. Er sollte pauken! Schon immer hatte es ihn unheimlich angeweht, wenn sie mit ihren Stöcken in der Luft ihm die Schläge vorgeführt hatten, die sie einander beigebracht haben wollten; oder wenn einer von ihnen eine schwarze Mütze um den Kopf hatte und nach Jodoform roch. Jetzt dachte er gepreßt: 'Warum bin ich dabeigeblieben und Konkneipant geworden! Nun muß ich ran.'

Er mußte. Aber gleich die ersten Erfahrungen beruhigten ihn. Er war so sorgsam eingewickelt, behelmt und bebrillt worden, daß ihm unmöglich viel geschehen konnte. Da er keinen Grund hatte, den Kommandos nicht gerade so willig und gelehrig nachzukommen wie in der Kneipe, lernte er fechten, schneller als andere. Beim ersten Durchzieher ward ihm schwach: über die Wange fühlte er es rinnen. Als er dann genäht war, hätte er am liebsten getanzt vor Glück. Er warf es sich vor, daß er diesen gutmütigen Menschen gefährliche Absichten zugetraut hatte. Gerade der, den er am meisten gefürchtet hatte, nahm ihn unter seinen Schutz und ward ihm ein wohlgesinnter Erzieher.

(pp. 30–34)

Diederich's entry into the Neuteutonen marks the beginning of his increasing self-confidence and his rise to a position of social domination and esteem, the subject of the rest of the novel. The student society of our extract may, therefore, be taken as a microcosm of the Wilhelminian society of which Diederich is a typical representative—he is later specifically described as such. Thus the fraternity is based on a strict hierarchy of masters and servants and commands given and implicitly obeyed—Diederich is proud to serve as personal attendant of one of the older students, performing the most menial of tasks with masochistic zeal. Its ideology too anticipates that of society in the wider sense: its chauvinism suggested in the name of the fraternity, its devotion to pseudo-traditions reflected in the décor of their meeting-place ('altdeutsch'). The anti-feminist stance of this exclusively male club anticipates the attitude to women evinced elsewhere in the novel: women are simply objects, whether of lust, of barter (Diederich's sister is married off to the man who would otherwise have ruined his business) or merely of social status. The virtues extolled here are worth looking at in detail. Beer, for example, is not like the 'kokette Weiber', but 'treu und gemütlich'. 'Treue' is one of the virtues that ideologists from medieval times onwards have liked to describe as peculiarly German. Diederich's 'treue, blaue Augen' are a *leitmotiv* of the novel. But they are never as 'treu'-looking as when he is on the point of committing or has just committed some abomination. Much of the novel is concerned with the underhand transactions involved in having a statue built to Kaiser Wilhelm I; Diederich is as much involved in the machinations as anyone, but rages none the less at the 'Treulosigkeit' of the age when he finds himself on the receiving end of a piece of treachery. 'Gemütlich' is a still more 'German' adjective; just what barbaric customs it can conceal is amply demonstrated in our extract. The 'Mannhaftigkeit' and 'Idealismus' which are the professed goals of the fraternity are similarly unmasked. Diederich is a coward and remains one throughout his life. One of the central scenes shows the trial for lèse-majesté of a man whom Diederich had provoked into saying something which might be construed as insulting the Kaiser; when at first everything seems in favour of the accused and damaging for Diederich, Diederich retracts his evidence; but after the turning-point, when a conviction appears certain, he changes his mind, asks to be allowed to make a statement and unleashes a tirade of chauvinistic, reactionary propaganda which seals the fate of his opponent. This characteristic is anticipated in our extract: the ritual face-slashing is carefully organized so that those who undergo it run no real risks and yet take all the honour. Of 'idealism' as such our extract shows no trace, rather the opposite—a complete submission to the lowest, least intellectual sides of man's activities. And just as the talk of 'Mannhaftigkeit', 'Idealismus' and 'innere Freiheit' is merely a cover for a shameless and repulsive orgy of beer-drinking, so in the rest of the novel the ideals which Diederich constantly has in his mouth—'Ordnung', 'Opfer', 'echt deutsches Wesen', 'Christentum', 'Vaterland'—conceal what is really a struggle for power, and especially economic power.

This power is available to the individual who is prepared to conform, to identify himself with the prevailing tendencies in society. *Der Untertan* is a novel in which the individual most obviously is meaningful only in a social group. With the Göppel family Diederich was merely a private person and, having no individuality, he remained a nonentity. With the support of the herd he is irresistible. The Bucks and Lauers, the representatives of an earlier, more liberal age, are doomed. But Heinrich Mann goes even further in suggesting that Diederich experiences a masochistic pleasure in submitting to authority. Towards the end of the novel the author makes this—perhaps unnecessarily—

explicit when he describes a scene of sexual masochism between Diederich and his wife Guste. But throughout the novel we are constantly aware of the delight he takes in degrading himself, nowhere more clearly perhaps than in the scene in which he tries to make Lieutenant von Brietzen marry his sister, whom he has seduced. Rejected, Diederich nevertheless finds himself admiring the lieutenant as he drives past: 'Den macht uns niemand nach', he thinks. By depicting the perversion at the heart of the social group in power Heinrich Mann expresses his criticism of society, and this too is foreshadowed in the 'Mensur' scene described in our extract. In this deeply pessimistic novel, with scarcely a hint of better things to come, the ruling tendency in society is portrayed much as we see it in the scenes with the Neuteutonen: alcoholic, brutal, repulsive and perverted.

11 Man and Nature

Ach, daß die innre Schöpfungskraft
Durch meinen Sinn erschölle!
Daß eine Bildung voller Saft
Aus meinen Fingern quölle!

Ich zittre nur, ich stottre nur
Und kann es doch nicht lassen;
Ich fühl', ich kenne dich, Natur,
Und so muß ich dich fassen.

For the young Goethe there was almost no distinction between external nature and nature as an inner force. External nature meant the natural as opposed to the man-made environment, while man's inner natural aspect was his instinctive creative powers, the pure life of his emotions uncorrupted by artificial social conventions. But even in his most storm-and-stressful moments Goethe remained aware that such an ideal correspondence between inner and outer nature is unattainable; *Künstlers Abendlied* takes the form of a prayer, its verbs are subjunctive in mood or future in tense. Goethe's work as a whole seeks to reconcile natural man with man as a self-aware, moral and social creature. The original simple equation becomes infinitely complex, the destructive as well as the creative aspect of nature and of 'human nature' is fully realized. But nature remains a supreme value. This is true not only of Goethe but of most German literature in the nineteenth and into the twentieth century.

In the twentieth century nature as an inner value predominates, rather than external nature. Many writers, whether explicitly or implicitly, judge society against an ideal of what could or should be the *natural* mode of human intercourse, while most political ideologies make some claim to correct the unnatural distortions of modern society. Brecht's Puntila, for example, becomes humane when drunk. The pressures of the capitalist system make him a wicked man when sober. Human beings, it is implied, are alienated from their true nature by a corrupt social order. Brecht does not suggest, however, that man can only live a natural life in a natural environment. As a Marxist, he is committed to the belief that technology can be harnessed to serve man's natural impulses, to express his natural creativity. And this is true of many other writers, whether Marxist or not. Total repudiation of urban and industrial civilization has not been common in serious literature. None the less, external nature has not completely disappeared from the pages of fiction. This chapter will look at some examples of 'Naturdichtung' in the circumscribed sense of novels where external nature is significant, whether intrinsically or symbolically.

At its simplest, nature means the countryside as opposed to the town. The impact of industrialization resulted in widespread revulsion against mass urban civilization which found expression in the tradition of *Heimatdichtung*. The works of Ernst Wiechert, for example, continue in this tradition in the inter-war period and express an ideal of the simple life governed by the natural round of the seasons in a rural setting, as suggested by the title of one of his works *Das einfache Leben*. Wiechert's work up to the Second World War is essentially escapist. It takes little account of the impact of industrialization, nor of the realities of class exploitation, racialism and political gangsterism which impinged even on the countryside of twentieth-century Germany, now willy-nilly an industrial great power. No countryside was remote enough to bring escape from the problems this entailed. Wiechert was never a Nazi and indeed spent some time in a concentration camp during the war, but his work has some affinities with the more dubious types of *Heimatdichtung* with their cult of *Blut und Boden*, their appeal to instinct and rejection of reason.

Hermann Broch, who himself propounds a religion of nature in his Alpine novel *Der Versucher*, was highly critical of what he considered the dangers inherent in the cult of nature. In the first part of his trilogy *Die Schlafwandler*, *Pasenow oder die Romantik*, Broch analyses the fear and confusion which give rise to latter-day pastoral longings. The following passage shows how Joachim von Pasenow's longing for the simple life comes from his fear of the great man-made city with its new frightening class of industrial workers, its strange underworld of corruption and exploitation. Joachim is going to visit the parents of his fiancée Elisabeth in their town residence in a Berlin suburb:

Manches war in den letzten Tagen unsicher geworden ... und es wuchs die Sehnsucht nach Festigkeit, Sicherheit und Ruhe. Nun, diese wohlhabende Villengegend mit ihren schloßartigen Gebäuden in trefflichstem Renaissance-, Barock- oder Schweizerstil, umgeben von wohlgepflegten Gärten, aus denen man das Harken der Gärtner, den Strahl des Gartenschlauches, das Plätschern der Fontänen vernahm, strömte große und insulare Sicherheit aus ... Aus offenen Fenstern tönten Etüden von Stephen Heller und von Clementi: wohlgeborgen können die Töchter dieser Familien ihren Studien nachgehen; gutes Geschick der Sicherheit und der Sanftheit, von Freundschaft erfüllt, bis Liebe die Freundschaft ablöst und die Liebe wieder in Freundschaft verklingt. Von ferne, nicht von allzu ferne her krähte ein Hahn, als wollte auch er die Ländlichkeit dieses gepflegten Aufenthaltes andeuten ... Schön wäre es, mit Elisabeth durch die Felder zu gehen, das reifende Korn zwischen die prüfenden Finger zu nehmen ... Aber zu alldem war es für ihn ja zu spät, für ihn, den man zum Fremdling gemacht hatte, und er ist — nun fiel es ihm ein — heimatlos wie Bertrand. (*Pasenow* I, pp. 31–2).

The conjunction of Joachim's dream of the country and the countrified suburb he so admires shows how easily pastoral idyll can become sentimental *Kitsch* far from the stylishness of the eighteenth-century variety. The backward-looking architecture with its aristocratic pretensions is an attempt to deny the reality of urban squalor and mass civilization. This is the visual equivalent of literary *Kitsch*. Elsewhere in the novel Broch provides a depressing counter-image of the countryside and the life of Joachim's family of Prussian landowners, scarred by the madness of a rigid inhuman code of behaviour. Pastoral *Kitsch* closes its eyes not just to the city, but to the all too real sufferings of country life as well. Such *Kitsch*, Broch argues elsewhere, is evil.[1] The illusions it purveys only compound the fear and confusion of people caught up in great economic and social upheavals.

In a later novel, *Die Schuldlosen*, Broch argues that guilt for the crimes of the Third Reich lies not just with members of the Nazi party, but with the apparently guiltless too. Through ostrich-like refusal to become involved in political activity, they allowed the Nazis to seize power. This broad theme is conveyed symbolically through the personal failings of the central character,

---

[1] 'Das Böse im Wertsystem der Kunst', in *Dichten und Erkennen, Gesammelte Werke* Volume 6, (Zürich, 1955), p. 347.

Andreas. Significantly the 'guiltless' Andreas moves to a lonely house in a forest, apparently a refuge of purity and safety in an evil world. But though Andreas lives surrounded by nature, his life is highly unnatural: inner and outer nature are *not* in harmony. Andreas has betrayed and deserted Melitta, the girl he loved. He has chosen the unnatural role of a prolonged childhood in the company of an elderly substitute mother. Though he lives in the depths of nature, he does not go so far as to indulge in any natural toil, but continues at long distance to make money on the stock-exchanges of the world. On the other hand, he certainly indulges in the natural functions of eating and sleeping. It is as if in this way he has tried to merge into nature, to escape out of the human condition into a state of nature. But such a state of 'nature' is not natural for a human being.

Retribution comes to Andreas in the shape of the grandfather of the dead Melitta, who calls Andreas to account. The numinous grandfather, a bee-keeper, is portrayed as at once supremely human and totally in harmony with nature. Andreas is sitting in his study writing cables to his banker when he is disturbed by sounds of strange singing, heralding the approach of the grandfather:

> Wußte der Sänger nicht, wie viel es gerade jetzt hier noch zu erledigen gab? Zudem war nach dem reichlichen Essen der Nachmittagsschlaf bereits dringlich notwendig geworden; ohne ausgeruhten Kopf — weiß der Kuckuck, warum er gerade heute so schläfrig war — lassen sich keinerlei Entschlüsse fassen. Die Axthiebe störten nicht; die waren ein natürlicher Teil des Waldes, das Singen hingegen war unnatürlich, auch wenn es, wie eben jetzt, sich ins ganz Dunkle herabdämpfte und dem Tiefgesumme von Bienenschwärmen glich. Bienensummen ist kein Gesang, ist etwas Natürliches, hat ihn noch niemals gestört und wird ihn auch heute nicht stören. Unsinn, schwärmende Bienen im März! Im Sommer ist's natürlich, im Winter ist's Gesang.... Kamen die Axtschläge und der Gesang nicht aus verschiedenen Richtungen, voneinander getrennt, dennoch aufeinander abgestimmt? Das klang fast wie ein Choral vieler Stimmen. Nichtsdestoweniger, es war eine einzige Stimme, die das Chorhafte bewältigte, und dies wurde merkbar, sooft sie, gewissermaßen über sich selbst hinausschwingend, zu einer Art Arie wurde... (*Steinerner Gast*, p. 313)

The single voice crystallizing out of the natural sounds symbolizes the proper relationship between man and nature. Man's individuality, his consciousness, his gift of reason, his moral sense, preclude for ever a total immersion in nature, in a purely instinctive or sensual existence. On the other hand, Broch suggests that man should never try to rationalize away his nature, as Andreas has done in choosing a eunuch-like existence on the grounds that he was acting as protector to an elderly woman. Brought at last to recognize that his condition is both unnatural and inhuman, Andreas confesses:

> Das ist meine wiedergefundene Erinnerung und es ist die Rechenschaft, die ich abzulegen habe. Rechenschaft für den Ich-Verlust, Rechenschaft für die Vertierungsgefahr, unter der ich stehe, unter der die Welt steht, die Welt mich, ich die Welt bedingend, in gemeinsamer Gefahr. (p. 334)

and further down:

> Ich glaubte die Verantwortungslosigkeit zu fliehen, und in Wahrheit war es die Verantwortung, die ich geflohen habe. Das war meine Schuld. (p. 335)

Broch implies here that the active violence of mass hysteria, racial hatred, rabid nationalism and the passive indifference of a man like Andreas are equally 'bestial.' Both represent the same 'Vertierungsgefahr'. Both types of behaviour arise from a reduction of human nature. Animals are not 'bestial', only man can be that, for he is born with the gifts of reason and awareness. If in his confusion and fear he tries to escape from these into irrational instinct or a vegetable-like torpor then he will become monstrously destructive or half-dead, like Andreas.

To return to our point of departure, in *Die Schuldlosen* Broch attacks both the Nazi cult of nature of the *Blut und Boden* variety and what might be seen as the escapist tendencies in a writer such as Wiechert; he suggests an inner identity between them. Broch's equation is surely overdrastic, influenced perhaps by the Jewish doctrine of collective responsibility—'ich die Welt, die Welt mich bedingend'. But it is understandable in the apocalyptic atmosphere of the aftermath of the war.

In the posthumous novel *Der Versucher* the theme of false and true relationships between man and nature receives full orchestration. Broch treats at greater length than in *Die Schuldlosen* the actively violent and hysterical side of that general 'Vertierungsgefahr', exemplified in Nazism, which he felt threatened mankind. The novel is set in a remote Alpine village. A newcomer to the village, Marius Ratti, preaches a form of barbaric earth-worship. According to Marius no single individual matters, only the community as a whole; as a peasant community, the village lives from the bounty of the earth and finds its identity in worshipping the towering grandeur of the Alps and the fructifying rain drawn down by the mountains from the clouds above. The climax of the novel comes when, whipped up by Marius to mass hysteria, the villagers carry out a human sacrifice. The blood of a young girl is spilt in tribute to the earth. According to Marius the highest fate a human being can achieve is return to the earth as a willing sacrifice. The villagers also attack a scapegoat figure, a newcomer to the village, on whom they blame all their troubles. He is a man from the city who, according to Marius, can never therefore become part of the community since he does not live by the old ways. On the other hand, Marius and the villagers accept new ways such as modern medicine when it suits them. They are not quite prepared to die of the old natural diseases, as the logic of their creed would demand. The parallel with the Nazi cult of Germanic earth and the Germanic *Herrenvolk*, the hatred of the Jew as an outsider polluting the purity of the race, is clear. So too is the allusion to the inconsistency between ideological rejection of degenerate modern civilization and ruthless exploitation of modern technology to wage war.

Corresponding to the mythical figure of the grandfather in *Die Schuldlosen* is the equally mythical Mutter Gisson, in *Der Versucher*. She embodies natural wisdom. Through her and through the narrator's descriptions of the Alpine scenery, Broch expresses an alternative natural religion in opposition to Marius's blood-cult. Towards the end of the novel Mutter Gisson goes up into the mountains to die. Her dying is a sinking into nature quite different from the violence of the blood sacrifice. In the following extract the narrator, the village doctor, describes what he saw as he follows her to talk to her for the last time before her death:

> Kein Laut ist zu hören, kein Duft zu spüren; ich schmecke die Luft, sie ist wie destilliert. Nur das Sichtbare ist vorhanden, erfüllt von der Stille, körperlos, als sei es das Weltall selber. Wie die Wände eines ungeheueren hohlen Baumes ragen die Felsen um den Kessel, eines Baumes, der keine Außenseite mehr hat, und wie Wurzelsaft dunkel ruht der Teich inmitten, tiefer noch dringend sein Wurzelgehäuse in noch tiefere Stille, tiefer noch reichend bis zu dem Mittelpunkt der Welt. So ruht er inmitten. Das Echo der

Wände singt Schweigen, und Schweigen singt des Echos Quell aus der Tiefe. So träumt das Sterben, und in seinen ruhenden Wellen spiegeln sich die mittäglichen Sterne, die über dem Brunnenrand blinken —, mittäglich die Nacht, auf deren Grund der Sterbliche um den Kristall wandelt. Traum wohnt in Traum, Unendliches in Unendlichem, Unsichtbares in Unsichtbarem, doch das Auge des Sees und das Auge des Himmels spiegeln einander. (Chapter XII, pp. 542–3)

The doctor describes here a mystical experience, a transformation of the visible and natural into a vision of the invisible and spiritual. Marius's cult of nature is perverse. It is a form of idolatry, a worship of the physical sign instead of the spiritual essence. For the narrator, and for Broch, the great mountains—indeed all of visible nature—are but symbols. The physical is an echo or a reflection, to use the metaphors of our extract, of a metaphysical or spiritual order. Similarly human salvation lies not in any particular *outer* mode of life more 'natural' than others. All human beings partake of the spirit and so it is a great crime to make of anyone a scapegoat, an outsider to be destroyed.

Ultimately Broch's response to the horrors of war and modern industrial society is the religious answer of faith, faith in an indestructible metaphysical order. Here is a final example of how Broch links unique historical events and final transcendent order through nature symbolism. The passage comes from the opening of the chapter following the bloody climax of the novel:

Wie Großstadtschmutz im Flusse vermündet und, wieder rein geworden, ins Meer getragen wird, so läuft alles Elend, durchsichtig und rein geworden, wieder ins Leben zurück, wird wieder zu dem, was es gewesen ist, was es war und ist, was es bleiben wird: Leben, ein Teilchen des Ganzen, unerkennbar in der Ganzheit, aufgesaugt von ihr, unerkennbar in ihr, untergegangen im Unwandelbaren. Selbst die Scham, dieses heilige Gut des Menschen, das tiefer in ihm hinabreicht, als er es oft wahrhaben möchte, die Scham, die länger währen wollte als der Schmerz, auch sie wird wieder durchsichtig und zum unerkennbaren Leben, wird zu einer Linie der Abendröte, zu einem Gedanken im Meer des Gedachten. (Chapter XI, p. 480)

In nature man finds images for underlying harmony; but these images are only symbols, and the harmony they symbolize is spiritual and embraces man and nature alike. The reader who does not share Broch's religious belief in a metaphysical order may find this resolution of human and historical problems rather

E

arbitrary. Broch's portrayal of ideal characters, such as Mutter Gisson and the bee-keeper grandfather in *Die Schuldlosen*, comes dangerously close to the ludicrous: bare-footed old ladies gathering herbs and old gentlemen with odd vocal powers. Though these characters are not intended realistically as model citizens of the new Europe, the symbolism in this personified form is so remote from present-day Europeans and their concrete problems that it becomes incongruous at times.

Broch's *Versucher* is in the Romantic tradition. His view of nature has close affinities with the Romantic concept of a world-spirit: the soul of which nature is the body, just as man is body and spirit. Another Alpine novel, Thomas Mann's *Der Zauberberg*, has affinities with *Renaissance* nature symbolism. The naïve pastoral tradition suggests man would be happy were he to flee. the artifice of town and court and live in nature. But it is not so much this tradition Mann draws on. It is rather that more sophisticated pastoral which saw parallels between human social order and the order or hierarchy of nature. As the sun rules the heavens, so the monarch the state, and so on. The descriptions of the mountain landscape of *Der Zauberberg* imply analogies between the organization of nature and human values. But unlike the logical parallelism of Renaissance correspondences, Mann's analogies are negative ones: the organization of nature demonstrates what ought *not* to happen in the human sphere.

In the chapter entitled *Schnee* Hans Castorp sets off into the snowy Alpine landscape to climb higher up the mountain than ever before. The narrator comments on two aspects of snow as they impinge on Hans. The first is the individual snowflake. No single snowflake is identical with another. But:

> ... in sich selbst war jedes der kalten Erzeugnisse von unbedingtem Ebenmaß und eisiger Regelmäßigkeit, ja, dies war das Unheimliche, Widerorganische und Lebensfeindliche daran; sie waren zu regelmäßig, die zum Leben geordnete Substanz war es niemals in diesem Grade, dem Leben schauderte vor der genauen Richtigkeit ...
> (*Schnee*, p. 663)

The other aspect of snow is the mass of snowflakes together as a storm or a great blanket obliterating outlines, obscuring vision:

> Die nichtige Atmosphäre geriet in Aufruhr, sie war so ausgefüllt von Flockengewimmel, daß man nicht einen Schritt weit sah. Böen von erstickender Stärke versetzten das Gestöber in wilde,

treibende, seitliche Bewegung, sie wirbelten es von unten nach oben, von der Talsohle in die Lüfte empor, quirlten es in tollem Tanz durcheinander, — das war kein Schneefall mehr, es war ein Chaos von weißer Finsternis, ein Unwesen, die phänomenale Ausschreitung einer über das Gemäßigte hinausgehenden Region, worin nur der Schneefink, der plötzlich in Scharen zum Vorschein kam, sich heimatlich auskennen mochte. (*Schnee*, p. 652)

These twin images of deadly or *inhuman* regions—the microscopic world of formal perfection, the huge formless chaos of the storm—become associated symbolically with what is dangerous or *inhumane* in human affairs. The geometric perfection of the snow-crystals is associated particularly with totalitarian political systems. An excess of law and order can too easily become rigid tyranny. Similarly, traditional social or moral codes may become dead convention crushing all individual freedom. On the other hand, the wild chaos of the snow-storm is associated symbolically with the irrational passions of the human heart if unrestrained by any sense of ethical or social responsibility. The crystals and the storm are aspects of the same phenomenon. The implication is clear. Excessively logical political or moral systems and anarchic rejection of all order, whether political or personal, have the same end-effect: the destruction of humane values.

These are negative symbolic analogies. Mann also draws parallels of a more positive sort between human life and the order of nature, but, not surprisingly, they are rather different from Renaissance parallels. Mann is writing in the twentieth century in a scientific culture. The order of nature is expressed now by predictive laws, based on mathematical quantification and measurement. Such laws do not apply to huge areas of human life, to the body politic or aesthetics, for example. But they certainly apply to some areas of human life, particularly to the physical processes of life and death. All the medical sections of the book go to show this. Mann acknowledges too that the workings of the mind are to some extent physiologically determined and, paradoxically, that the body is to some extent a function of the mind. The doctors Krokowski and Behrens are agreed that disease may be psychosomatic. But Krokowski takes the view that such illness is psychological in origin, while Behrens argues that the psychological disturbance is itself physical or chemical in origin. Mann comes down on neither side in this argument. But he does suggest that the predictive laws of nature stretch far into the combined working of body and mind, though they by no means *wholly* determine human behaviour. For example, when Hans Castorp sets out to climb higher up the mountain and comes close to death he observes in himself all the known symptoms of exposure. But he is not quite far enough gone to be completely at the mercy of this particular law of nature:

> Für sein natürliches Teil war er sehr geneigt, sich der Unklarheit zu überlassen, die mit zunehmender Müdigkeit Besitz von ihm ergreifen wollte, nahm jedoch von dieser Geneigtheit Notiz und hielt sich gedanklich darüber auf. 'Das ist die modifizierte Erlebnisart von einem, der im Gebirge in einen Schneesturm gerät und nicht mehr heimfindet', dachte er arbeitend und redete abgerissene Brocken davon atemlos vor sich hin, indem er deutlichere Ausdrücke aus Diskretion vermied. 'Wer nachher davon hört, stellt es sich gräßlich vor, vergißt aber, daß die Krankheit — und meine Lage ist ja gewissermaßen eine Krankheit — sich ihren Mann schon so zurichtet, daß sie miteinander auskommen können. Da gibt es sensorische Herabminderungen, Gnadennarkosen, Erleichterungsmaßnahmen der Natur, jawohl ... Man muß jedoch dagegen kämpfen, denn sie haben ein doppeltes Gesicht, sind zweideutig im höchsten Grad; bei ihrer Würdigung kommt alles auf den Gesichtspunkt an. Sie sind gut gemeint und eine Wohltat, sofern man eben nicht heimkommen soll, sind aber sehr schlimm gemeint und äußerst bekämpfenswert, sofern von Heimkommen überhaupt noch die Rede ist, wie bei mir, der ich nicht daran denke, in diesem meinem stürmisch schlagenden Herzen nicht daran denke, mich hier von blödsinnig regelmäßiger Kristallometrie zudecken zu lassen ...' (pp. 669–70)

The 'blödsinnig regelmäßige Kristallometrie' is the hexagonal regularity of snow-crystals. The shape of snow-crystals and the mental and physical effects of exposure are equally laws of nature. But, as Hans realizes, man is not wholly subject to the laws of nature. It is ridiculous to call snow-crystals 'blödsinnig', but the comic incongruity makes a serious point. It asserts man's superiority over nature, it reveals a human attitude, an unquantifiable factor which prevents human behaviour from being wholly predictable.

Der Zauberberg is full of scientific information, whether on crystallography or metabolic processes, and Mann argues that human beings are subject to natural laws, albeit to a limited extent. But he does not argue in the manner of a textbook. He is less concerned with the facts as such than with how these facts affect his hero emotionally, how they affect his sense of identity. One element in Hans's sense of identity is his sense of himself in relation to nature. He is a child of his age in that he looks at nature from a scientific point of view. But he learns as the novel goes on that there is no necessary conflict between such rational knowledge and the emotional value nature continues to have for him. Man may know the laws of physics and still feel joy, awe or defiance in the face of the beauty, grandeur, or threatening inexorability of nature. He may find in nature symbols for matters of human concern, while still acknowledging the *literal* application of natural laws to human life. Mann's descriptions of the Alpine scenery do full justice to these very different attitudes which coexist in the human mind. They combine scientific analysis, symbolic suggestion and sheer celebration.

The religiosity of Broch and Mann's humanism have this in common: both place human life, in part at least, in a natural context. Even in the highly artificial industrial civilization of today, both writers see the individual's sense of identity, his sense of relation to reality beyond himself, as profoundly affected by awareness of nature as an environment and of the natural in himself. Broch and Mann, in differing ways, attempt to harmonize man as nature and man as a self-conscious thinking creature. Another striking experiment in this direction is Döblin's *Berlin Alexanderplatz*. Döblin constantly draws analogies between the interaction of man and city and the interaction of animal and environment. Franz Biberkopf's wild outbursts of violence are compared with the instinctive terror and aggression of any threatened animal. As Biberkopf comes closer to death, so the different layers of his body and mind are uncovered: human consciousness, animal instinct, the plant-like metabolism of the body's chemical processes. But like Broch and Mann, Döblin asserts human superiority over the purely natural, for man *knows* himself and his environment, he is not simply instinct and reflex. He must recognize his own nature without fear and so learn to control it.

In contrast to such works which try to integrate nature and culture, nature and morality, nature and spirit, are those which in varying ways emphasize the disharmonies and tensions of modern man. The work of Hermann Hesse, for example, often presents a vision of man alienated from nature and torn within himself. It expresses a profound sense of a *lost* unity of man and nature. Max Frisch's *Homo Faber* shows man as engineer surrounded

by his own artefacts, who has lost contact with nature as an inner
force and an external environment (see *Register*). Or there is
Kafka's profoundly ambivalent view of nature. At times it is a
threatening or simply alien force, at other times an image of
perfection from which man is forever excluded through his self-
consciousness. Here, for example, is the ape in *Bericht für eine
Akademie* describing human acrobats:

> Oft habe ich in den Varietés vor meinem Auftreten irgendein
> Künstlerpaar oben an der Decke an Trapezen hantieren sehen. Sie
> schwangen sich, sie schaukelten, sie sprangen, sie schwebten einander
> in die Arme, einer trug den anderen an den Haaren mit dem
> Gebiß. 'Auch das ist Menschenfreiheit', dachte ich, 'selbstherrliche
> Bewegung.' Du Verspottung der heiligen Natur! Kein Bau würde
> standhalten vor dem Gelächter des Affentums bei diesem Anblick.
> (*Erzählungen*, p. 158)

Even artistic self-expression, that highest expression of human
freedom, is but a travesty of 'holy nature'. For the conscious
artistry of the human acrobat can never equal the unconscious
perfection of movement of the untamed beast.

In conclusion, here is a piece of simple celebration of nature.
It comes from the Swiss writer Robert Walser's novel *Der Gehülfe*:

> Das waren Tage das, nasse und stürmische, und doch war ein
> eigener Zauber dabei. Das Wohnzimmer wurde auf einmal so weh-
> mütig-gemütlich. Die Nässe und Kälte draußen machten die Zimmer
> freundlicher. Man heizte jetzt schon. Durch das neblige Grau der
> Landschaft brannten und leuchteten fiebrig die gelben und roten
> Blätter. Das Rot der Kirschbaumblätter hatte etwas Glühendes und
> Wundes und Wehes; aber es war schön, das versöhnte und erheiterte
> wiederum. Oft erschien das ganze Wiesen- und Baumland in Schleier
> und nasse Tücher eingehüllt, oben und unten und in der Ferne und
> Nähe alles grau und naß. Wie durch einen trüben Traum schritt man
> durch das alles hindurch. Und doch drückte auch dieses Wetter und
> diese Art Welt eine geheime Heiterkeit aus. Man roch die Bäume,
> unter denen man ging, man hörte reifes Obst in die Wiese und auf
> den Weg fallen. Es schien alles doppelt und dreifach still geworden zu
> sein. Die Geräusche schienen zu schlafen oder sich zu fürchten, zu
> tönen. An den frühen Morgen und späten Abenden drang über den
> See der langdahingeatmete Ton der Nebelhörner, die einander da
> draußen, Schiffe ankündigend, das warnende Signal gaben. Sie
> erklangen wie Klagelaute von hüflosen Tieren. Ja, Nebel gab es
> genug. Dazwischen gab es einmal wieder einen schönen Tag. Und
> Tage gab es, echt herbstliche, weder schöne noch wüste, weder

besonders freundliche noch besonders trübe, weder sonnige noch
dunkle Tage, sondern solche, die ganz gleichmäßig licht und dunkel
blieben von morgens bis abends, wo vier Uhr nachmittags dasselbe
Weltbild bot wie elf Uhr vormittags, wo alles ruhig und mattgolden
und ein bißchen betrübt dalag, wo die Farben still in sich selber
zurücktraten, gleichsam für sich sorgenvoll träumend. Solche Tage,
wie liebte sie Joseph! Alles kam ihm dann schön, leicht und vertraut
vor. Diese leichte Traurigkeit in der Natur machte ihn sorglos, beinahe
gedankenlos. Es war dann vieles nicht schlimm, vieles nicht mehr
schwer, was ihm vorher schlimm und schwerfällig erschienen war.
Eine angenehme Vergeßlichkeit trieb ihn in solchen Tagen die
hübschen Dorfstraßen entlang. Die Welt war ruhig, gelassen und gut
und gedankenvoll anzusehen. Man konnte überall hingehen, es blieb
immer dasselbe blasse und volle Bild, dasselbe Gesicht, und das
Gesicht blickte einen ernst und zart an.

Zu dieser Zeit wurde unter dem verschwiegenen Aufruf: Geld her!
ein neues Inserat 'Fabrikbeteiligung gesucht' in die Zeitungen gedruckt.
Die kleinen Geschäftsleute des Dorfes hatten Geld haben wollen,
waren aber abgewiesen und auf spätere Zeiten vertröstet worden.
Im Dorfe wurde infolgedessen laut gesprochen: Tobler zahlt nicht!
Die Frau wagte sich kaum noch recht in die innere Ortschaft; sie
fürchtete, beleidigt zu werden. Die hauptstädtische Schneiderin
ersuchte brieflich um Einsendung des Preises für das angefertigte
Kleid. Der Betrag belief sich auf rund hundert Franken, eine dem
Frauengedächtnis nur zu gut sich einprägende Summe.

(pp. 111–12)

Passages such as these add to the novel an important dimension
of simple pleasure in nature in contrast to the perplexing
ambiguities of human relationship. *Der Gehülfe* tells of the half-
year or so Joseph Marte spends as apprentice in the Tobler
household. Herr Tobler has set up on his own to make his fortune
from his inventions, a clock, an invalid chair, an automatic
dispenser of cartridges for Swiss *Schützenfeste*. By the end of the
novel Tobler is about to go bankrupt and Joseph leaves without
ever receiving any salary. He leaves reluctantly, for he has grown
fond of the family. Nothing much happens. Joseph spends a lot
of time drinking coffee in the garden with Frau Tobler and
playing cards in the evening. He visits an old friend in Zürich,
he goes for walks.

On the surface the novel is comic in tone. The young man
swings rather ludicrously between nervous fear of his employer,
noble outrage at injustice done him, and a yearning affection.

The Tobler family's complacent kindness and superiority, their bourgeois solidity is laughable in view of their very unsolid financial position. They comically persist in a patronizing manner when they have no patronage to dispense and cannot even pay the gardener. Underlying the comic surface, however, is a deep unease. Joseph's shifting feelings come not just from immaturity, they reflect radical uncertainty about himself and others. He is not sure whether he really feels what he seems to. Are his pride, his indignation, his love real? He determines consciously to love his work and be happy, yet all the time his life remains rather strange and, as it were, external to him, a role with which he cannot quite identify. It is this inner isolation which causes him to love and envy the unreflecting self-assurance of the Toblers. The erosion of the Toblers' apparent security, culminating in a depressing Christmas Eve when the lonely people, the Toblers and Joseph, sit playing cards to dull their misery, is not funny at all, but frightening.

Beneath the surface events, the novel moves through a series of shifting moods and ambiguous emotions. But the uncertainty of the human relationships, the constantly threatening sense of unreality in Joseph are counterbalanced by the indubitable reality of sense impressions. The delicious coffee with its deep brown colour, the tendrils of hair on Frau Tobler's neck, the delicate yellowish colour and savoury taste of *Kalbsbraten*, the feel of water sliding over the skin during a swim, the velvet surface of the lake—all these provide an anchor in reality for Joseph's consciousness. The link between inner mood and external cause is unproblematic. It is above all the Swiss landscape in all its seasonal changes that Joseph can love with simplicity. In the passage above sense impressions and emotional reactions intertwine harmoniously. Sounds, colours, smells, brisk movement, warmth, cold elicit pleasurable melancholy, exhilaration, joy, familiarity, a sense of being at home in one's skin. It is perhaps this mixture of estrangement from, yet loving attachment to life that caused Kafka to see in Walser a kindred spirit.

12   Politics, History and Utopia

This chapter will look at novels concerned with the recent history of Germany, a history of vast political upheavals. It will look too at some Utopian and historical novels, because a setting in the future or the past turns out very often to be a distancing device in works really concerned with the present. To turn from nature to politics seems a move from one extreme to its opposite. Nature implies all that is unchanging, inborn, timeless; politics all that is changing and contingent. But, as the last chapter showed, even attitudes towards nature may have political undertones. This is true of the other two topics discussed in this section, *Character* and Man and Society. An important element in one's sense of identity is the feeling of belonging to a particular community or cultural tradition. In an unstable society everything tends to take on political colouring. The troubled history of Germany since the foundation of the Reich in 1870 has meant that all kinds of attitudes, from the overtly political to the apparently non-political, can be seen as politically significant.

The unification of Germany was partly a gradual evolution brought about by economic and cultural pressures. But the actual political unit of the Reich resulted from a violent solution to the struggle between Austria and Prussia for dominance over the German states. The new nation-state by no means satisfied all her citizens. Some objections were straightforwardly political: to the undue power of Prussia over the other territories, for example, or to an undemocratic, indeed unrealistic constitution which failed to reflect the real forces in a rapidly industrializing Germany. But there were other objections, often expressed in apparently un-political terms. The trouble was that the Reich failed to give real political shape to that amorphous notion of Germany as a cultural sphere. Many Germans looked back to narrower provincial loyalties and considered the nation-state as such to be un-German. Many hated the economic and social transformations brought

E*

about by Germany's industrial revolution, a reaction leading
often to political apathy. Many had wider ambitions for a greater
Germany whose political contours would coincide with the German
linguistic-cultural sphere in Europe, or simply defined Germany
in cultural terms, ignoring the dangerous political implications
such a view might have. Such feelings were of course not limited
to Germany. In *Der Mann ohne Eigenschaften* Robert Musil shows
the clash in Austria between pan-German nationalism and the
old supranational ideals of the Habsburg Empire. Musil's novel
is set in 1913, but it is clear how a cultural sense of 'Germanness'
could lead later to Austrian sympathy with Hitler's National
Socialism. The Nazi cocktail of *Blut und Boden* was an intoxicating
brew. It satisfied local attachment to a lost rural provincialism,
grandiose dreams of pan-Germanic empire, and specific grudges
such as the loss of Alsace. By linking mystic *Blut* to all too real
political *Boden* it justified an aggressive expansionist policy. Not
all conservative proponents of a cultural rather than a political
definition of Germany betrayed their own principles by succumbing to a myth with such crude political overtones. But with
hindsight it is easy to see why so many did.

There is then, especially before the last war, a spectrum running
Apparently non-political or anti-political attitudes in Germany
were also fuelled by a strong intellectual tradition of metaphysical
speculation. Many Germans saw the cataclysm of the First World
War as inevitable, as part of the logic of history itself. Oswald
Spengler, for example, wrote of war as a symptom of the inevitable
decline of Western civilization and of history as a process analogous
to the biological cycle of growth, maturity and decay. Politics in a
pragmatic sense clearly could have little significance in such a
philosophy.

There is then, especially before the last war, a spectrum running
from overtly political works at one extreme to the completely
unpolitical, even anti-political at the other. But many of the
latter had, willy-nilly, political implications. The quarrel between
Heinrich and Thomas Mann at the time of the First World War
was a clash between the two extremes of the spectrum. Heinrich
Mann was one of the most trenchant critics of Wilhelminian
Germany. His political satire *Der Untertan* (1918) is a far-seeing
study of the disastrous course on which Germany was set (see
Man and Society). In the essay *Zola* (1915), Heinrich Mann
implied that literature should be politically committed and
expressed his own commitment to the ideals of democratic

socialism. In what is perhaps the most striking document of German conservative thinking, *Betrachtungen eines Unpolitischen* (1917), Thomas Mann attacked his brother, the 'Zivilisationsliterat'. To the Western democratic ideal of 'civilization' he opposed a German ideal of 'culture', a culture he saw threatened by the attempt to make of Germany a liberal democratic nation-state. In a chapter entitled 'Einiges über Menschlichkeit' he writes:

> Vor allem schien mir niemals eine Meinungsverschiedenheit darüber möglich, daß 'Menschlichkeit', eine menschliche Denk- und Betrachtungsweise selbstverständlich den Gegensatz aller Politik bedeutet. Menschlich denken und betrachten heißt unpolitisch denken und betrachten, ein Satz mit dem man sofort in schärfsten Widerspruch zur Demokratie gerät.[1]

As the last phrase indicates, Mann's rejection of dehumanizing dogmatic politics in favour of a kind of suprapolitical humanism is disingenuous. His advocacy of a musical, philosophical and spiritual tradition is tainted by an all too political nationalism, which leads him to some highly political conclusions, such as support of an authoritarian system and of the war against the western democracies.

At the unpolitical end of the scale, however, there were enormous differences of attitude. Hermann Hesse, for example, was deeply pessimistic about the threat modern mass civilization presented to inner spiritual values and patrician culture. But, more clear-sighted than the Thomas Mann of the *Betrachtungen*, Hesse consistently rejected the cultural propaganda of German nationalism. He never made the mistake of seeing the war as a spiritual crusade. In complete contrast is Ernst Jünger. Jünger shares with Hesse a tendency towards mysticism: to seek through ever deeper probing into the self ultimate self-transcendence. But Jünger saw the violence and suffering of war as an extreme situation which could intensify mystic experience. Jünger's work demonstrates particularly clearly how an apparently non-political concern with spiritual values may take on disturbing political overtones. *Die totale Mobilmachung* (1931), for example, extends the notion of personal self-transcendence into a totalitarian vision of a state where the individual is completely absorbed into the collective body of society.

[1] *Betrachtungen eines Unpolitischen* (Frankfurt a.M., 1956), p. 420.

Particularly interesting is Hermann Broch's attitude towards the First World War. Broch believed the war was symptomatic of an inevitable historical process. But unlike Spengler's writings glorifying war as the birth-pangs of a new age, Broch's novel *Die Schlafwandler* (published between 1931 and 1933) is a lament for the suffering caused by historical change. He altered the basic conception of the third part of the trilogy, *Huguenau oder die Sachlichkeit,* because horror of the war and recognition of the Nazi threat proved stronger than the logic of his theory. He found it impossible to make the protagonist Huguenau at once the agent of the violent dissolution of the old order *and* the herald of the new order. A new character, a child, takes on the latter function and Huguenau survives the war to remain as a threat of renewed chaos. Broch believed in the historical inevitability of certain large-scale changes which he explained in metaphysical terms. But he came to believe that the *manner* in which historical transitions occurred was not uncontrollable and so a political dimension comes increasingly into his work. In *Die Schuldlosen* (completed in 1949) the main character's name begins with A. Andreas's crime is that of indifference and political apathy. At the other end of the alphabet is the Nazi *Z*acharias. Andreas sees clearly that he is living in an age of profound historical change and withdraws from all action out of a sense of despairing defeatism. Zacharias acts violently out of mindless panic in the face of a changing world he cannot comprehend. He is a mathematics teacher, and for a while his hatred and fear are focused on the new 'Jewish' physics of Einstein! Neither Andreas nor Zacharias can be absolved of guilt, both personal and political, on the grounds that the historical situation was opaque and beyond control. The rise of National Socialism and the war may have been symptoms of a vast change ultimately beyond control, but the symptoms could have been modified through rational and humane political activity.

Broch's work exemplifies a major tendency in German literature of the inter-war period and since 1945. This is the call not so much for any specific political action as for political awareness as such, and a concern with the political consequences of apparently non-political attitudes. This tendency is evident in the development of three major writers, Thomas Mann, Döblin and Hesse. The transition from the bitter polemics of Mann's *Betrachtungen eines Unpolitischen* to the conciliatory humour of *Der Zauberberg*

(1924) is not as illogical as it at first sight appears. The very fact that Mann was led to advocate political steps to defend unpolitical values was proof that the unpolitical stance could not be maintained. Mann remained a cultural conservative all his life and *Der Zauberberg* celebrates the same cultural traditions as the *Betrachtungen*. But there is this essential difference: *Der Zauberberg* recognizes that all culture has a political dimension. This recognition removed the whole basis of Mann's anti-democratic stance. It enabled him to espouse political ideals more in keeping with his professed humanism than the aggressive nationalism of the *Betrachtungen*. The hero of *Der Zauberberg*, Hans Castorp, learns to be critical of any tradition which becomes mere authoritarian formalism inimical to all change. He preserves a sceptical distance from bloodless abstractions which justify crushing real human beings in the name of abstract humanity. As the novel progresses, so Hans's typical activity of 'Dösen', an unreasoning trance-like condition, gives way to a new mental state he calls 'Regieren'. 'Regieren' involves a critical and analytical exercise of his powers of reasoning in all spheres from the most private to the public and political. To be sure, he never accepts the view of his democratic mentor, Settembrini, that music is 'politisch verdächtig' and remains to the end under the spell of Schubert's *Lindenbaum*. This song symbolizes for him all that is inward-looking, unpolitical, nostalgic in the German Romantic tradition. However, Hans consciously recognizes his own irrational tendencies and the need, not to suppress them, but to complement them with responsible thinking and activity. In social rather than personal terms, the implication of Mann's novel is the need for political responsibility in Germany if what is best in her cultural tradition is to survive. Mann adds a humorous twist to this counterbalancing of music by politics, for Hans continues his 'Regieren' even while listening to music. For example, the high priest's call of 'Rechtfertige dich' in *Aida* becomes a call to responsibility he feels himself bound to answer. Whether he will or not once the holocaust of the Great War is over is left an open question at the end of the novel, but there can be no doubt as to Mann's hopes.

Der Zauberberg is a work by a German who, under pressure of political events, profoundly modified his earlier attitudes and in particular recognized early the political dangers threatening the Weimar Republic. A rather similar reappraisal of past attitudes marks Döblin's *Berlin Alexanderplatz* (1929). In earlier novels such as *Die drei Sprünge des Wang-lun* (1915), which shows the influence of Eastern contemplative philosophy, and the historical novel *Wallenstein* (1920), of which the true hero is not Wallenstein but the passive figure of the emperor Ferdinand II, Döblin expressed a philosophy of passive contemplation. He suggested that all evil results from human enmeshment in action aimed at controlling and possessing the material world. Truth lies in a spiritual reality to be reached not through action, but through contemplation.

Berlin Alexanderplatz marks a shift away from this quietist, unpolitical position to a more active philosophy. At the end of the novel the narrator sums up the lessons his hero Franz Biberkopf has learnt:

> Wach sein, wach sein, es geht was vor in der Welt. Die Welt ist nicht aus Zucker gemacht. Wenn sie Gasbomben werfen, muß ich ersticken, man weiß nicht, warum sie geschmissen haben, aber darauf kommts nicht an, man hat Zeit gehabt, sich drum zu kümmern.
>
> Wenn Krieg ist, und sie ziehen mich ein, und ich weiß nicht warum, und der Krieg ist auch ohne mich da, so bin ich schuld, und mir geschieht recht. Wach sein, wach sein, man ist nicht allein. Die Luft kann hageln und regnen, dagegen kann man sich nicht wehren, aber gegen vieles andere kann man sich wehren. Da werde ich nicht mehr schrein wie früher: das Schicksal, das Schicksal. Das muß man nicht als Schicksal verehren, man muß es ansehen, anfassen und zerstören.
>
> Wach sein, Augen auf, aufgepaßt, tausend gehören zusammen, wer nicht aufwacht, wird ausgelacht oder zur Strecke gebracht.
>
> Die Trommel wirbelt hinter ihm. Marschieren, marschieren. Wir ziehen in den Krieg mit festem Schritt, es gehen mit uns hundert Spielleute mit, Morgenrot, Abendrot, leuchtest uns zum frühen Tod. (pp. 500–01)

Döblin's novel demonstrates the indivisibility of personal, social and political morality. No man is an island. He both affects and is affected by his social environment. If he closes his eyes to this fact of life, then he will become no better than an animal in the jungle which cannot foresee danger and can only react with terrified aggression when it is already too late. When Franz Biberkopf comes out of prison at the beginning of the novel, he determines to ignore the world around him and concentrate on leading his own life honestly. But external pressures defeat him. The lesson is clear. Political upheavals, wars, economic disasters affect good and evil men alike. The former must accept political responsibility to make the good life possible.

The second two paragraphs delineate a political position which requires on the one hand solidarity: alone the individual is helpless. On the other hand, merely to belong to a collectivity is not enough. The individual must retain personal responsibility. When Franz fails in his attempt to go it alone, he falls into the opposite error of blind adherence to a group. The herd instinct is as dangerous as a narrow individualism, especially if the herd you join is a gang of criminals. Franz comes to grief again. And Döblin prophetically warns that Germany too will come to grief if her citizens band together into a criminal political party out of self-righteous resentment against the injustice of the Versailles Treaty and panic in the face of economic problems. This is the way not to safety in numbers but to self-destruction. Döblin's general warning is all the more authoritative because his portrayal of the specific details of the social and political situation in Germany is so clearsighted, his analysis of the threat to peace so accurate and prophetic.

Döblin's political imperative rests on a moral imperative grounded finally on a religious or metaphysical basis, so that his later conversion to Christianity is no surprise. None the less, there are good grounds for calling *Berlin Alexanderplatz* a political novel since the political dimension of human behaviour is so emphasized. This is less true of Hesse's work. But he too, if more ambiguously, modified earlier attitudes under the impact of political events. In his case the change comes later than with Mann or Döblin. Hesse's *Steppenwolf*, published in 1927, and *Das Glasperlenspiel*, published during the war in 1943, are a striking contrast.

At the end of *Steppenwolf*, the hero Harry Haller enters a magic theatre and comes face to face with all the contradictory facets of his personality. He recognizes, for example, that there is no bestiality of which he is incapable. Along with horrifying self-recognition goes deep cultural pessimism. In the magic theatre he meets Mozart, the last great composer unflawed by modern decay. Harry expresses his disgust of the modern world when he hears the music of Handel painfully distorted by a radio. But Mozart teaches him how to come to terms with his inner contradictions and the decadence of the world around him:

> Und nun hören Sie ja nicht bloß einen durch das Radio vergewaltigten Händel, der dennoch auch in dieser scheußlichsten

Erscheinungsform noch göttlich ist, — Sie hören und sehen, Wertester, zugleich ein vortreffliches Gleichnis alles Lebens. Wenn Sie dem Radio zuhören, so hören und sehen Sie den Urkampf zwischen Idee und Erscheinung, zwischen Ewigkeit und Zeit, zwischen Göttlichem und Menschlichem. Gerade so, mein Lieber, wie das Radio die herrlichste Musik der Welt zehn Minuten lang wahllos in die unmöglichsten Räume wirft, in bürgerliche Salons und in Dachkammern, zwischen schwatzende, fressende, gähnende, schlafende Abonnenten hinein, so, wie er diese Musik ihrer sinnlichen Schönheit beraubt, sie verdirbt, verkratzt und verschleimt und dennoch ihren Geist nicht ganz umbringen kann — gerade so schmeißt das Leben, die sogennante Wirklichkeit, mit dem herrlichen Bilderspiel der Welt um sich, läßt auf Händel einen Vortrag über die Technik der Bilanzverschleierung in mittleren industriellen Betrieben folgen, macht aus zauberhaften Orchesterklängen einen unappetitlichen Töneschleim, schiebt seine Technik, seine Betriebsamkeit, seine wüste Notdurft und Eitelkeit überall zwischen Idee und Wirklichkeit, zwischen Orchester und Ohr. Das ganze Leben ist so, mein Kleiner, und wir müssen es so sein lassen, und wenn wir keine Esel sind, lachen wir dazu. Leuten von Ihrer Art steht es durchaus nicht zu, am Radio oder am Leben Kritik zu üben. Lernen Sie lieber erst zuhören! Lernen Sie ernst nehmen, was des Ernstnehmens wert ist, und lachen über das andre! (pp. 409–10)

Perhaps Hi-Fi would have reconciled Harry to modern times, but it is doubtful. Mozart advocates a remote stance of humorous and aesthetic contemplation vis-à-vis the world. He devalues so-called reality, an object of laughter, as against the timelessly beautiful. As important as what he says is his tone— of aristocratic contempt for the ugly citizens of the modern world and their petty and contemptible concerns. The trouble is that aesthetic contemplation may be rudely interrupted and even Hesse's Mozart might have found difficulty in raising a laugh at some imminent developments in European reality. Paradoxically, it is the 'positive' final message of *Steppenwolf* which arouses doubts, not the preceding pessimistic study of a tormented individual. Literature is not bound in a crude way to be morally or politically committed, and in any case it is sometimes the most seemingly private statements which seem to later generations most precisely to measure the pulse of history. But if a work purports, as does *Steppenwolf*, to provide a solution to moral and social dilemmas, then the critic is justified in judging that solution on moral and political criteria.

Das Glasperlenspiel, if rather ambiguously, turns away from the aesthetic stance of *Steppenwolf*. The novel explores a Utopian realization of the kind of aesthetic and contemplative life to which Harry Haller presumably aspires. The hero Josef Knecht finally leaves Utopian Castalia. He does so for many reasons. The urge to action is an aspect of personality which must be subdued in Castalia and so he decides to go into the world fully to develop himself. He becomes critical too of the unquestioning aristocratic assumptions of Castalia, and recognizes that the high aesthetic culture it preserves was originally rooted in the world of practical activity. He sees too how static the culture of Castalia is. It is backward-looking, cut off from the present, and so cannot develop. Its aesthetic products may be the supreme expression of a culture, but Castalia preserves the past rather than expressing the present. And so Josef Knecht answers the call to action and involvement in the world's affairs, not because he has turned against aesthetic and contemplative values, but the more truly to serve them.

It would be perverse to call *Das Glasperlenspiel* a political novel. It is much too oblique for that. Knecht dies before he ever reaches the outside world; the effect of his example remains in the realm of legend. But none the less, in the context of Hesse's work, and of German literature generally, *Das Glasperlenspiel* is symptomatic of an increasingly pragmatic approach to the real problems of the present, a move away from metaphysics and hankering after the past. Josef Knecht meditates on his conversion thus:

> Es ging, so schien es, beim 'Erwachen' nicht um die Wahrheit und die Erkenntnis, sondern um die Wirklichkeit und deren Erleben und Bestehen. Im Erwachen drang man nicht näher an den Kern der Dinge, an die Wahrheit heran, man erfaßte, vollzog oder erlitt dabei nur die Einstellung des eigenen Ich zur augenblicklichen Lage der Dinge. (*Die Legende*, pp. 490–91)

Since 1945, especially among the younger generation of writers, the trend away from metaphysical speculation towards a more empirical spirit is evident. A main preoccupation has been the Nazi past. Some writers emphasize political questions, others confront the past in personal moral terms. Günter Grass's *Die Blechtrommel*, for example, is an oblique indictment of its hero Oskar of political irresponsibility. Oskar hated the Nazis from the start, made one or two personal gestures of defiance, but he accepted some of the more dubious compromises of the 'inner emigration', kept out of involvement in any organized resistance, such as that of the young Communist workers, and generally went his own way. Grass is *not* advocating art as propaganda, but he is suggesting that art, especially if it portrays society, always expresses, implicitly if not explicitly, value judgments of some kind. In that sense all art is committed. Oskar's claim to stand totally outside society is spurious. And, in any case, artistic freedom is one thing, irresponsible artists *qua* citizens quite another.

Different in emphasis is Alfred Andersch's novel *Sansibar oder der letzte Grund* (1957). It is set in 1938. Four characters confront the moral dilemma of how to behave faced by the *fait accompli* of the Third Reich. For the fifth, a young Jewess, there is no choice. She must leave Germany. The Nazis are simply 'die Anderen'; specific historical details are not emphasized; the situation becomes, as it were, an abstract test, a *Grenzsituation*. The four characters are called upon to decide who they truly are, in what their human integrity lies. Significantly, two are lapsed Communists, their reasons for action are specifically *not* political. The fisherman agrees to risk his life to preserve his self-respect, his manhood, the priest to bear witness to God and to life as something meaningful. The young boy returns home to danger to prove himself in the adventure of life and the great adventure is not in 'Sansibar', but at home in Germany. The former Communist party official risks his life to save a religious statue from destruction by the Nazis. The statue symbolizes for him the principle of freedom. Grass and Andersch both call for responsibility in the individual, but the emphasis is different: Grass is the more social writer, Andersch more concerned with the isolated moral gesture. The difference is evident too in the mood of the two novels: *Die Blechtrommel* is more satiric, *Sansibar* more pathetic.

Most of the novels mentioned, if not all political novels, have touched on politics in the sense of portraying some aspects of the political history of Germany this century. But not all. *Das Glasperlenspiel*, for example, is set in a Utopia sometime in the future. Utopias often have an element of imaginative play, but where play predominates they shade off into what might more properly be called science fiction. Other less playful characteristics of Utopian fiction bring it close to the main concerns of this

chapter. Utopias often isolate and develop significant tendencies
in the present. They warn or exhort, more commonly these days
warn of what the future may hold. Huxley's *Brave New World* and
Orwell's *1984* are of this type. So are Döblin's *Berge, Meere und
Giganten*, Ernst Jünger's *Gläserne Bienen* and Hermann Kasack's
Die Stadt hinter dem Strom, a despairing vision of dehumanized
collective existence in a world governed by the demands of the
machine. *Das Glasperlenspiel* is not quite of this type. It is less
concerned with warning about what might develop out of the
present, than with isolating and enlarging aspects of the present,
in this case certain cultural presumptions. Often, of course, the
two concerns are combined. Jünger's *Gläserne Bienen*, for example,
is at once a rather ambivalent warning of the potentially dehumanizing aspects of a technological culture. At the same time it is
an uncomfortable apologia for an earlier fascination with war
and totalitarian social order, an oblique comment on the recent
German past.

Utopia in the traditional sense of the ideal society is rare in
twentieth-century literature. In this sense, Utopia sometimes
appears as a dimension in otherwise non-Utopian novels: the
author judges the present from the Utopian standpoint of what
man or society ideally could be. But Utopia generally remains
unrealized, an ideal from which reality always falls short. Since
1848 and the first big wave of German emigration, America—
the New World—has often served as a cypher for a Utopian
society. Kafka's novel *Amerika* opens thus:

> Als der sechzehnjährige Karl Roßmann, der von seinen armen
> Eltern nach Amerika geschickt worden war, weil ihn ein Dienst-
> mädchen verführt und ein Kind von ihm bekommen hatte, in dem
> schon langsam gewordenen Schiff in den Hafen von New York
> einfuhr, erblickte er die schon längst beobachtete Statue der
> Freiheitsgöttin wie in einem plötzlich stärker gewordenen Sonnen-
> licht. Ihr Arm mit dem Schwert ragte wie neuerdings empor, und
> um ihre Gestalt wehten die freien Lüfte. (p. 7)

The beginning of the first sentence tells of the corruption of
innocence. It suggests too the tragic confusion of the Old World.
The guilty are so often also the victims—the seducing maid left
with her illegitimate baby—and the victims are guilty—the
seduced Karl who fathers and deserts a child. The authority
exercised by the parents has nothing to do with order and justice,
it simply sets the seal on a confused situation. Then comes in

contrast the image of the Statue of Liberty holding the sword of justice, the insignia of the New World. But the impetus of this opening paragraph with its transition from the troubled European past to the Utopian American future is not maintained. Indeed, even in this paragraph a certain delaying movement is evident in the slowing down of the ship as it enters the harbour. Karl's landing in America is strangely delayed. He returns to the bowels of the ship and is immediately caught up in the hatreds, the injustice, the misery of Europe. When he does land, he brings with him into the New World all the problems of the Old. A spirit of pessimistic scepticism undermines the American Utopia except in the final dreamlike episode. Broch's *Die Schlafwandler* also introduces the motif of the American Utopia. In the second part, *Esch oder die Anarchie*, Esch dreams of escape into the New World away from the disorder and injustice of Europe. But the means he employs to get there involve him even deeper in guilt. Günter Grass too looks back to the dream of America at the beginning of *Die Blechtrommel* when he tells of the legend of Oskar's fire-raising, revolutionary grandfather who perhaps drowned, but perhaps escaped the authorities and swam all the way to America. But if he did reach the land of the free, his revolutionary fervour is sadly transformed there:

> Joe Colchic soll er sich genannt haben. Holzhandel mit Kanada gab man als sein Gewerbe an. Aktien bei Streichholzfirmen. Begründer von Feuerversicherungen. Schwerreich und einsam beschrieb man meinen Großvater: in einem Wolkenkratzer hinter riesigem Schreibtisch sitzend, Ringe mit glühenden Steinen an allen Fingern tragend, mit seiner Leibwache exerzierend, die Feuerwehruniform trug, polnisch singen konnte und Phönixgarde hieß. (p. 27)

Utopia lies in the future. Sometimes the ideal may lie in the mythical past, for example the Christian Garden of Eden, or the classical Golden Age. Hans Castorp has a vision on the magic mountain of a mediterranean paradise, a Golden Age of humanity. Broch's *Tod des Vergil* takes up the motif of the Golden Age from the *Aeneid*, but it looks forward into the future too through the dying Virgil's prophetic vision of Christianity. The vision is in mythical garb; the Christ child, a symbol of rebirth and regeneration, is simply a new embodiment of the ancient myth of the holy child. But the projection into the future makes it, from Virgil's point of view, a Utopian vision. Here myth and Utopia coincide.

But *Der Tod des Vergil* uses history as well as myth and Utopia to express human ideals and aspirations, and to comment obliquely on the present. Broch believed the twentieth century to be an age of transition, at the end of the Christian era and on the threshold of a new era which would establish an as yet unknown system of values. Transitions are opaque and incomprehensible until complete. A writer who tries to analyse the present as a transition risks usurping the role of prophet only to be proved wrong. He invites the accusation of wishful thinking if he tries to look into the future or of pessimism if he writes only of the collapse of past values. Broch gets over this difficulty by portraying an analogous transition in the past, from the Classical to the Christian era, so that he has inbuilt, as it were, the dimension of a future known to the reader and towards which Virgil's speculations are angled.

The following is an extract from Hans Erich Nossack's short novel *Das Testament des Lucius Eurinus* (1964). The novel is set in the first century A.D. and, like Broch's *Der Tod des Vergil*, is an oblique comment on the present. The narrator, Lucius Eurinus, is a Roman magistrate whose wife has just become converted to the new disruptive creed of Christianity.

Ja, da stand sie, ein paar Meter entfernt, eine gutaussehende, gepflegte Dame in der ihr angemessenen Atmosphäre unseres Hauses und Speisesaals. Von draußen hörte man — und das auch nur, weil eine ganz ungewöhnliche Stille zwischen uns herrschte — einen der Bedienten in der Küche beim Geschirrspülen singen. Da stand eine Frau in ihren besten Jahren, eine Frau von tadellosen Manieren und aus altem Geschlecht. Da stand meine Frau, mit der ich seit zwanzig Jahren zusammen lebte, die Mutter meiner Kinder, und sagte: 'Übrigens, was ich dir noch mitteilen wollte ...' und so weiter.

Ganz unglaubhaft! Auch jetzt noch beim Niederschreiben der Tatsachen will es mir scheinen, als berichte ich nach Altweiberart über einen Traum, in dem ich mich quäle, das Unsinnige mit einer Handbewegung beiseite zu schieben und aufzuwachen.

Das Unglaubhafte liegt darin, daß es meine Frau war, die mir das mitteilte.

Die Christen rekrutieren sich fast ausschließlich aus kleinen Leuten. Aus Bedienten, Freigelassenen, Kleinbürgern, Handwerkern und ehemaligen Bauern, die in die Stadt gezogen sind, da das Land sie nicht mehr ernährt. Die überwiegende Mehrzahl der Anhänger sind keine gebürtigen Großstädter, sondern stammen aus der Provinz. Als Richter hat man sich das dauernd vor Augen zu halten. Man hat mit Leuten zu tun, die keine Tradition besitzen und daher alle

Tradition als Schranke empfinden, durch die sie am Aufstieg gehindert werden. Nur so läßt sich die sonst unbegreifliche Wirkung der christlichen Propaganda verstehen. Sie spricht die Neidgefühle und den Haß derer an, die ohne Herkunft sind oder den Boden ihrer Herkunft verlassen haben. Es schmeichelt denen, die sich für benachteiligt halten, und denen es an Fähigkeiten und selbständigem Streben fehlt, wenn man ihnen einredet, daß es nur an der bestehenden Gesellschaftsordnung liege, wenn sie zu kurz kämen. In äußerst geschickter Weise wird ihnen vorgespielt, daß die Zukunft ihnen gehöre, sobald erst einmal alles Herkömmliche beseitigt sei. Die Negation wird als Verdienst und positives Verhalten verkündet.

Das alles wird oberflächlich mit mystischen Unklarheiten verbrämt, doch die Wirkung der Propaganda ist allein in diesem Kunstgriff oder dieser dialektischen Verdrehung zu sehen. Es ist ein eindeutiger Appell an die Instinkte der Masse. Der kleine Mann fühlt sich gehoben, wenn man ihm immer von neuem erzählt, daß alle Menschen gleich seien und daß er genau so viele Rechte habe wie jemand, der nur durch Familie und Wohlstand an leitender Stelle stehe.

Daß es mehr auf Tüchtigkeit und persönliche Eignung ankommt als auf Familienbeziehungen, ist richtig. Kein vernünftiger Römer wird das in Zweifel ziehen. Engstirnige Weiber, wie die Mutter Claudias, zählen nicht. Falsch ist der Gedanke nur, wenn er als Motiv des Zerstörens gebraucht wird, statt zur Verbesserung der Zustände, also nicht mit der Bereitschaft, höhere Verantwortung zu übernehmen. Niemand ist der Übernahme von Macht würdig, der sie durch Zerstörung erwerben will.

Die zerstörerische Tendenz liegt schon im Ursprung der christlichen Lehren begründet. Sie stammen aus dem Orient, das heißt, aus Ländern, die despotisch regiert wurden und wo daher von den Unterdrückten Freiheit mit Aufsässigkeit gleichgesetzt wird. Die Juden, das weiß man, sind ein besonders streitsüchtiges Volk und die Christen sind eine jüdische Sekte. Mögen sie sich jetzt auch bis aufs Messer bekämpfen, die Rechthaberei haben die Christen von den Juden übernommen. Das sind allbekannte geschichtliche Tatsachen, doch ist es gut, sie sich immer wieder klarzumachen, wenn man das Problem richtig sehen will.

(pp. 37–40)

Lucius Eurinus is a member of what is now called the Establishment, faced by a radical challenge to the *status quo*. The obvious present-day parallel to the Christian threat is any revolutionary and egalitarian political doctrine, most obviously Communism. Lucius Eurinus analyses the attitudes and psychological needs he sees as underlying the Christian movement. In so doing this liberal conservative reveals, sometimes unconsciously, his own prejudices and psychological needs. The novel as a whole, then, explores a gamut of attitudes and in effect reduces politics, the dynamics of social change, to psychology. The parallel between social unrest in the first and twentieth centuries suggests that the same psychological factors underlie all political struggle and large-scale historical revolutions. The unconscious self-revelation of the narrator adds immediacy and drama to what could otherwise have seemed a historical essay rather than a novel.

In our extract Lucius Eurinus considers some sociological factors favouring the rise of Christianity. The shift of population into the cities as a result of economic pressures is reminiscent of the industrial revolution in nineteenth-century Europe. He suggests that social unrest causes the success of Christianity rather than Christianity causing the social unrest. What might be considered the core of Christianity is reduced to mere 'mystische Unklarheiten'. Similarly, in our own day it is a common conservative accusation against radical political movements that their ideology is a mere smokescreen of obscure and illogical notions concealing envy and lust for power. Above all Lucius Eurinus rejects ideology as such, without quite realizing that his own position has its ideology too. He claims that the Christian ideology ignores human nature and would disturb the slow organic process of social change. Men cannot establish a condition of complete equality; the nearest approach is a moderate élitism, based preferably on talent rather than inheritance.

But this analysis of the part-sociological, part-psychological factors underlying a political movement cannot quite account for the conversion of his wife, Claudia. She is not a displaced peasant with a grudge. Nor can it account for his final decision to commit suicide. Nor can it explain the character of the other main protagonist. The climax of the novel is a conversation between Lucius Eurinus and a great teacher and prophet of the movement, probably St. Paul. It is a confrontation between two elemental human types, or perhaps between two poles in human nature, Lucius Eurinus the proponent of classical order and balance, Paul the romantic. Both men see future disaster. For Lucius Eurinus the disaster is the overthrow of traditional culture. The Christian movement might just be contained were it simply a matter of social tensions. Reactionary forces might be tamed, the grievances of the underprivileged slowly removed. True, a perfect realization of classical harmony in the body politic is impossible. Reality always lags behind the ideal, historical change will always lead to temporary tensions and injustices. But at least the reformist approach would prevent the ultimate evil of chaos. The irresistible impetus of the movement does not come from such grievances. Lucius Eurinus recognizes in Paul that thirst for absolutes, that demand for pure truth, that existential assertion of selfhood beyond all myths, social conventions, traditions, constructs of reason which, if once set in motion in the right conditions, must overthrow all established order. Paul calls for an inner transformation, but inevitably, through action, the revolution will become external.

But Paul too sees future disaster. He sees how Christianity will itself become a myth, a constraining law, an institution, a *status quo*. For he recognizes in Lucius Eurinus a force bound finally to triumph over the absolute call for human emancipation. This force is not just human greed and stupidity. It is the inability of human beings to bear the burden of absolute freedom. It is their need for a sense of objective order independent of themselves and within which they may find certainty and security. Such order is given, so Lucius Eurinus thinks, by 'die Unsterblichen', the law of 'die Unsterblichen' he calls nature. For him the law of life has a metaphysical status, but whether it be metaphysical or simply a projection of psychological needs, this order or need for order will always reassert itself after every revolution. And it will lead to institutions tending to the rigid protection of vested interests.

All the excellencies of the novel, the elegance of its ironies, the concision and objectivity of its presentation, derive from the historical setting. For Lucius Eurinus the Christians represent a threat to natural piety and religion—they are the atheists! They disturb the relations of the sexes, they cause women to forget their natural role in the illusory search for a new identity. Thus they undermine marriage, that institution on which all social order is based! The oblique light cast by such ironic reversals illumines the whole novel. The twin disasters of the decline and fall of the Roman order and the rise and institutionalization of Christianity are twin triumphs as well, depending on the point of view. It is the proponent of an objective order who makes a supreme and absurd personal gesture by committing suicide in the name of truth, while the radical prophet bows to necessity.

PART IV   MODES

13   Realism

Realism is probably the oldest critical concept. Plato disapproved, Aristotle approved of art's imitating life; they did agree, however, that art is imitation. Realism is also the most widespread concept. The naïve person judges the work of art solely on the criterion of how far it conforms to 'real life'. At the same time, at least in literary criticism, the term is one of the emptiest, since it has so many, often mutually exclusive, connotations.

Realism relates to the 'real', but the latter term is even emptier than the former. One might think of the real as the empirical, actual, matter-of-fact, outward form, that which immediately impinges on our senses and which appears to have an existence independent of our conception of it: 'real estate', economic pressures, concrete objects. In practice, however, one also speaks of the 'reality behind appearances', the real contrasting with the ostensible. In another sense the real contrasts with the ideal. Now the ideal itself has two meanings, the desirable ('Ideal Homes Exhibition') or that which exists only in the mind, as an idea. Ideas, however, whether desirable or not, have a reality of their own: anti-semitism, for example, was real enough to lead to the deaths of seven million Jews, patriotism has resulted in the catastrophe of wars. The real may further be opposed to the imaginary: imaginary dangers are not real, ghosts are not real. But the imaginary danger is real enough to the person who imagines it and may influence his behaviour significantly; ghosts were real to previous generations and are still so for a large number of people. Reality, in other words, is a very subjective affair; each generation has its own reality, each individual has his own conception of what is real. This is reflected in literature: in a way, every successful work of literature, whether it concerns itself with the ostensible or the reality behind it, with ideas or objects, with the desirable or the factual, is an image of the reality of its author or the times in which he lived.

In philosophy, realism is the opposite of nominalism, but it may also be the opposite of idealism. In the first case it denotes the belief that universals, rather than particulars, are 'real'; in the second, the reverse is implied, namely one or other variety of empiricism, materialism or positivism, the belief that the empirical rather than abstractions are 'real'. Inasmuch as this raises the question of the typical in relation to the individual, it is relevant to literary criticism: does realistic literature concern itself with the particular, even pathological case, or ought the writer rather to find and portray the general tendency of the age? Are, for example, Kafka's novels merely bizarre, the product of a diseased mind, the reflection of a unique experience, or are the apparently unparalleled happenings in them symptomatic of what is going on in twentieth-century life? The medieval controversy between the realists and the nominalists appears to recur in contemporary Marxist writings on realism: 'realist' writings are those which show the universal (Marxist) law of history; they are distinguished from the works of 'naturalism' or 'impressionism' (cf. nominalism), which content themselves with registering surface realities. Naturalist writers, on the other hand, considered themselves to be 'consistent realists'. They were influenced by nineteenth-century positivism, the belief that events can be explained according to scientific principles; they abandoned the idealist concept of free will. Realism in literary criticism may be a value judgment, a description of style, a reference to content (the depiction of lower-class life) or to ideology (socialist realism), or may denote a fairly arbitrarily selected period in the history of European literature, the years 1830–1900, including in Germany such disparate names as Büchner, Grillparzer and Raabe. 'Ideally' one would like to abandon the terms 'real', 'realist' and 'realistic'; in practice, the terms are in such current use that one has to attempt to make them meaningful even at the risk of creating distinctions which are quite arbitrary.

In the first place, realism raises the question of objectivity. A realistic description might be thought to be one which describes events as objectively as possible. But it is an epistemological truism that we can never know things as they objectively are, only as they appear to us. As the chapter on Point of View demonstrated, the novel is an admirable illustration of this, since every novel incorporates or implies a person to whom events and people appear in the way in which they are being described.

But are there degrees of objectivity? Can one kind of perspective
be termed more realistic than another? Consider the following
extracts:

Am folgenden Abend gab man im Stadttheater den 'Lohengrin',
und alle gebildeten Leute waren anwesend. Der kleine Raum war
besetzt von oben bis unten und erfüllt von summendem Geräusch,
Gasgeruch und Parfüms. Alle Augengläser aber, im Parkett wie
auf den Rängen, richteten sich auf Loge dreizehn, gleich rechts
neben der Bühne, denn dort waren heute zum ersten Male Herr
von Rinnlingen nebst Frau erschienen, und man hatte Gelegenheit,
das Paar einmal gründlich zu mustern.

Als der kleine Herr Friedemann in tadellosem schwarzen Anzug
mit glänzend weißem, spitz hervorstehendem Hemdeinsatz seine
Loge — Loge dreizehn — betrat, zuckte er in der Tür zurück,
wobei er eine Bewegung mit der Hand nach der Stirn machte und
seine Nasenflügel sich einen Augenblick krampfhaft öffneten. Dann
aber ließ er sich auf seinem Sessel nieder, dem Platze links von
Frau von Rinnlingen.

Sie blickte ihn, während er sich setzte, eine Weile aufmerksam an,
indem sie die Unterlippe vorschob, und wandte sich dann, um mit
ihrem Gatten, der hinter ihr stand, ein paar Worte zu wechseln. Es
war ein großer, breiter Herr mit aufgebürstetem Schnurrbart und
einem braunen, gutmütigen Gesicht.

Als die Ouvertüre begann und Frau von Rinnlingen sich über
die Brüstung beugte, ließ Herr Friedemann einen raschen, hastigen
Seitenblick über sie hingleiten. Sie trug eine helle Gesellschafts-
toilette und war, als die einzige der anwesenden Damen, sogar
ein wenig dekolletiert. Ihre Ärmel waren sehr weit und bauschig,
und die weißen Handschuhe reichten bis an die Ellenbogen. Ihre
Gestalt hatte heute etwas Üppiges, was neulich, als sie die weite
Jacke trug, nicht bemerkbar gewesen war; ihr Busen hob und senkte
sich voll und langsam, und der Knoten des rotblonden Haares fiel
tief und schwer in den Nacken. (Thomas Mann, *Der kleine Herr
Friedemann*, p. 88)

Ja, applaudieren wir mit. Der neben mir klatscht wie verrückt. Ob's
ihm wirklich so gut gefällt? — Das Mädel drüben in der Loge ist
sehr hübsch. Sieht sie mich an oder den Herrn dort mit dem blonden
Vollbart? ... Ah, ein Solo! Wer ist das? Alt: Fräulein Walker,
Sopran: Fraülein Michalek ... das ist wahrscheinlich Sopran ...
Lang' war ich schon nicht in der Oper. In der Oper unterhalt' ich
mich immer, auch wenn's langweilig ist. Übermorgen könnt' ich
eigentlich wieder hineingeh'n, zur 'Traviata'. Ja, übermorgen bin
ich vielleicht schon eine tote Leiche! Ah, Unsinn, das glaub' ich

selber nicht! Warten S' nur, Herr Doktor, Ihnen wird's vergeh'n,
solche Bemerkungen zu machen! Das Nasenspitzel hau' ich Ihnen
herunter ...

Wenn ich die in der Loge nur genau sehen könnt'! Ich möcht'
mir den Operngucker von dem Herrn neben mir ausleih'n, aber
der frißt mich ja auf, wenn ich ihn in seiner Andacht stör' ... In
welcher Gegend die Schwester vom Kopetzky steht? Ob ich sie
erkennen möcht'? Ich hab' sie ja nur zwei- oder dreimal gesehen,
das letztemal im Offizierskasino ... Ob das lauter anständige
Mädeln sind, alle hundert? O jeh! ... 'Unter Mitwirkung des
Singvereins'! — Singverein ... komisch! Ich hab' mir darunter
eigentlich immer so was Ähnliches vorgestellt, wie die Wiener
Tanzsängerinnen, das heißt, ich hab' schon gewußt, daß es was
anderes ist! ... Schöne Erinnerungen! Damals beim 'Grünen Tor'
... Wie hat sie nur geheißen? Und dann hat sie mir einmal eine
Ansichtskarte aus Belgrad geschickt ... auch eine schöne Gegend!
— Der Kopetzky hat's gut, der sitzt jetzt längst im Wirtshaus und
raucht seine Virginia! ...

Was guckt mich denn der Kerl dort immer an? Mir scheint, der
merkt, daß ich mich langweil' und nicht herg'hör' ... Ich möcht'
Ihnen raten, ein etwas weniger freches Gesicht zu machen, sonst
stell' ich Sie mir nachher im Foyer! — Schaut schon weg! ... Daß
sie alle vor meinem Blick so eine Angst hab'n ... (Arthur Schnitzler,
Leutnant Gustl, pp. 337–8)

Both passages concern a public musical event; in both the occa-
sion is more important than the music; in both we find a man
fascinated by an unknown lady in the audience. In the first
passage everything is related from outside, by the cold, rather
mocking observer, who first sets the scene with all the necessary
details, so that we can picture it exactly, down to the number of
the box in which Herr Friedemann and Frau von Rinnlingen
meet. In the second the point of view is that of one of the participants, and no precise details are given, only the fleeting impressions which he has and which spark off his thought processes.
The first is apparently objective, inasmuch as objects, exteriors,
appearances are most important and seem to speak for themselves;
the second is 'subjective', since the scene is relayed through the
subjectivity of a particular person, which is itself the centre
of attention. But is the first passage more 'realistic' than the
second? Does anybody ever experience a concert or opera in the
way Thomas Mann describes it? Does not the technique used
by Schnitzler more closely render the reality of a concert-goer's

experience? Few of us could afterwards describe people and places in the detail given by Thomas Mann. And, in any case, the 'objectivity' of Thomas Mann's description is only apparent. Some one is describing events for us, but he remains anonymous. With Schnitzler's story we become Gustl, the reader is present at the concert and registers its atmosphere with the central character. In a sense, therefore, Schnitzler's description is also more 'objective', inasmuch as the perspective is firmly within one of the 'objects' of the story, the hero himself. And that the most objective standpoint also dissolves reality into the most subjective of impressions is part of the dialectics of the novel.*

Related to the necessary subjectivity of all realism is the question of selectivity, how much and what kind of reality is to be reproduced. If *Leutnant Gustl* transmitted everything that passes through Gustl's consciousness in the nine hours of narrative-time, it would be several times longer than it is; Thomas Mann selects only *some* of the details of the opera house and of the appearance of Frau von Rinnlingen. Even the camera has to be pointed in a certain direction, started and stopped again. And the effect will be quite different depending on whether it is pointed at a carefree middle class family living in the country or at a poverty-stricken working class one in a city tenement. On the face of it, there is no reason why the one picture should be termed more realistic than the other. Historically and arbitrarily, however, realism has always been associated with the depiction of scenes of lower class life, often unpleasant, unhappy scenes, and with a concentration on the lower aspects of human nature, body and instinct rather than mind and spirit. Thus *Bahnwärter Thiel* is about an inarticulate railway worker who is driven to insanity by an accident in which his son is killed by a train; *Papa Hamlet* is about an unemployed actor, who finally kills his child and drinks himself to a miserable death in the gutter. The ugly and repulsive (the eel scene of *Die Blechtrommel*, for example), the physiological or medical (in *Berlin Alexanderplatz* Döblin's account of the workings of the human digestive system after a meal, Thomas Mann's clinical description of the symptoms of typhus in *Buddenbrooks*) are realistic in this sense.

---

* Realism, as already noted, can be a value judgment. It must be emphasized, however, that our analysis is in no way intended as an evaluation of the success or failure of the respective passages, but merely to point out the baselessness of this particular criterion.

But again, far from being more 'objective' than the portrayal of noble sentiments would be, these themes imply a particular, subjective conception of humanity, one, for example, which sees man as the prisoner of his bodily frame or of the economic system. A sneeze in real life indicates that a person is catching a cold; a sneeze in literature will usually imply the Frailty of Human Life.

Thematically, therefore, the realist mode can be defined only arbitrarily. It tends to concern itself with the social, rather than the individual, man in society rather than man vis-à-vis the infinite (*Buddenbrooks* rather than *Der Zauberberg*, *Die Schlafwandler* rather than *Der Tod des Vergil*). An overt political element is often present: concentration on working class conditions or class conflicts will generally imply a particular social stance on the part of the author. Since realist writers believe the city to be more typical of modern life than the country, realist novels generally depict urban rather than rural life. They treat the present directly rather than by way of historical parallels or utopian visions. Otherwise one has to be content with negative definitions: the realist novel avoids the fantastic (the hallucination scenes of *Der Steppenwolf*), the supernatural (the devil in *Doktor Faustus*, the dance of death in *Berlin Alexanderplatz*), the absurd or empirically impossible (the glass-destroying voice of Oskar in *Die Blechtrommel*, Gregor Samsa's metamorphosis in *Die Verwandlung*), or the generally implausible (many of the events of *Amerika*, *Der Prozeß* and *Das Schloß*). A glance at these titles suggests that very little remains!

A further obstacle in the path of literary realism lies in the nature of a work of literature. While painting and sculpture may claim to reproduce exactly the forms, outlines, colours of objects, literature operates by means of words, and words themselves are abstractions. Pygmalion could not so conveniently have been satisfied in his desires if his creation had been a character in a book. In this respect drama is closer to life than the novel and there have been cases in which members of the audience have become so caught up in what they were viewing that they were moved to interfere. The dramatized consciousness most closely approaches this in the field of the novel; the distancing voice of a narrator, anonymous or not, has the opposite effect. This type of realism is perhaps better called illusionism. In fact, of course, life does depend to some extent on written documents; hence, for example, the widespread use of the fictitious biography; the novel in letters (*Werther*) or diary form (*Malte Laurids Brigge*) is another example of this kind of illusionism. On the other hand, the reproduction of fragments of reality in the shape of written documents—summonses, posters, advertisements, newspaper cuttings—in *Berlin Alexanderplatz* has a rather different tendency. Their lack of context, their juxtaposition with so many fictional items, results in their taking on a poetic life of their own, while at the same time vouching for the 'reality' of the story of Biberkopf. The so-called 'scientific approach', the 'experimental novel' of Zola and his followers, is very much a nineteenth-century matter, reflected perhaps most clearly in the number of shorter prose works published about the turn of the century as 'Studien' (*Bahnwärter Thiel, Papa Hamlet,* some of the early short pieces of Thomas Mann); the twentieth century in general has been less concerned with this type of fictional realism.

However, the claim to be reproducing life by means of words will give rise to certain textural or stylistic features. Register will approximate as far as possible to what would be expected of a similar person in a similar situation in the real world; dialect, for example, is a common feature of the realist mode; the historical novel may like to introduce archaisms into the direct speech of its characters, although clearly it can never be consistent without running the risk of being quite incomprehensible to the twentieth-century reader who is not a historical philologist. Imagery will be sparingly used, preference being given to the simile, which keeps clear the borderline between fact and fancy, rather than to the metaphor, which creates a poetic world of its own. Dialogue will often dominate over narrative, since in dialogue it is easier to approximate to the sounds and statements of reality—this at least was the theory of Arno Holz:

'Hä? Was? Was sagste nu?!'
'Was denn, Nielchen? Was denn?'
'Schafskopp!'
'Aber Thiiienwiebel!'
'Amalie?! Ich ...'
'Ai! Kieke da! Also döss!'
'Hä?! Was?! Famoser Schlingel! Mein Schlingel! Mein Schlingel, Amalie! Hä! Was?'
Amalie lächelte. Etwas abgespannt.
'Ein Prachtkerl!'

'Ein Teufelsbraten! Mein Teufelsbraten! Mein Teufelsbraten!
Hä! Was, Amalie? Mein Teufelsbraten!'
Amalie nickte. Etwas müde.
'Ja doch, Herr Thienwiebel! Ja doch!'
Aber Frau Wachtel mühte sich vergeblich ab. Herr Thienwiebel,
der große, unübertroffene Hamlet aus Trondhjem, wollte seinen
Teufelsbraten nicht wieder loslassen.
'Hä, oller Junge? Hä?'
'In der Tat, Nielchen! In der Tat, ein ... ein ... Prachtinstitut!
Ein Prachtinstitut!'
'Hoo, hoo, hoo, hopp!! Hoo, hoo, hoo, hopp!! Bumm!!!'
Der große Thienwiebel schwelgte vor Wonne. Er hatte sich jetzt
sogar auf ein Bein gestellt. Hinten aus seinem karierten Schlafrock
klunkerten die Wattenstücken.
'Aber Thiiienwiebel!'—
(Arno Holz and Johannes Schlaf, *Papa Hamlet*, pp. 19–20)

In general one expects a matter-of-fact tone in the realist mode.
Caricature is normally avoided, although in practice such clearly
realist novels as *Der Untertan* make frequent use of it. Irony,
however, as might be expected, is an important feature: the
juxtaposition of man and the concrete conditions of his existence
invites this device. Martin Walser's reproduction of the minutiae
of a social evening, for example, is not neutral, but satirical:

Susanne saß im Sessel, als habe man sie hineingebunden. Gerade,
daß sie noch den Kopf bewegen konnte. Den drehte sie immer ganz
deutlich zu dem, der sprach. Dadurch will man, wenn man nicht
zuhört, beweisen, daß man zuhört. Jetzt spricht schon wieder der
da drüben. Sollte sie, nein, sie durfte ihren Kopf nicht in einem
deutlichen Ruck herumwerfen, also schwenkte sie langsam, führte
die aufmerksam schnuppernde Nase schön das Gesicht, schön und
doch zügig, dem mit der Halbglatze zu. Hieß der nicht Justus?
Gerade noch rechtzeitig nahm sie im Augenfeld wahr, daß Josef-
Heinrich lächelte. Also sagte Justus etwas, worüber man lächelte,
also lockerte sie ihren Mund, erlaubte den Mundwinkeln, ein
bißchen aufs Geratewohl ins Gesicht zu schwimmen, holte sie aber,
jetzt sprach Edmund, gleich wieder zurück, weil sie das ganze
Gesicht brauchte, um Edmund zuzuhören. Erich füllte ihr Glas.
Kurzes Abfallen zu ihm hin. Rasch und zerstreut danken. Aller-
aufmerksamste Rückkehr zum sprechenden Edmund, eine zarte
Entschuldigung für den Abstecher zu Erich, jetzt bin ich aber
wieder ganz da, bitte, fahren Sie fort. Mit uhrzeigerhafter Unmerk-
lichkeit gruppierte sie ihre Beine um, weil sie die Augen der Männer
nicht aus dem Gespräch reißen wollte. Das linke war's, das voller

Stacheln stak. Sie rieb, ich sah hin, sie erschrak ein bißchen, ich
nickte freundlich. Es ist doch Ihre Verlobung. (*Halbzeit*, Part I,
Chapter 2, p. 298)

It is further worth noting that some of the most interesting effects
are gained by combining realism of texture with non-realism
of content. This, for example, is what gives the novels of Kafka
their uniqueness, that the basically absurd events are related in
a highly plastic manner. For example, in *Der Prozeß* Josef K. is
summoned to appear before a mysterious commission of investiga-
tion which meets in a particularly disreputable part of the town;
the description of the district is as graphic as that which any so-
called realist author might supply; the working class, clearly
Jewish, and frequently repulsive milieu is also ideologically
irreproachable. That an investigating body should assemble on
this day and in one of the tenements of this district—that is the
premise which conflicts with the realism of the description.

Realism is thus a highly ambiguous concept, whose definition
ultimately requires quite arbitrary distinctions. Doctrinaire
realism reached its peak in the Naturalist manifestoes of the late
nineteenth century, but regularly raises its head every twenty
years or so: *Neue Sachlichkeit* in the 1920s, *reportage* in the 1940s,
neorealismo, cinéma vérité. One further point, however, is worth
making. Literature is concerned with truth; it may occasionally
find truth in beauty, it may more often find it in the ugliness of
the so-called real. Realism has its conventions, like any other
-ism; the forms it uses are, as Käte Hamburger puts it, as much
'symbols' as are the trappings of conventional symbolism.[1]
Consistent realism would eventually become identical with
aestheticism, historically its diametrical opposite. For very few
works of art content themselves with 'reproducing life'; they
set out rather to instruct, exhort, admonish—even entertain.

One particular kind of realism, related to the 'chosime' of the
French writer Robbe-Grillet, is exemplified in Peter Handke's
novel *Die Hornissen*. *Die Hornissen* has no story which might be
retold; it has elements of a story—a boy is drowned, a mother
dies, another son becomes blind—but these elements are not
arranged in such a way that the reader is able to construct a
meaningful pattern out of them; the order in which they occur
and even the relationships between the characters, some of whom

[1] *Die Logik der Dichtung*, p. 249.

F

apparently are figures out of a book which the blind narrator read some time earlier, are nowhere made clear. This technique, one might say, is realistic, inasmuch as we do not experience the structures in life, only the textures. 'Life', as Virginia Woolf put it, 'is not a series of gig lamps symmetrically arranged';[2] there is in life no plot, no patterns, no beginnings and endings— these are all imposed on it by the writer. This the conventional 'realist' novel ignores—indeed, one of the first principles which the naïve reader would choose in order to recognize the realist novel would be that it 'tells a good story'.

Instead of trying to impose a pattern on life in this way, Peter Handke concentrates on the details. His novel consists of a series of 'snapshots', in which single, often trivial events are described in the minutest detail, the beginning of a meal, a kitchen sink, a farmer trying to get his horse to pull its load of rushes up a hill, the congregation leaving church, a man getting dressed:

Das Ankleiden
Inzwischen hat sich Gregor Benedikt (so oder ähnlich ist sein Name) für den Sonntag gekleidet.

Er ist auf dem Bett gesessen und hat die Schuhe gebürstet. Er hat sich rasiert und gewaschen. Er ist zum Bett gegangen und hat mit der weichen Bürste das Leder poliert. Er ist zum Tisch gegangen und hat sich neben dem Tisch auf einen Schemel gesetzt.

Er hat die Socken über die Füße gezogen. Er ist aufgestanden und zum Schrank gegangen.

Mit dieser Tätigkeit hat er viel Zeit vertan. Mit dem Ankleiden der Socken hat er weniger Zeit vertan.

Er hat den Schlüssel gedreht und den Flügel des Schranks geöffnet. Er hat dem Schrank den Anzug entnommen. Er hat die Hose vom Bügel gestreift und den Rock auf das Bett gelegt. Er hat sich neben den Rock gesetzt. Er ist mit dem linken Bein in die Hose gestiegen. Er ist mit dem rechten Bein in die Hose gestiegen. Er hat, nicht weil er blind ist, darauf eine lange Zeit verwendet.

Er ist aufgestanden und hat die Hose hinaufgezogen. Er hat sie zugeknöpft. Er hat den Gürtel durch die Schnalle gesteckt. Er hat den Gürtel festgeschnallt. Er hat mit dem Daumen den Stachel der Schnalle durch das gewohnte, im Vergleich mit den andern erweiterte Loch geschoben. Er hat das Ende des Gürtels nach und nach durch die Laschen gesteckt.

Auch darauf hat er beträchtliche Zeit verwendet.

Er ist jetzt zwischen dem Tisch und dem Bett gestanden.

[2] 'Modern Fiction', in *The Common Reader* (First Series, London, 1925), p. 189.

Er ist aus dem Stand zum offenen Schrank gegangen. Er hat aus dem Schrank die Krawatte genommen.

Er ist ans Fenster gegangen. Er hat unterwegs die Schlinge über den Kopf gezerrt. Er hat das Hemd verschlossen und den Kragen ans Kinn gestellt. Er hat den Knoten der Schlinge zwischen zwei Fingern gehalten und die Schlinge mit der anderen Hand um den Hals gezogen.

Das Knüpfen der Schlinge hat ihn lange beschäftigt.

Er ist zum Bett gegangen und hat den Rock genommen. Er hat den Rock über die Schulter geworfen und ist zum Schrank gegangen. Er hat die Flügel des Schrankes geschlossen und den Schlüssel gedreht.

Er hat den Rock von der Schulter geschwungen. Er hat ihn mit dem Arme von sich gestreckt.

Zu dieser Zeit ist er inmitten des Zimmers gestanden.

Er ist mit der rechten Faust unter den linken Arm und in den Rock gefahren. Er hat den Rock über die rechte Schulter gezogen. Er hat mit der linken Faust den Rock auf der rechten Schulter befestigt. Er hat die Faust von der Schulter gelöst.

Das Lösen der Faust hat den Blinden viel Zeit gekostet.

Er hat mit dem linken Arm hinter sich gegriffen. Er ist mit der linken Faust in den Rock gefahren. Er hat den Rock hinauf und über die Schulter gezogen.

Er ist zum Bett gegangen. Er hat sich nach der Bürste gebückt. Er hat die Bürste in die gehörige Schachtel getan. Er ist mit der Schachtel zum Tisch gegangen. Er hat sie unter den Tisch geschoben.

Diese Handlung hat ihm einige Zeit genommen.

Er ist zum Waschbecken gegangen und hat durch den Ausguß aus der Schüssel das Wasser gegossen.

Er ist daneben gestanden.

Er hat mit dem Rücken der Hand das Kinn geschabt.

Dann ist er in einer langen Zeit zu der Tür gegangen, ist in einer längeren Zeit durch den Flur gegangen, ist die längste Zeit vom Haustor die Stufen hinabgestiegen.

Er ist schnell durch den Hof gegangen.

Er ist zurückgekommen.

Er lehnt jetzt, die Hände weit in den Taschen der Hose, neben den Stufen an der Mauer des Hauses. Man stellt sich ihn rauchend vor, mit großem, feierlich geneigtem Kopf, den Hals und den Arm, der mit der verkrampften Hand wie immer den unteren Rocksaum umgreift, noch im Schatten, das Gesicht darüber schon in der Sonne; mit nichts beschäftigt, es sei denn, aus dem Mund und aus den Höhlen der Augen den Rauch zu stoßen.

Die Gedanken kommen und gehen.

Er macht sich ein Bild von einem fahrenden Zug.

(*Die Hornissen*, pp. 65–8)

Such descriptions are not symbolic, as the stage sneeze tends to be. The circumstances described do not refer to anything beyond themselves—they are there and told for their own sake. Gregor Benedikt's dressing is of no significance for a story, for our understanding of society or of man's relationship to the infinite. Nor is the description satirical, as the social small talk in *Halbzeit* is. At most we laugh at the supposed naïvety of a writer who thinks it worth while describing something which we all do every morning. All that Handke claims to do by means of such descriptions is to raise the trivial aspects of life into our consciousness, to make us more aware of them. Gregor is blind; this is one device which Handke uses to 'alienate' the actions described and thus heighten our awareness of everything he does. This, Handke believes, is as far as literature can go. So-called *littérature engagée* is not literature at all. Nevertheless, it is not that Handke has no concern for the events of the real world. Awareness is not the supreme value; but it alone makes actions to change the real world possible.

Some of his descriptions of complicated activities, such as the accident in which the horse stumbles and is dragged with its load downhill again, show very great technical skill. Indeed, much of our enjoyment of the book springs from admiration of the virtuoso—whether his music is worth listening to is more dubious. And yet even in this apparently realistic description of the process of dressing is the stylization which is the mark of all creative writing. At first sight there seems to be a deliberate attempt not to stylize: the repetition of the same sentence form, the sentences beginning with the same words, the exclusively paratactical constructions are features which we are all taught at school to avoid. But when it is done so consistently as here it becomes a conscious mannerism, a litany, reminiscent of some of the Psalms. This itself is a further alienation effect. But attention is thereby inevitably drawn to the sentences which do not follow the normal pattern and which almost invariably refer to the time taken to perform each action. Why? To underline the difficulties experienced by a blind man? At one point this is explicitly denied. The alternative explanation is that his thoughts are elsewhere, indeed *that he is thinking*. Ancient associations of the blind man as seer are now evoked. And so even *Die Hornissen* turns out to be less concerned with surface realities than at first sight appeared.

14 Symbolism

The German term 'Sinnbild' catches neatly the central notion of symbolism. A symbol is a 'meaning-picture'. A symbolic novel is one whose 'pictures', or concrete events, characters and locations, convey some further meaning. Of course all serious novels convey meaning, are significant statements in one way or another. What matters is *how* this meaning is conveyed. The philosophical novel comments most directly through an authorial persona, through discursive conversations or meditations of characters. The symbolic novel works less directly to suggest that there is more in the novel than meets the eye. The realistic novel in the naïve sense of the term has no further intrinsic meaning beyond its representation of human beings in action. These representations may be in themselves of a significant sort: the author may have presented such a range and depth of human experience in such an organized way that the reader may recognise what Goethe called 'die Wahrheit des Realen'.[1] But in a realistic work this truth concerns primarily the immediate representations of the novel—that is, it is a 'truth to life'. Any extension beyond the action of the novel, that is a 'truth about life', the reader must make for himself. It is different with symbolism. By some means other than discursive comment, the author must himself suggest within his work what general truth or meaning is implied by the action of his novel.

Such distinctions between the realistic, the symbolic and the philosophical novel are notional. Most novels are a mixture of two or three kinds. The essayistic novel is generally if not realistic then at least mimetic to some extent: it conjures up an imaginable, coherent 'world' of its own. Few realistic novels are wholly devoid of discursive comment in one guise or another. Moreover, a basically realistic novel may use a lot of what might be called internal symbolism—repeated motifs, patterns of events and so on—to link together in an associative or aesthetic way its various parts. The symbolic novel tends to flesh out its symbolic structure

[1] *Gespräche mit Eckermann*, 25 December 1825.

F*

with a realistic texture. Placing novels within a category is a matter of emphasis.

Much of this book has already been concerned with symbolism in one way or another. In an age of vast intellectual revolutions and violent political upheavals, so often centred on Germany, it is not surprising that many German writers have tried to integrate into the basically realistic novel form complicated 'truths about life'. In so doing they have created works remarkable for a wealth of formal inventiveness and experimentation in symbolic devices designed to extend the reference of their work beyond the portrayal of individual fates to embrace broad social, political and philosophical issues. Clearly it is impossible to give an exhaustive account of the technicalities of symbolism: each work constitutes its own unique meaning in its own unique way. But some of the preceding chapters have tried to show that critical generalizations are possible about how major aspects of the craft of novel-writing, such as patterns or time-structure, may be so handled as to imply symbolic meanings. Others have touched on some of the major issues which German writers have again and again confronted and sometimes treated symbolically. This chapter will deal first with three broad types of symbolism and then consider the distinction between public or traditional as against private or individual symbolism.

Within the symbolic mode three different types are what might be called the exemplary novel, the allegorical novel and the symbolic novel. They differ from each other in that the relationship between concrete symbol and meaning is in each case different. In the exemplary novel the individual characters, events and locations are examples of some general principle, be it sociological, psychological or whatever. The relationship of symbol to meaning is that of particular to general. The borderline between this type of novel and pure realism is fluid (see *Realism*). Many realistic novels seem to go beyond the particular case. Their characters appear typical of an age or a social milieu, or their author unconsciously reveals attitudes and prejudices which make his work historically revealing. But unless such typicality is emphatically part of the purport of the novel, it does not come into our category.

An interesting example of the exemplary novel is Döblin's *Berlin Alexanderplatz*, which tells the story of a named individual called Franz Biberkopf and the particular city of Berlin. Döblin makes clear, to the extent of quoting statistics, that it is also about man in the city, about the interaction of consciousness and environment. It might well be argued that such a novel is just dressed-up social psychology, and prophets of doom have argued that the new social sciences have delivered a death-blow to the novel. Yet, although Döblin presents Biberkopf as virtually a walking statistical norm, he implies too that unless unreasoning stupidity makes a man the victim of his instinctive reactions and so a creature of his environment, statistics cannot grasp the whole man. Man in the city is not quite as predictable as an animal in the jungle, if he uses his gifts of reason and moral awareness. Döblin shows a typical case but one who in the end transcends his own typicality, becomes truly an individual.

It is common to distinguish between two other types, symbolism and allegory. Allegory involves a clearly defined body of abstract principles quite separable from concrete symbols of little intrinsic significance. With symbolism the meaning can less easily be defined and is more bound up with the concrete symbol which is in itself significant. This distinction is not very important for the novel. The wholly allegorical novel is a rare phenomenon: the abstraction of allegory conflicts with that realism which is the life-blood of the novel as a form. Historically, too, allegory flourishes in a religious culture. Where life is but a shadow of transcendental reality, so literature may mirror such a dualism through the clear allegorical distinction between image and meaning. Nowadays, even the most convinced propagandist cannot assume that others share his beliefs, and so rather than just codify them through allegory, he will try to prove their validity through the action of his novel. Thus 'allegorical' tends now to be a pejorative term implying that a writer has imposed an arbitrary meaning on the action of his novel. None the less, the distinction between allegory and symbolism is still a useful one, since writers do sometimes deliberately use allegorical effects in an aesthetically satisfying way, even at the risk of irritating the sceptic. It is a mark of the strong didactic intent of *Berlin Alexanderplatz*, for example, that it has an element of allegory, notably in the figure of death, a cypher standing in part for Franz's conscience, in part for the psychological impact of imminent death, in part for Döblin's own moral and metaphysical beliefs.

No writer has provoked more allegorical interpretation than Kafka. It is easy to see why. Take *Das Schloß* for example. It

tells the story of a man called K. who arrives in a village dominated by a castle and its bureaucracy of officials. He wishes the castle
to confirm his appointment as official land-surveyor, to settle in
the village, perhaps to marry, and to be recognized as a free
individual with inviolable rights. Various elements in the novel—
the hero, other characters, the setting—at first sight suggest
allegory. K. is scarcely personalized. His past is virtually unknown. His emotional and moral motivations, the impact of his
social background, his upbringing, all that we normally call
psychology, is left obscure. His name is scarcely a name, just an
initial. Perhaps, then, it does not matter who he is, just as it does
not matter who Bunyan's Christian is in *The Pilgrim's Progress*—he
is anyone in all Christendom. The setting is similarly indefinite,
a village, a castle somewhere, anywhere. And when is it? Electric
lights and telephones are oddly disconcerting in an otherwise
pre-industrial atmosphere. Those details of interiors, objects,
the trappings of everyday life which in a realistic novel go to
create the flavour of a particular here and now have the opposite
effect in Kafka's novel. We are Anytime, Anywhere and so
expect a struggle of timeless forces of which the places and characters are mere analogies. The characters K. meets have little depth
of personality in their own right, but appear largely in terms of
their role in K.'s quest to reach the castle as helpers or obstacles,
perhaps like the characters Christian meets in his quest for the
good life.

Yet *Das Schloß* is a very odd sort of allegory, if it is one, since
it lacks the defining characteristic of allegory, namely a body of
doctrine, a set of principles for which the action and characters
stand. K. and Bunyan's Christian are anonymous, but in a radically different sense. Christian needs no personal characteristics,
they would merely diminish his representative nature. His identity
is sufficiently defined in his Christianity: his role and function,
his direction and aim in life are given by Christian doctrine,
which in Bunyan's work is presented as objectively valid. K., on
the other hand, is anonymous because he lacks a clear sense of
identity. The novel offers no objective solutions to K.'s final
questions about his own identity and role in life; the nature of the
other people he meets; the rationale of the putative 'laws' govern-
ing the community he has entered. Much of the deceptively
allegorical atmosphere comes from K.'s own attitude: he behaves
rather as if he believed life to be an allegory with himself as chief

character. Thus he has a sense of ultimate purpose, but is not very clear as to what this is. One of K.'s aims, for example, is to get binding confirmation from the castle that he is an official land-surveyor, but this he never receives. And as the castle teases K. on this point, so Kafka teases his readers, since we are given conflicting hints that K. is perhaps a land-surveyor, but equally perhaps not. This desire for the security of a fixed social role conflicts with his individualistic assertion of total freedom.

The muddled contradictoriness of his sense of purpose finds its counterpart in his contradictory interpretations of the nature of the castle. Its officials appear to him now majestic, grand and threatening, now sordid, farcical and timid. A similar confusion marks the character and role of the village people he meets. Barnabas, for example, a young man whom he thinks has connections with the castle, appears at first like a messenger of light, but then as a disappointing and irritating obstacle. K. might have found simply a friend in Barnabas, but he reduces people to their function in relation to his muddled sense of purpose. Minor achievements of his own are devalued because they do not lead to ultimate success. Kafka is perhaps suggesting that he who goes through life looking for signs and portents is unlikely to appreciate things and people in themselves. A critic has suggested that some of Kafka's work comes into the category of *anti-Märchen*.[2] An appropriate label for *Das Schloß* might be anti-allegory.

Of course even in plotting the absurd contradictions in K.'s quest, in revealing the pointlessness of questions to which there are no answers, Kafka gives potent expression to that perennial human longing that the world be somehow meaningful: that individual life have shape and pattern. No doubt the resultant tension between an extreme of scepticism and a thirst for certainties accounts for the continuing fascination of Kafka's work for sceptics and believers alike. *Das Schloß* does have a general meaning, but not the sort that stands in allegorical relation to the concrete details of the work. It is a symbolic novel with a misleadingly allegorical surface.

Apart from such differences of type, the flavour of a work may depend on whether it uses symbols valid only within that one work or recognized symbols drawn from myth, legend, history,

[2] Clemens Heselhaus, 'Kafkas Erzählformen', in *Deutsche Vierteljahrsschrift für Literaturwissenschaft und Geistesgeschichte* 26 (1952), pp. 353–76.

or perhaps from other literary works (see also *Patterns*). It is easy
to miss the first sort because of superficial reading. An author
must by one means or another, through emphasis of particular
motifs, multivalence of vocabulary and so on, indicate that his
text has symbolic import, and he must work harder at this than
if he adopts some traditional symbolic motif. If a novel about a
musician of the twentieth century is called *Doktor Faustus* it obviously
purports to be symbolic in some sense and so the reader is alerted.
But traditional symbolism has pitfalls too. A work may depend
too much on extrinsic, esoteric knowledge in its readers. On the
other hand, knowledge of the original may be no help, even a
hindrance to correct understanding, if an author has so transformed what he has borrowed as to make it entirely his own.

Doktor Faustus is a case in point. The title alone indicates that
part of the novel's symbolic meaning is a parallel between Adrian
Leverkühn and Faust. But Faust himself in his many legendary
and literary incarnations is a symbolic figure, and the meaning
of his life and pact with the Devil shifts from work to work.
To say that Leverkühn is a Faust figure is simply to push back
the question of the significance of Leverkühn's life and works
by one step, to ask now what Faust and the Devil mean in the
context of Mann's restatement of the legend.

If the novel were an allegory, then the Devil would simply be
the principle of evil, God's adversary in the struggle for man's
soul. Is Mann implying that the fate of Leverkühn and the horrors
of Nazi Germany can be interpreted in timeless terms as an
instance of the evil wreaked by a metaphysical force of evil
personified as the Devil? Hardly. The matter is further complicated by Zeitblom's presentation, which makes use of terms such
as 'das Dämonische'. This, along with other motifs such as Adrian's
syphilis and the many submerged references to syphilitic artists,
notably Nietzsche, introduces a whole complex of notions including Romantic versions of demonic natural forces and a link
between disease, crime and genius. The religious interpretation
of Faust's pact with the Devil is in competition, then, with other
part-psychological, part-metaphysical, though not Christian,
views.

Mann's Devil is in the end none of these things. He is very
much a historical, cultural and social Devil, with some psychological undertones. He is the whole historical situation and Leverkühn's pact is the attempt of a man of insight to 'come to terms'

with this situation without succumbing either to despairing silence or false solutions. The Devil is those other things only in the sense that one of the dilemmas Leverkühn faces is the German intellectual tradition, which has been 'bedevilled' by a tendency to mythologize history, to despise rational political discourse, to overvalue irrational instinct, to explain human affairs by metaphysics and so absolve human beings from responsibility. It is too easy to blame the Devil. Mann has achieved the super-ironic coup of implying that the Devil is belief in the Devil.

Mann, then, uses traditional legend and myth. He does so to extend the scope of his novel so as to embrace wide social and historical perspectives and, perhaps paradoxically, to promote thereby a demythologizing interpretation of reality. This twin tendency is perhaps most striking in his *Joseph* tetralogy which uses a vast arsenal of mythology to dramatize a shift in consciousness away from a timeless, impersonal, mythical view of life towards an ethical, humanistic and historical outlook.

Doktor Faustus very obviously draws on public symbolism, though in an ironic way. It also has a highly organized set of symbolic motifs peculiar to this work alone. The descriptions of the semi-scientific experiments of Adrian's father Jonathan Leverkühn, for example, are an oblique introduction to all the political, social and historical problems developed later in the novel:

> Ein verwandtes Gefallen fand er an Eisblumen, und halbe Stunden lang konnte er sich an Wintertagen, wenn diese kristallischen Niederschläge die bäuerlich kleinen Fenster des Buchelhauses bedeckten, mit bloßem Auge und durch sein Vergrößerungsglas, in ihre Struktur vertiefen. Ich möchte sagen: alles wäre gut gewesen und man hätte darüber zur Tagesordnung übergehen können, wenn die Erzeugnisse sich, wie es ihnen zukam, im Symmetrisch-Figürlichen, streng Mathematischen und Regelmäßigen gehalten hätten. Aber daß sie mit einer gewissen gaukelnden Unverschämtheit Pflanzliches nachahmten, aufs wunderhübscheste Farrenwedel, Gräser, die Becher und Sterne von Blüten vortäuschten, daß sie mit ihren eisigen Mitteln im Organischen dilettierten, das war es, worüber Jonathan nicht hinwegkam, und worüber seines gewissermaßen mißbilligenden, aber auch bewunderungsvollen Kopfschüttelns kein Ende fand. Bildeten, so lautete seine Frage, diese Phantasmagorien die Formen des Vegetativen *vor*, oder bildeten sie sie *nach*? Keines von beidem, erwiderte er wohl sich selbst; es waren Parallelbildungen. (Chapter 3, pp. 31–2)

The questions: what came first, what caused what, what was simply coincidence, turn up again and again in the novel, notably regarding the relationship between social and political upheavals and artistic or intellectual ones. Do revolutions in thought cause social change or result from it, or are they simply 'Parallelbildungen'? How far were German intellectuals to blame for the course of German history? How far were they its victims?

The indirectness of symbolism brings it close to irony. Irony offers two points of view, an ostensible usually false one and a hidden true one. Symbolism is one method the ironist may use, in that the symbolic significance of an event may contradict its apparent significance. *Doktor Faustus* is a good example. The action of the novel is coloured throughout by the narrator's attitudes, but his interpretation of events conflicts, at points radically, with the symbolic significance Mann invests in them. But not all symbolism is ironic, since generally there is no tension between the symbol and its meaning. Nor, of course, is symbolism the only means the ironist has at his disposal to induce his double vision.

Between the extremes of public symbolism and individual symbolism comes a grey area where symbolism and realism, symbolism and simple atmospheric effects may easily overlap. Life is full of archetypal events and contrasts. We all emerge from the womb; we all open and close doors to get inside and outside; we all experience successions of light and darkness; we are all masculine, feminine or at least mixed; most of us still know that there is a revolution of seasons. It is not always easy to decide whether some object, action or motif has no special significance, or contributes to a particular mood; whether it is significant, but only in the sense of illuminating the attitudes and psychology of a character, or whether it is fully symbolic, radiating some broad if not easily definable meaning extending beyond the particular context. Such distinctions are not very important and cannot be laid down rigidly, but they are useful if they help to avoid the excesses of some schools of criticism like the Freudian or the Jungian, yet on the other hand alert us to subtle, understated effects. Kafka's treatment of the weather, light and darkness in *Das Schloß* is an example of effects which hover between the atmospheric and the symbolic. The novel opens in darkness:

Es war spätabends, als K. ankam. Das Dorf lag in tiefem Schnee. Vom Schloßberg war nichts zu sehen, Nebel und Finsternis umgaben ihn, auch nicht der schwächste Lichtschein deutete das große Schloß an. Lange stand K. auf der Holzbrücke, die von der Landstraße zum Dorf führte, und blickte in die scheinbare Leere empor. (Chapter 1, p. 481)

The next morning K. sees the castle in daylight and Kafka conjures up the brilliant outlines things assume on a snowy day of sunshine:

> Nun sah er oben das Schloß deutlich umrissen in der klaren Luft und noch verdeutlicht durch den alle Formen nachbildenden, in dünner Schicht überall liegenden Schnee. (p. 486)

But this first brilliant impression is perhaps illusory. Only a few lines down we read:

> Aber im Näherkommen enttäuschte ihn das Schloß, es war doch nur ein recht elendes Städtchen, aus Dorfhäusern zusammengetragen, ausgezeichnet nur dadurch, daß vielleicht alles aus Stein gebaut war; aber der Anstrich war längst abgefallen, und der Stein schien abzubröckeln. (p. 487)

If K.'s impressions are so contradictory even in bright daylight, it is not surprising that things are even more confused when the atmosphere literally darkens by the opening of the second chapter a few pages later:

> Als sie — K. erkannte es an einer Wegbiegung — fast beim Wirtshaus waren, war es zu seinem Erstaunen schon völlig finster. War er so lange fort gewesen? Doch nur ein, zwei Stunden etwa nach seiner Berechnung, und am Morgen war er fortgegangen, und kein Essenbedürfnis hatte er gehabt, und bis vor kurzem war gleichmäßige Tageshelle ʒewesen, erst jetzt die Finsternis. 'Kurze Tage, kurze Tage!' sagte er zu sich, glitt vom Schlitten und ging dem Wirtshaus zu.
>
> Oben auf der kleinen Vortreppe des Hauses stand, ihm sehr willkommen, der Wirt und leuchtete mit erhobener Laterne ihm entgegen. Flüchtig an den Fuhrmann sich erinnernd, blieb K. stehen, irgendwo hustete es im Dunkeln, das war er. Nun, er würde ihn ja nächstens wiedersehen. (Chapter 2, p. 495)

But K. is wrong. It is someone else who coughed—the mistake is not surprising in view of the darkness lit only by the weak rays of a lantern. Throughout the rest of the novel the great majority of references to natural conditions set a scene of dusk or total darkness. With few exceptions, references to light are not to the natural light of day, but to sometimes harsh, sometimes dim electric light, or occasionally candles, in haze-filled interiors with dark corners. Taken singly, such references contribute to the atmosphere at that point in the texture of the novel: they create a mood of gloom, of uncertainty or of harsh bare ugliness. Cumulatively they become structural and assume symbolic significance which occasionally comes close to the surface as in the following passage. K. is waiting at night in the courtyard of an inn, determined to assert himself and force an interview with a castle official:

> Und als nun, nach Beendigung der Arbeit im Stall, der Kutscher quer über den Hof ging, in seinem langsamen, schaukelnden Gang, das große Tor zumachte, dann zurückkam, alles langsam und förmlich nur in Betrachtung seiner eigenen Spur im Schnee, dann sich im Stall einschloß und nun auch alles elektrische Licht verlöschte — wem hätte es leuchten sollen? — und nur noch oben der Spalt in der Holzgalerie hell blieb und den irrenden Blick ein wenig festhielt, da schien es K., als habe man nun alle Verbindung mit ihm abgebrochen und als sei er nun freilich freier als jemals und könne hier auf dem ihm sonst verbotenen Ort warten, solange er wolle, und habe sich diese Freiheit erkämpft, wie kaum ein anderer es könnte, und niemand dürfe ihn anrühren oder vertreiben, ja kaum ansprechen; aber — diese Überzeugung war zumindest ebenso stark — als gäbe es gleichzeitig nichts Sinnloseres, nichts Verzweifelteres als diese Freiheit, dieses Warten, diese Unverletzlichkeit. (Chapter 8, p. 575)

The alternation of light and darkness in Kafka's novel, then, does *not* follow the archetypal pattern of day and night in natural succession, just as the seasons seem, to say the least, a bit odd. As one character tells K., in retrospect the village seems to have only two days of summer and sometimes it snows even then. Daylight is occasionally mentioned, but by the end of the novel the overall impression is of constantly threatening darkness, broken only by not very effective, man-made light. K.'s experience in the village is of a place where total darkness may descend at any time, where the puny lights which scarcely pierce it bring little illumination or security. To put it crudely, the world is a dark place and man's efforts to illumine it, to enlighten himself, are frail.

An odd confusion of traditional associations brings together light and darkness, interiors and out-of-doors, freedom and constriction. Normally prisons are associated with darkness, freedom with light. In the last quotation K. experiences a sense of freedom out-of-doors—is not imprisoned—but in darkness, so that the normal positive connotations of freedom are turned into black threatening emptiness. On the other hand K. spends much time in little stuffy rooms or narrow corridors and is finally offered refuge by a serving-girl, Pepi, in the maids' room in an inn. She describes the maids' life, in constant artificial light, as she puts it, while the maids' room sounds like a narrow prison, even a trap when at night unknown threatening presences creep about outside the door. Yet she presents it too as a sanctuary and perhaps even the artificial light of a prison is better than the real darkness of freedom outside.

By the end of the novel these effects of light and darkness— perhaps the most archetypal contrast there is—become more than simply atmospheric, become symbolic though in an un- traditional way. The exaggeration of darkness suggests this, even if no specific meaning can be ascribed to each instance. The exaggeration could just be explained away on a number of occasions: it might just be K.'s impression that darkness has fallen after only two hours of day; Pepi says it is only in retrospect that summer seems so short; K. did not notice the daytime because he slept right through it. But the cumulative effect is exaggerated to a grotesque degree. The novel as a whole is pervaded by gloomy darkness and, alas, by equally comfortless electric light. A most striking contrast could be made with Goethe, to whom Kafka stands as an opposite pole, Goethe whose poetry is pervaded by the serene light of the moon, the life-giving radiance of the sun; whose works seeks to reconcile freedom and order, where Kafka's seems to show the emptiness of freedom, the slavery of a false order.

And yet a certain humour lightens at times the darkness—a black humour to be sure. Compare the last two excerpts quoted above. The last one is undoubtedly deeply depressing in mood; the slow inexorable movements of the coachman; the bleakness of the single track in the snow; the sense of futility in the question, 'Wem hätte es leuchten sollen?'; the progression from light to darkness; the terrible disillusionment in the final clause after the energetic build-up of the preceding phrases. In the preceding excerpt, after the initial anxiety of the realization that darkness has fallen, the movement is towards light and a welcoming figure; a mistake is made, shortly to be corrected, however, with the help of a lamp. And surely K. is unconsciously comic when he mutters to himself: 'Kurze Tage, kurze Tage!' What an understatement! Such touches of sardonic humour, above the head of his creature K., and the subtle patterns such as the effects of light and darkness, reveal the guiding intelligence of Kafka in this most impersonal of works.

15   Essayism

Alfred Döblin's last novel, *Hamlet*, tells the story of Edward Allison, a young man who returns home to England after the Second World War, crippled and haunted by the memory of the death of his friend in a kamikaze attack by Japanese airmen. His experiences cause him to question everything: the justification of the war, the relations between his parents, man's responsibility for his actions. He begins to read Kierkegaard, whose demand for complete intellectual honesty seems a striking parallel with his own preoccupations. But in his ruthless quest for truth he makes life unbearable for the people around him, brings out the hidden conflicts in his family and ultimately destroys it; war, he discovers, corresponds to the eternal war between the sexes and within the family.

As a kind of therapy his father, Gordon Allison, a writer, earlier proposes a series of social evenings at which the family and some friends should come together and tell each other stories, stories which should have a bearing on the problems raised by Edward:

> Ich will auf meine Weise die Diskussion aus dem Gebiet der bloßen Abstraktion entfernen und der Wahrheit annähern, die in der Tat, wie Edward annimmt, stark an Personen, an menschlichen Schicksalen hängt und davon nicht zu trennen ist. Aber wie, das ist die Frage. Also ich plane, als erster hier meine Auffassung an einem Beispiel, an einer Geschichte, zu entwickeln. Ich will erzählen und sehen, ob es überzeugt. Danach sollen auch die anderen erzählen. Sie können immerhin, wenn es ihnen beliebt, eine andere Methode wählen. (pp. 36–7)

Hamlet is a novel of ideas, the story of a quest for truth; but the ideas are expressed for the most part indirectly, by means of parables, the story of the Princess of Tripoli, of King Lear, of Pluto and Proserpina. This is always Döblin's method; even *Unser Dasein*, an anthropological treatise, contains a number of stories, dialogues, passages in rhyme. But, as Gordon Allison puts it, there are other methods. Döblin's polar opposite would be

Gottfried Benn, whose *Roman des Phänotyp* is probably the purest example of the essayistic mode, the novel as essay. It is a novel narrated by one who envies 'mit wilder Wehmut' the old sea-dogs spinning their yarns over a glass of grog, whom he cannot emulate because he no longer believes in the meaningfulness of the conventions of fiction.

The role of ideas in literature has always been controversial. On the one hand we find Goethe's maxim: 'Bilde, Künstler, rede nicht.' Ironically, Goethe himself was later taken to task by the novelist Spielhagen, who attacked *Die Wahlverwandtschaften* for the narrator's reflections expressed in it. On the other hand we find Friedrich Schlegel's definition of Romantic poetry:

> Ihre Bestimmung ist nicht bloß, alle getrennte Gattungen der Poesie wieder zu vereinigen, und die Poesie mit der Philosophie und Rhetorik in Berührung zu setzen. Sie will, und soll auch Poesie und Prosa, Genialität und Kritik, Kunstpoesie und Naturpoesie bald mischen, bald verschmelzen, die Poesie lebendig und gesellig, und das Leben und die Gesellschaft poetisch machen, den Witz poetisieren, und die Formen der Kunst mit gediegnem Bildungsstoff jeder Art anfüllen und sättigen, und durch die Schwingungen des Humors beseelen.[1]

A little thought will demonstrate at once that literature has never restricted itself to 'telling a story'; essayistic passages—moralizing, meditation, historical review, analysis, commentary—have always played a part in fiction, not only in third-person 'omniscient' narrative, but even within the dramatized consciousness. Nevertheless, it does seem that the twentieth century has seen the *poeta doctus* in greater numbers and insistency than earlier times, not only in Germany and Austria, but also in France (Proust, Gide) and even in England (Joyce, Huxley, Shaw). His reflections, moreover, are no longer merely 'interruptions' or 'digressions'. Reasons for the intellectualization of the novel are similar to those suggested in Chapter 9 on the changing attitude to character: depersonalization, the increasing complexity and abstractness of life. As Brecht put it:

> ... ich benötige die Wissenschaften. Und ich muß sogar zugeben, ich schaue allerhand Leute krumm an, von denen mir bekannt ist, daß sie nicht auf der Höhe der wissenschaftlichen Erkenntnis sind,

[1] Athenäums-Fragment 116.

daß heißt daß sie singen, wie der Vogel singt, oder wie man sich vorstellt, daß der Vogel singt.[2]

One might add that the compartmentalization seen not only in the natural sciences, but in every aspect of life, has meant that literature is almost the only field in which the attempt to present a whole picture of life can be made. The idea that art and the novel in particular—in this respect the *Roman* is rather different from the *novel*, as the words themselves imply—should present a total picture of life has indeed been prevalent in German thinking at least from Friedrich Schlegel onwards. And it may well be felt that this 'Totalität' can nowadays be expressed only reflectively, by essayistics rather than by narrative.

Ideas can appear in the novel in two main ways. They can be 'dramatized', that is to say, expressed in dialogue (the disputes of Naphta and Settembrini in *Der Zauberberg*), as the thoughts of an identifiable person belonging to the fictional world (Zeitblom's reflections in *Doktor Faustus*, Ulrich's diary entries in *Der Mann ohne Eigenschaften*) or as emanations of the stream of consciousness of a fictional character (the meditations of Broch's Virgil). Alternatively they can appear 'straight', as commentary by an anonymous narrator. The ideas may be present as part of the world of the novel and of no greater or lesser standing than other aspects of this world; on the other hand, they may be the end to which the novel is being written. For example, there is clearly a difference between a novel about an intellectual for whom ideas are as important and as natural as sex for Casanova, and a novel about an industrial worker whom the narrator's commentary puts into his place in the development of human civilization. Strictly speaking, the essayistic mode covers only the second of the two categories in each case. However, since *Doktor Faustus* is clearly essentially different from the more 'realistic' *Buddenbrooks* both in its treatment of and in the scope allotted to ideas, it seems unwise to exclude it from this category. Furthermore, the difference between 'dramatized' and 'straight' essayism is a fleeting one: as was noted in *Point of View*, the 'omniscient' narrator is himself a fiction, part of the world of the novel. Thomas Mann was at pains to emphasize this in a lecture on *Joseph und seine Brüder*:

[2] 'Vergnügungstheater oder Lehrtheater?', in *Gesammelte Werke*, (Frankfurt a.M., 1967), Volume 15, p. 268.

Die Erörterung gehört hier zum Spiel, sie ist eigentlich nicht die Rede des Autors, sondern die des Werkes selbst, sie ist in seine Sprachsphäre aufgenommen, ist indirekt, eine Stil- und Scherzrede, ein Beitrag zur Schein-Genauigkeit, der Persiflage sehr nahe und jedenfalls der Ironie ...[3]

The terms 'Spiel' and 'Scherz' underline a further point. The essay, as distinct from the philosophical tract, contains to a greater or lesser degree the element of play, playing with ideas, 'trying them out', experimenting with them in various contexts. This is not to diminish their importance; play can be a very serious matter indeed.

Of this Hesse's novel *Das Glasperlenspiel* is, as its title suggests, a straightforward illustration. The focus of the Utopian order of Castalia is the 'glass bead game', 'ein Spiel mit sämtlichen Inhalten und Werten unsrer Kultur' (*Einführung*, p. 84), a game which seeks to establish hidden correspondences between all aspects of human life and science, one which demands great intellectual stamina and universal culture and which originated in the attempt to overcome the dilettantism and materialism of the twentieth century. External action in *Das Glasperlenspiel* is slight. It is a novel of ideas, ideas on the relative importance of the *vita activa* and the *vita contemplativa* and of the religious and secular spheres, ideas on education and on music, critical ideas on the disease at the root of twentieth-century life, and suggested remedies. To a large extent these ideas are dramatized, inasmuch as they are associated with individual characters; for example, the conflict between activity and contemplation is fought out in terms of Plinio Designori and Fritz Tegularius. The clearest example of essayism, however, is the long introduction with its ponderous title 'Das Glasperlenspiel. Versuch einer allgemeinverständlichen Einführung in seine Geschichte'. Here the ideas are presented in a straightforward manner, as ideas, as history. But are they? The ponderousness of the title at once suggests irony, a dual perspective on the ideas expressed. The ideas are, moreover, distanced by being put in the mouth of a fictitious biographer and being placed in a future moment of time. And the ideas on Castalia expressed in the introduction are not completely vindicated by the rest of the novel; the tension between the establishment view and the anti-establishment view is illustrated by

[3] *Neue Studien*, (Stockholm, 1948), pp. 165–6.

Knecht's career. In these ways, therefore, Hesse's ideas are 'fictionalized'; they suggest the 'game' itself; the novel is in fact a kind of 'glass bead game'. For this reason it is wrong to identify the views expressed in the novel with Hesse's own convictions. For example, the rejection of Romantic and post-Romantic music is symbolic, serving to underline certain ideals of harmony, the reconciliation of opposites, 'Maß'. It is precisely the danger of attempting to stop the clock at 1800 which is the message of the novel. Hesse is playing with ideas, as other novelists play with characters and events. The weakness of his novel is that the ideas are not sufficiently original or interesting to bear the weight of a long novel; one feels that they really belong to the 'feuilletonistisches Zeitalter' which they purport to be castigating.

Thomas Mann's *Doktor Faustus* might similarly be described as a 'Spiel mit sämtlichen Inhalten und Werten unsrer Kultur'. Here too we find the attempt to sum up human life in the twentieth century under all its aspects. But how much more profound and at the same time how much more alive are the ideas! Here if anywhere Friedrich Schlegel's demand that art should be satiated 'mit gediegnem Bildungsstoff jeder Art' is fulfilled. Essayistic are the protracted discussions of musical theory, history, theology, politics, even oceanography, with which the book abounds. All of them nevertheless relate to the central preoccupation, the balance-sheet of twentieth-century life in the light of National Socialism and the Second World War. Two features of Mann's essayism stand out. In the first place his knowledge is comprehensive and exact, based on a thorough study of the relevant sources, which he occasionally reproduces word for word. But in the second place all of the ideas are completely integrated into the fiction. This is done by distancing them not merely by one narrator, as in *Das Glasperlenspiel*, but by two, since Zeitblom in most cases is reporting the lectures or conversations of other people. This can be a question of register and tone, personal and individual, rather than the neutral, abstract language of the scientific treatise. More strikingly, the ideas are fictionalized by their association with the eccentric individuals who expound them: the stuttering Wendell Kretschmar on Beethoven's last sonata, Eberhard Schleppfuß's theology, not least the 'Devil', to whom are allotted some of the central ideas on music and society. Mann, unlike for example Broch, is not an original thinker. What makes the essayism of his novels so much more satisfying than his essays proper is the use of ideas as aesthetic symbols beside and on a level with the figures and events of the novel.

In this method Thomas Mann remains within the framework of the traditional novel: he is presenting a picture of the world, a world in which ideas are important while remaining parts of the world. This 'democratic' outlook can be contrasted with the 'hierarchical' outlook of Hermann Broch, for whom literature is a means to knowledge and philosophy the pinnacle of a world graded according to its degree of rationality. In a letter to his publisher Broch criticized the methods of Gide, Musil, Mann and Huxley:

> Bei den meisten dieser Autoren steht die Wissenschaft, steht die Bildung wie ein kristallener Block neben ihrem eigentlichen Geschäft, und sie brechen einmal dieses Stückchen, ein andermal jenes Stückchen davon ab, um ihre Erzählung damit aufzuputzen.[4]

The third part of *Die Schlafwandler* consists of a montage of eighty-eight segments, in which various loosely connected stories are intertwined with ten essayistic sections entitled 'Zerfall der Werte'. In the latter Broch expounds his ideas on contemporary society in relation to his theory of history—the parallel with *Das Glasperlenspiel* and *Doktor Faustus* is evident. Broch's intention, however, was that the various strands of the trilogy should each present the same problem—roughly speaking, the relation of the individual to his age between 1888 and 1918—at various levels ranging from the unconscious and irrational to the completely rational; the latter is represented by the theoretical essay. The principle of this novel might, therefore, be described as one of 'vertical totality' rather than the 'horizontal totality' of *Doktor Faustus*.

The essays of *Die Schlafwandler* are much more independent of the rest of the novel than those of Mann and Hesse. Indeed, the editors of Broch's collected works included them also in one of the volumes devoted to his theoretical writings. Nevertheless, even here we find a degree of aesthetic distance: they are the work of an identifiable fictional character, a person who has conversations and encounters with other fictional people, although he has no part to play in the main strand of the novel, that concerning Huguenau. They also raise a number of questions of general interest relating to the essayistic mode. Broch's claim that

[4] *Briefe von 1929 bis 1951*, ed. Robert Pick (Zürich, 1957), p. 60.

the novel illustrates the same problem on various levels including the rational seems to reject the axiom that a work of art must always be more than its rational interpretation; in other words, if the novel explains itself completely in the sections on the 'Zerfall der Werte', then the rest is mere illustration and dispensable. Yet 'illustration' may indeed be valuable for the less philosophically minded; the whole question of parables, didactic and propagandist literature would seem to be raised here. Furthermore, are the essayistic sections wholly satisfying as an 'explanation' of the rest? For example, it is disturbing that the impression given of Huguenau in the essays is more favourable than that which we receive of him in the narrative. There is perhaps a fruitful tension between essay and narrative. And finally, is not the philosophy its own justification? The loss of individuality, the lack of a unified style, the 'Sachlichkeit' of contemporary man, which are the themes of the essay, mean precisely that traditional aesthetic notions are no longer valid.

Essayism of a kind rather different from that of either Mann or Broch characterizes Robert Musil's *Der Mann ohne Eigenschaften*. Once again we find the attempt to present in depth the state of a particular society at a given moment in time: 1913–14. Once again the novelist appears to be striving after totality, in the range of his characters and the variety of human experience and activity he depicts. This ironically reflects one of his themes: the search, conscious or otherwise, on the part of the characters in the novel, for the wholeness of life, a search which is in most cases quite misguided; 'totality' is not even achieved in the novel, which remained a gigantic torso. An exhaustive analysis of Musil's essayism is beyond the scope of the present book. However, the following points seem particularly relevant. *Der Mann ohne Eigenschaften*, to a degree far greater than that of any of the other novels discussed, is one protracted essay. In time it covers a year; but the reader completely loses sight of the passing of time except towards the end when the events surrounding the liberation of Moosbrugger are narrated. Time is hardly a category which can usefully be applied to this novel, since it is not about a sequence of events; ideas are timeless. Nevertheless, it remains fiction since most of the reflections either concern fictitious people —speculation concerning the responsibility of criminals for their actions takes the psychopath Moosbrugger as its starting-point— or come from fictitious people themselves, notably Ulrich, whose ideas are presented in various ways, as indirect speech merging into *erlebte Rede*, in direct speech when he expounds them to other people, or as the entries in his diary. Even the commentary of the anonymous narrator does not lack the element of essayistic play: a strong flavour of irony pervades his attitude to his hero and the other characters of the novel. But the most original and fruitful feature of the 'Essayismus' of *Der Mann ohne Eigenschaften* is that it is not only the form of the novel, but the form of life of its central character:

> Ungefähr wie ein Essay in der Folge seiner Abschnitte ein Ding von vielen Seiten nimmt, ohne es ganz zu erfassen, — denn ein ganz erfaßtes Ding verliert mit einem Male seinen Umfang und schmilzt zu einem Begriff ein — glaubte er, Welt und eigenes Leben am richtigsten ansehen und behandeln zu können. (Book I, 62, p. 257)

The 'essay' is thus the adequate expression of the 'Möglichkeitsmensch' discussed in Chapter 13.

As *Der Mann ohne Eigenschaften* consists to a large extent of essay it is perhaps otiose to choose an illustrative passage from it—in the Sahara sand is less interesting than water. Here instead is a passage from a comparable but rather more conventional novel, Thomas Mann's *Der Zauberberg*.* Appropriately enough, in view of the importance of time to narrative techniques, it is from the sub-chapter *Exkurs über den Zeitsinn*, the very title of which implies the scientific treatise rather than the novel. On his third day at the sanatorium Hans Castorp has bought two blankets in order to be able to spend the prescribed amount of time lying outside on his balcony:

Und so war denn Zufriedenheit in Hans Castorps Herzen darüber, daß zwei leere und sicher gefriedete Stunden vor ihm lagen, diese durch die Hausordnung geheiligten Stunden der Hauptliegekur, die er, obgleich nur zu Gaste hier oben, als eine ihm ganz gemäße Einrichtung empfand. Denn er war geduldig von Natur, konnte lange ohne Beschäftigung wohl bestehen und liebte, wie wir uns erinnern, die freie Zeit, die von betäubender Tätigkeit nicht vergessen gemacht, verzehrt und verscheucht wird. Um vier erfolgte der Vespertee mit Kuchen und Eingemachtem, etwas Bewegung im Freien sodann, hierauf abermals Ruhe im Stuhl, um sieben das Abendessen, welches,

---

* *Der Zauberberg* could, of course, have been chosen to illustrate the symbolic mode and is discussed in *Irony*. These terms are seldom mutually exclusive, least of all in such a 'universal' novel as this.

wie überhaupt die Mahlzeiten, gewisse Spannungen und Sehens-
würdigkeiten mit sich brachte, auf die man sich freuen konnte,
danach ein oder der andere Blick in den stereoskopischen Guckkasten,
das kaleidoskopische Fernrohr und die kinematographische Trommel
... Hans Castorp hatte den Tageslauf bereits am Schnürchen, wenn
es auch viel zuviel gesagt wäre, daß er schon 'eingelebt', wie man es
nennt, gewesen sei.

Im Grunde hat es eine merkwürdige Bewandtnis mit diesem Sichein-
leben an fremdem Orte, dieser — sei es auch — mühseligen Anpassung
und Umgewöhnung, welcher man sich beinahe um ihrer selbst willen
und in der bestimmten Absicht unterzieht, sie, kaum daß sie vollendet
ist, oder doch bald danach, wieder aufzugeben und zum vorigen
Zustande zurückzukehren. Man schaltet dergleichen als Unter-
brechung und Zwischenspiel in den Hauptzusammenhang des Lebens
ein, und zwar zum Zweck der 'Erholung', das heißt: der erneuernden,
umwälzenden Übung des Organismus, welcher Gefahr lief und schon
im Begriffe war, im ungegliederten Einerlei der Lebensführung sich
zu verwöhnen, zu erschlaffen und abzustumpfen. Worauf beruht dann
aber diese Erschlaffung und Abstumpfung bei zu langer nicht aufge-
hobener Regel? Es ist nicht so sehr körperlich-geistige Ermüdung und
Abnutzung durch die Anforderungen des Lebens, worauf sie beruht
(denn für diese wäre ja einfache Ruhe das wiederherstellende Heil-
mittel); es ist vielmehr etwas Seelisches, es ist das Erlebnis der Zeit,
— welches bei ununterbrochenem Gleichmaß abhanden zu kommen
droht und mit dem Lebensgefühle selbst so nahe verwandt und
verbunden ist, daß das eine nicht geschwächt werden kann, ohne
daß auch das andere eine kümmerliche Beeinträchtigung erführe.
Über das Wesen der Langenweile sind vielfach irrige Vorstellungen
verbreitet. Man glaubt im ganzen, daß Interessantheit und Neuheit
des Gehaltes die Zeit 'vertreibe', das heißt: verkürze, während
Monotonie und Leere ihren Gang beschwere und hemme. Das ist
nicht unbedingt zutreffend. Leere und Monotonie mögen zwar den
Augenblick und die Stunde dehnen und 'langweilig' machen, aber
die großen und größten Zeitmassen verkürzen und verflüchtigen sie
sogar bis zur Nichtigkeit. Umgekehrt ist ein reicher und interessanter
Gehalt wohl imstande, die Stunde und selbst noch den Tag zu verkürzen und zu beschwingen, ins Große gerechnet jedoch verleiht er
dem Zeitgange Breite, Gewicht und Solidität, so daß ereignisreiche
Jahre viel langsamer vergehen als jene armen, leeren, leichten, die
der Wind vor sich her bläst, und die verfliegen. Was man Langeweile
nennt, ist also eigentlich vielmehr eine krankhafte Kurzweiligkeit der
Zeit infolge von Monotonie: große Zeiträume schrumpfen bei ununter-
brochener Gleichförmigkeit auf eine das Herz zu Tode erschreckende
Weise zusammen; wenn ein Tag wie alle ist, so sind sie alle wie einer;
und bei vollkommener Einförmigkeit würde das längste Leben als

G

ganz kurz erlebt werden und unversehens verflogen sein. Gewöhnung ist ein Einschlafen oder doch ein Mattwerden des Zeitsinnes, und wenn die Jugendjahre langsam erlebt werden, das spätere Leben aber immer hurtiger abläuft und hineilt, so muß auch das auf Gewöhnung beruhen. Wir wissen wohl, daß die Einschaltung von Um- und Neugewöhnungen das einzige Mittel ist, unser Leben zu halten, unseren Zeitsinn aufzufrischen, eine Verjüngung, Verstärkung, Verlangsamung unseres Zeiterlebnisses und damit die Erneuerung unseres Lebensgefühls überhaupt zu erzielen. Dies ist der Zweck des Orts- und Luftwechsels, der Badereise, die Erholsamkeit der Abwechslung und der Episode. Die ersten Tage an einem neuen Aufenthalt haben jugendlichen, das heißt starken und breiten Gang, — es sind etwa sechs bis acht. Dann, in dem Maße, wie man 'sich einlebt', macht sich allmähliche Verkürzung bemerkbar: wer am Leben hängt oder, besser gesagt, sich ans Leben hängen möchte, mag mit Grauen gewahren, wie die Tage wieder leicht zu werden und zu *huschen* beginnen; und die letzte Woche, etwa von vieren, hat unheimliche Rapidität und Flüchtigkeit. Freilich wirkt die Erfrischung des Zeitsinnes dann über die Einschaltung hinaus, macht sich, wenn man zur Regel zurückgekehrt ist, aufs neue geltend: die ersten Tage zu Hause werden ebenfalls, nach der Abwechslung, wieder neu, breit und jugendlich erlebt, aber nur einige wenige: denn in die Regel lebt man sich rascher wieder ein als in ihre Aufhebung, und wenn der Zeitsinn durch Alter schon müde ist oder — ein Zeichen von ursprünglicher Lebensschwäche — nie stark entwickelt war, so schläft er sehr rasch wieder ein, und schon nach vierundzwanzig Stunden ist es, als sei man nie weg gewesen und als sei die Reise der Traum einer Nacht.

Diese Bemerkungen werden nur deshalb hier eingefügt, weil der junge Hans Castorp Ähnliches im Sinne hatte, als er nach einigen Tagen zu seinem Vetter sagte (und ihn dabei mit rotgeäderten Augen ansah):

'Komisch ist und bleibt es, wie die Zeit einem lang wird zu Anfang, an einem fremden Ort. Das heißt ... Selbstverständlich kann keine Rede davon sein, daß ich mich langweile, im Gegenteil, ich kann wohl sagen, ich amüsiere mich königlich. Aber wenn ich mich umsehe, retrospektiv also, versteh mich recht, kommt es mir vor, als ob ich schon wer weiß wie lange hier oben wäre, und bis dahin zurück, wo ich ankam und nicht gleich verstand, daß ich da war, und du noch sagtest: "Steige nur aus!" — erinnerst du dich? —, das scheint mir eine ganze Ewigkeit. Mit Messen und überhaupt mit dem Verstand hat das ja absolut nichts zu tun, es ist eine reine Gefühlssache. Natürlich wäre es albern, zu sagen: "Ich glaube schon zwei Monate hier zu sein", — das wäre ja Nonsens. Sondern ich kann eben nur sagen: "Sehr lange".'

'Ja', antwortete Joachim, das Thermometer im Munde, 'ich habe auch gut davon, ich kann mich gewissermaßen an dir festhalten, seit du da bist.' Und Hans Castorp lachte darüber, daß Joachim dies so einfach, ohne Erklärung, sagte.

(pp. 146–9)

Four types of essayism can be distinguished in *Der Zauberberg*: the ideas or information imparted one-sidedly to Hans Castorp by a fictitious individual (Behrens on physiology, Settembrini on humanism, Peeperkorn on quinine), the ideas expressed and contradicted in the arguments of Naphta and Settembrini, those which he gleans from books, and finally the reflections of the narrator. The first three correspond to the 'gediegner Bildungs-stoff' demanded by Friedrich Schlegel, and imply the position of *Der Zauberberg* in the *Bildungsroman* tradition; all the ideas expressed in these passages impinge directly on Hans Castorp's consciousness and influence his outlook and behaviour in varying degrees; all three types are 'dramatized' in different ways, although the third comes closer to the standpoint of the external narrator than the other two. The fourth is the essayistic type in the strict sense, and it is this type which the extract illustrates. It is striking that the extended discursive passages related by the narrator deal exclusively with time. This at once underlines how central the question of time is to this novel. And since, as distinct from the educative influences which Hans Castorp undergoes in the other essayistic passages, the discussion of time is beyond his horizon—although not completely so, as we shall see—it would seem that precisely what Hans Castorp misses, in spite of his insatiable hunger for knowledge, is the central point of the novel.

It is clearly appropriate that the narrator should be preoccupied with time. 'Die Zeit ist das Element der Erzählung,' as he points out elsewhere (*Strandspaziergang*, p. 748), and the problem of time is of practical importance for the story-teller. This aspect has been discussed in Chapter 2: the psychological experience of time is reflected in the structure of the novel, so that the last years pass more quickly and are told more quickly than the first weeks; indeed the *Exkurs über den Zeitsinn* comes when not three days of narrative-time have elapsed since the beginning of the story, to which about one-seventh of the novel has been devoted; time indeed for the narrator to explain himself in this his first digression on the nature of time! The *Exkurs über den Zeitsinn* articulates an important aspect of the novel's structure; this is in keeping with the novel of ideas, which does not merely show but comments and explains. But time in this novel is not merely the 'element' in which narrative flows, but the theme of the narrative itself. *Der Zauberberg* is, as Mann puts it in several places, a 'Zeitroman' in two senses; it is about the age (the normal meaning of the term) and also about the nature of time. And the message of the novel—simplified—is that the age is too little concerned with the nature of time.

Time is a highly ambiguous 'element', and many of the paradoxes and ambiguities of the novel can be traced to this fact. The routine of life in the sanatorium blurs the experience of time and with the loss of the 'Erlebnis der Zeit' goes the loss of the 'Lebensgefühl' itself—the inmates of the Berghof are in a sense 'dead'. And yet death is the clearest reminder of the passage of time, a unique event in each life, a 'real' event and a diversion in the continuum of time. Death is all around them, but they ignore it; the corpses of the patients who die are disposed of discreetly. Irresponsibility is the keynote of life at the sanatorium; when time loses its meaning, actions, events in time, do so too. The Berghof patients are 'free' because they are living in a fool's paradise, and paradise is by definition 'timeless'. This applies in some measure also to Hans Castorp's search for erudition: timelessness is the feature of the other essayistic passages of the novel, even of the arguments of Naphta and Settembrini, which lead nowhere, least of all to agreement, which would mark a division in time. Now clearly the information which Hans Castorp gleans during the seven years in the sanatorium is not valueless, even although it is not fruitful. The basic dilemma in fact is the age-old dilemma, the conflict between thought and action. And the dilemma is not resolved at the close of the novel, when Hans Castorp like Rip van Winkle arouses himself from his slumbers, for it is only to devote himself to Death in another way, to take part in the Great War. Time becomes real again, but life may be extinguished still more radically than in the sanatorium.

Mann integrates his essayism into the narrative in an interesting way. The ideas in our extract come directly from the narrator, the 'Geist der Erzählung', as he calls himself at the end of the novel. It is a very personal, although anonymous narrator, who takes up at times the pose of the raconteur with his listeners gathered around him, who feels free to withhold information in the cause of propriety or tension, and to pass judgment on his characters. This in itself helps to integrate his discussions into the fiction of the novel. At the close of our extract this integration is strengthened by the words of Hans Castorp to Joachim. For while the narrator's reflections are beyond Hans Castorp's horizon, they in fact do little more than put into more coherent form one of his first discoveries on arrival at the sanatorium, that of the puzzling nature of time—a discovery which, however, he fails to follow up. The hero's cruder way of expressing ideas similar to those of the narrator brings those ideas down to earth, relativizes and thus fictionalizes them. This relativizing technique, akin to irony, is characteristic of the special essayistic qualities of the novel. For if the essay is defined as a playing with ideas, it is precisely this 'playing with ideas' of which Hans Castorp is 'guilty'—at least in the eyes of Settembrini. 'Placet experiri', he says, and castigates Hans Castorp's tendency to experiment with possible viewpoints (*Notwendiger Einkauf*, p. 139). Thus even the relativity of the essay is articulated in this novel, and Hans Castorp moves into the proximity of Ulrich, the 'man without qualities'.

16 Irony

The inclusion of *Irony* along with *Realism*, *Symbolism* and *Essayism* might seem to imply a fourth mode, the Ironic Novel: the realistic novel shows, the essayistic novel tells or explains, the symbolic and the ironic novels imply, though by different means. But this is not so. Irony is, rather, a technique which may pervade the other three modes and is fully compatible with them. Although irony is not of the same order as the other three modes, it has been included here simply because there is so much of it around. Works which appear in different categories by other criteria may none the less through their deployment of irony have much in common with one another as to mood and impact.

Irony is the simultaneous expression of two conflicting attitudes, opinions or meanings, in such a way that what is overtly stated purports to be the case, but the reader is induced by one means or another to see through the overt purport to a hidden true import. Irony at once mocks and flatters, it pretends that the reader is gullible but knows that he is not.

Often the overt purport and hidden true import stand in a relationship of some tension. The overt statement may not be immediately incredible, may not be false but only incomplete, or may be what the ironist wishes emotionally were the case but knows intellectually is not. In *Betrachtungen eines Unpolitischen* Thomas Mann calls such irony 'erotische Ironie'.[1] It is an irony with a strongly ambivalent element and tends to appear in any context where there is potential conflict between the emotions and the intellect. It is not surprising in an age of rapid social change and expansion of scientific knowledge that such irony should be common, since the emotions tend to lag behind the intellect in assimilating new knowledge. One generation tends to find the assumptions of its predecessor at once endearing yet naïve and so to present them with sympathetic irony. Likewise the intellectual observing his simpler fellows, as is so often the situation in Mann's work.

[1] *Betrachtungen eines Unpolitischen*, p. 561.

At the opposite extreme is destructive irony, a polemical expression of moral outrage at human baseness, political crime, gross social evil. Such irony sees the attitudes of an earlier generation not as endearing if outmoded, but as the root cause of present disaster. It is the stance of the enlightened observer towards not the naïve simplicity but the crass stupidity of his fellow men. Again, it is not surprising in the light of German history in this century that such irony is common. The darkening in tone from Mann's *Zauberberg* to *Doktor Faustus* results partly from a shift away from the 'erotic' to a more polemical brand of irony. These are rough generalizations. Each instance of irony must be examined for its own peculiar tone and effect. But as a general rule, whether it be 'erotic' or polemical, irony is a means of criticism, a way of adding comment to representation, which by its indirectness avoids the pedagogic or preaching tone.

This chapter is concerned with irony as structure, that is with whole novels which can be described as ironic. Manipulation of point of view and of time-structure are the two principal ways of inducing an ironic double vision. The double vision may lie within the overall narrative point of view itself, whether this be an implicit authorial stance, an omniscient narrator or a personalized narrator. The novel as a whole is ironic, then, because it is narrated in a pervasively ironic tone. More indirect still, the authorial stance may be concealed behind one or even a whole kaleidoscope of points of view which are ironically undermined by means other than narrative tone, though cumulatively such a novel can be called ironic in tone. Of course, such maintenance of the characters' points of view need not be ironic in effect, but simply a philosophical demonstration of how many-sided truth may be, or how ignorant is man, or whatever.

These are all ways of being ironic through playing off points of view against each other. Dramatic irony involves different vantage-points in time. The whole structure of a work may be inherently ironic so that earlier ignorance and later realization form a satisfying pattern, a surprising yet necessary logic of events. Unlike Greek plays, novels are not generally restatements of well-known myths and legends, and so unless the work is short with a very concentrated plot, the ironic structure must be highlighted in some way, perhaps by a fugal time-structure which directly juxtaposes the vantage-points in time to ironic effect. Often, too, ironic parallels with, or allusions to, traditional myths or legends, or ironic play with the realistic conventions of the novel form itself, may alert the reader to a hidden import. The rest of the chapter will look at some examples of different kinds of irony in works by Thomas Mann, Max Frisch and Günter Grass.

Thomas Mann's *Der Zauberberg* is an example of a work narrated throughout in an ironic tone by an omniscient narrator. It is reminiscent of eighteenth-century fiction, of Fielding perhaps or Wieland, but while exploiting it, Mann in the end ironizes the very convention of the omniscient narrator.

Der Zauberberg is a kind of adventure story, but it tells of an intellectual and moral adventure, not a physical one. Its theme is the struggle of the hero, Hans Castorp, to discover what is the properly humane attitude for a man of his times. Such a search must involve the attempt to formulate what is the human condition in the light of present-day knowledge, to integrate into a balanced whole its many aspects, and so harmonize the often apparently conflicting values by which we guide our activity. The tone of the narrator implies that he and of course the reader know the answers to these deep questions, but that he and the reader may enjoy the human comedy of entering sympathetically into Hans's struggles. The narrator frequently pretends to assume the point of view of Hans. At one point he even says he could not have put it better himself when Hans has been particularly clever. But at the same time he allows his own rather different, rather wiser point of view to shine through. Such irony has a didactic purpose. We are invited partially to identify with Hans, to recognize our own perplexities in his, but at the same time to maintain critical distance from Hans's story and so to learn as we cannot so easily from our own involving experience. Irony flatters and thus prevents resentment at a didactic tone, while the tug of the overt meaning and point of view prevents a too easy contempt.

Mann's irony extends even into the apparently autonomous direct speech of his characters.[2] The dialogue becomes depersonalized, half detached from the character speaking so that it reveals more than just his personality or opinions. We 'see through' what is said and perceive implications which transcend the understanding of the speaker, or in the case of the narrator, we are led to realize that he means more than he says. One way this

---

[2] cf. Ulrich Dittmann, *Sprachbewußtsein und Redeformen im Werk Thomas Manns* (Stuttgart, 1969).

is achieved is the use of jargon, a dead language of fixed phrases, dangerous because it reflects fixed, unthinking attitudes. Different sorts of jargon are mixed incongruously to suggest issues beyond the understanding of the speaker. Hans's cousin Joachim, a young Prussian officer, mixes the medical jargon of the sanatorium with the language of the military. In the sanatorium with its obligatory rest cures he talks of 'Liegedienst', as in the army he might talk of guard duty. Such a phrase does not just characterize in a comic way the naïve young soldier. Behind it is the ironic presence of the narrator reminding the reader that duty is an abstract concept, meaningless until translated into concrete terms. A military ethos which promotes this formal concept to an absolute is dangerous, because it gives no guidance as to what in any situation the human course of conduct should be.

Another character, the psychiatrist Dr. Krokowski, speaks a mixture of psychiatric jargon and romantic cliché, a style the narrator characterizes as a mixture of the lyrical and the scientific. This description is denigrating in tone, since Krokowski is a man who mixes science and magic in a way more appropriate to a witch-doctor casting spells than to a man of medical science devoted to mental and physical health. Yet behind the apparent denigration of Krokowski's particular brand of science and lyricism is an ironic apology for the narrator's own style, indeed for *Der Zauberberg* as a whole with its long philosophical dialogues, scientific discussions, yet finally poetic qualities.

A similar irony is at work in the characterization of the other doctor, Behrens. One of his favourite phrases is 'Gesegnete Nahrungsaufnahme!' a comic variation of the conventional 'gesegnete Mahlzeit!' and an appropriate joke for a doctor. In his case the grotesque juxtaposition of sacramental and scientific language is ironic in a double sense. His language purports to be the jocular manner of speech of a man dedicated to the good of mankind; it helps, he thinks, to bring a bit of common sense and medical insight to bear on mysteries and sacraments. But the narrator implies slyly, not least by lending to him such a grotesque manner of speech, that the good doctor has not quite succeeded in integrating his rational knowledge and his emotional or spiritual needs. A visual proof of his failure is his amateurish portrait of Clawdia Chauchat. Thanks to his knowledge of subcutaneous fat, it gives a marvellous representation of the epidermis of an attractive woman, but totally fails to convey the essence

G*

of her attraction. And yet there is the further ironic implication that the narrator too wants to integrate the scientific and the sacramental or emotional, though not in the grotesque fashion of Behrens, whose portrait is neither a good scientific diagram nor a celebration of beauty.

Often the ironic implications of such jargon are brought out through repetitions, a kind of internal quotation which extends into the narrator's language as well. He repeats his own turns of phrase in many different contexts: a way of hinting slyly that there is more in his language than meets the eye. The mixing of jargons brings out what are apparently clashes between different values. Other repetitions of phrases, however, often suggest possibilities of linking different areas of human experience in a positive way.

An example of ironic self-quotation by the narrator is the repetition of the phrase 'ehrbare Verfinsterung' towards the beginning of the novel. Hans as a child sees his dead grandfather lying out in what seems to him the immense and awful dignity of death. A fly lands on the dead man's forehead, bringing with it no doubt an uncomfortable reminder of the less dignified aspect of decaying flesh to which flies are attracted. The manservant Fiete brushes away the fly with an expression of 'ehrbare Verfinsterung' (*Von der Taufschale*, p. 44). In a completely deadpan way—on a first reading the repetition would scarcely be noticed—this phrase becomes the heading for the first section of the next chapter (p. 57). This time it is Hans Castorp who assumes an expression of 'ehrbare Verfinsterung' on hearing the noise of a couple making love next door. In both these cases there is offence at human physicality, a feeling that love and death are robbed of their dignity by their fleshly aspect. And yet Hans is fascinated by human physicality in love as in death, as witness his rather ghoulish investigations of the *moribundi* in the sanatorium or his acquisition, as a very odd love-token, of an X-ray picture of his beloved's breast. Hans, then, is at once over-idealistic, hence the 'ehrbare Verfinsterung', and ghoulish. He cannot transform these feelings into a third different attitude, which finds no contradiction between the spiritual and the physical. The phrase 'ehrbare Verfinsterung' is ironic, then, since it characterizes a quite unpraiseworthy attitude. Its repetition in different contexts, however, invites the reader to see inner connections, to draw conclusions, to learn from Hans's errors.

This common adolescent problem is expanded and linked with

analogous dilemmas of broader proportions. There is, for example,
the possible conflict between scientific or sociological analysis,
which seems to depersonalize individuals, just as the mechanics
of sex might seem to do, to turn people into economic units or
chemical processes ('gesegnete Nahrungsaufnahme!') and, on
the other hand, the mystical view of life Naphta sometimes
expresses, which denies material reality and is, potentially,
equally depersonalizing. He describes medieval art, for example,
as 'anonym gemeinsam', a phrase later taken up by Hans Castorp
and by the narrator in quite different contexts. Or there is a
potential clash between the values of individual experience such
as aesthetic experience or self-exploration, as indicated by Hans's
tendency to dreamy silence, with the values of political commitment and practical progress which Settembrini praises with such
eloquent rhetoric.

Mann employs an all-pervasive irony to make these points.
The narrator pretends to put the point of view of the characters.
But his ironic presence infiltrates even the direct speech of the
characters, since the repetitions and quotations blur the normally
sharp outlines between narration and dialogue.

The narrator scarcely ever breaks his ironic stance to teach
directly. Indeed, Mann ironizes the very convention of ironic
omniscience. His is a double irony in that the underlying truth
his narrator seems to imply is itself less than the whole truth.
The 'omniscient' narrator is not omniscient. The reader is invited
to enjoy the pretence of omniscience, to see the narrator as a kind
of god, the novel as his fictional world in which all is right. This
seems to hold good even of the famous statement: '*Der Mensch
soll um der Güte und Liebe willen dem Tode keine Herrschaft einräumen
über seine Gedanken.*' (*Schnee*, p. 686) For one thing, it is not a direct
statement by the narrator but part of Hans Castorp's dream in
the snowstorm. The very next words are: 'Und damit wache ich
auf', but on awakening Hans promptly forgets his dream. He
does not truly awake from the seven years of dreaming on the
magic mountain until the end of the novel, when the narrator
refuses to follow him into the trenches of the First World War.
If the dream is the narrator's 'message', it is a message the hero
does not learn in action within the fictional world of the novel,
as he would have in a proper *Bildungsroman*. Instead Mann
indirectly invites his readers to relate this fictional world to the
real world and its problems, to see that Thomas Mann in the

guise of the narrator cannot give final God-like answers. At the end of the novel the dream as a whole is recalled in a blandly anti-omniscient context, its remoteness from reality emphasized:

> Das junge Blut mit seinen Ranzen und Spießgewehren, seinen verschmutzten Mänteln und Stiefeln! Man könnte sich humanistisch-schönseliger Weise auch andere Bilder erträumen in seiner Betrachtung. Man könnte es sich denken: Rosse regend und schwemmend in einer Meeresbucht, mit der Geliebten am Strande wandelnd, die Lippen am Ohre der weichen Braut, auch wie es glücklich freundschaftlich einander im Bogenschuß unterweist. Statt dessen liegt es, die Nase im Feuerdreck ... (*Der Donnerschlag*, p. 992)

and further down:

> Fahr wohl — du lebest nun oder bleibest! Deine Aussichten sind schlecht; das arge Tanzvergnügen, worein du gerissen bist, dauert noch manches Sündenjährchen, und wir möchten nicht hoch wetten, daß du davonkommst. Ehrlich gestanden, lassen wir ziemlich unbekümmert die Frage offen. Abenteuer im Fleische und Geist, die deine Einfachheit steigerten, ließen dich im Geist überleben, was du im Fleische wohl kaum überleben sollst. Augenblicke kamen, wo dir aus Tod und Körperunzucht ahungsvoll und regierungsweise ein Traum von Liebe erwuchs. Wird auch aus diesem Weltfest des Todes, auch aus der schlimmen Fieberbrunst, die rings den regnerischen Abendhimmel entzündet, einmal die Liebe steigen? (p. 994)

The novel ends on a question, not a statement. Mann's irony thus extends into self-irony too, and, as Hans Castorp disappears out of the pages of fiction into the trenches of the First World War, indicates recognition of the proper boundary between art and prophecy.

Max Frisch's novel *Homo Faber* is an example of a work with a structure based on dramatic irony, but it highlights the dramatic irony by an ironic narrative technique as well. This takes the form of fictional autobiography, a device which lends itself to dramatic irony since it has inbuilt two vantage-points in time: the point of view of the character as actor in his own story and his point of view as narrator looking back, so that he can play off earlier ignorance against later realization.

Homo Faber is a Greek tragedy, but in modern dress. Psychology and moral laws replace Fate: the hero is guilty of hubris, against the laws of his own nature and the demands of common humanity. (See *Register*.) His guilt assumes visible form in an act of incest, though he is not aware at the time that his lover is also his daughter. The commenting chorus is replaced by his own comments as he narrates his story. These take the form of veiled hints, of touches of tonal irony so that the suspense of the plot is maintained, but the reader is prepared for a terrible revelation. More subtly, the irony means that we are involved simultaneously in the 'innocence' or ignorance of the hero—he does not know the girl he loves is his daughter—and his guilt, since his ignorance of the girl's identity is the direct result of deep human failure towards the mother, a German Jewess whom he allowed to disappear in the immediate prewar chaos. Ironically, his innocence, or ignorance, *is* his guilt. Unknowing incest seems a particularly appropriate objective correlative for such a paradox in that his love for the girl seems on the face of it to justify his role of lover, but points ironically to the hidden truth, his role of father. The plot of *Homo Faber* thus has that satisfying sense of logic and necessity, in its counterpoint of ignorance and knowledge, which is the mark of dramatic irony. In this sense, irony is a major tool in the job of artistic shaping. It is one of the means art uses to shape life, to deny the chaotic or the random. Alternatively, as the pessimist might argue, these beautiful ironies show the superiority of art over the shapeless absurdity of life.

The omniscient narrator of *Der Zauberberg* and the personalized narrator of *Homo Faber* are in these works the main source of irony. *Doktor Faustus*, on the other hand, is even more indirect, for Mann interposes an unironic narrator, Zeitblom, between himself and the action of his novel. This apparently dominant point of view is ironized in many ways. As the chapter on *Symbolism* argued, the symbolic import of the work stands in ironic tension with its purport as presented by Zeitblom. The hidden import is implied, for example, through the ambiguous descriptions of Jonathan Leverkühn's scientific experiments or Adrian's musical compositions in which the author's stance shines through Zeitblom's words. There is the ironic parallel with the Faust legend, and, as in *Der Zauberberg*, here too Mann undermines to ironic effect the formal conventions of his novel, in this case fictional biography. For example, Zeitblom protests at one point that he can tell us exactly what happened on occasions at which he was not present, because, he says, he knows Adrian so well. But his protest persuades us of the opposite from what it purports to. By gratuitously drawing attention to an inconsistency in the handling of point of view, Mann further undermines rather than bolsters up the illusion of a real biographer, Zeitblom. He reminds us, ironically, that the only person who 'knows' Adrian as well as that, is Thomas Mann, because Adrian and Zeitblom alike are his creations. By thus ironically reminding us of the fictional status of his characters, he alerts the reader to the true import of his *fiction*: the confessional account by a *real* German intellectual of the *real* history of Germany.

In his *Entstehung des Doktor Faustus*, an account of the writing of *Doktor Faustus*, Mann offers some reasons for interposing Zeitblom to mediate between himself and the theme of his novel, the moral collapse of Germany: 'überdies war die Maßnahme bitter notwendig, um eine gewisse Durchheiterung des düsteren Stoffes zu erzielen und mir selbst, wie dem Leser, seine Schrecknisse erträglich zu machen.'[3] He mentions too the dual plane of time of the novel:[4] the progress of the war as Zeitblom is writing, and the much longer course of events leading up to the war covered by Leverkühn's story, a device which brings into ironic juxtaposition earlier events and their later unforeseen horrible consequences—a form of heightened dramatic irony (see *Time*).

Rather similar motives may well have prompted Günter Grass to choose the form of fictional autobiography for *Die Blechtrommel*. As the novel opens, a dwarf called Oskar Matzerath, suffering from the aftermath of a nervous breakdown, is telling the story of his life up to the point of his breakdown. Oskar is an artist, a drummer, a kind of intellectual who has gone through life observing others, playing his drum, and otherwise apparently uninvolved in the events he narrates. He was born, he tells us, fully developed intellectually, decided to remain physically a three-year-old, and in this disguise of apparently innocent childhood sees the rise of Hitler, the war, and now the beginnings of the post-war *Wirtschaftswunder*. But it emerges in various oblique ways that he has contributed to the deaths of a number of people, and when the novel opens he is in a mental hospital after accepting guilt for the murder of a nurse, a crime he has not in fact committed.

Die Blechtrommel has a dual time-plane not unlike the time-structure of *Doktor Faustus*. As the novel goes on we move forward in time through Oskar's past history as he narrates it, but we also

---

[3] *Die Entstehung des Doktor Faustus* (Amsterdam, 1949), Chapter IV, p. 32.
[4] *Ibid.*, p. 29.

move forward with him in the mental hospital in which he is confined as he writes. There is thus an ironic counterpoint between his progress towards the breakdown and his progress towards a cure, which are narrated simultaneously. The guilt-ridden past which he narrates precipitates his breakdown, but the narrating of it helps towards his cure, is a therapeutic exercise. The point of view of Oskar as narrator is constantly played off against the point of view of Oskar as actor in his own history. The guilty conscience of the later point of view has a hard time to struggle through against the monstrous energy and vitality of the earlier Oskar who constantly asserts his innocence, asserts it indeed in the literally innocent shape of childhood. The later Oskar, torn by remorse, is separated from his earlier self by the abyss of his breakdown. Until the end of the novel Oskar is virtually a split personality with these different senses of identity struggling within him, a struggle reflected in his fluctuation between the first and third persons in referring to himself. Not until the end do these identities begin to grow together. Crippling remorse and hence denial of his earlier self turn to true acceptance of guilt and hence of himself as a continuous identity.

A multi-layered irony derives from this combination of fictional autobiography and dual time-plane, which the following passage may illustrate.

Es war einmal ein SA-Mann, der tötete vier Kater und wurde, da die Kater noch nicht ganz tot waren, von den Katern verraten und von einem Uhrmacher angezeigt. Es kam zu einem gerichtlichen Verfahren, und der SA-Mann mußte Strafe zahlen. Doch auch bei der SA wurde über den Fall gesprochen, und der SA-Mann sollte wegen unwürdigen Verhaltens aus der SA ausgestoßen werden. Selbst als sich der SA-Mann während der Nacht vom achten zum neunten November achtunddreißig, die man später die Kristallnacht nannte, besonders mutig hervortat, die Langfuhrer Synagoge im Michaelisweg mit anderen in Brand steckte, auch kräftig mittat, als am folgenden Morgen mehrere, zuvor genau bezeichnete Geschäfte geräumt werden mußten, konnte all sein Eifer seine Entfernung aus der Reiter-SA nicht verhindern. Wegen unmenschlicher Tierquälerei wurde er degradiert und von der Mitgliederliste gestrichen. Erst ein Jahr später gelang ihm der Eintritt in die Heimwehr, die später von der Waffen-SS übernommen wurde.

Es war einmal ein Kolonialwarenhändler, der schloß an einem Novembertag sein Geschäft, weil in der Stadt etwas los war, nahm seinen Sohn Oskar bei der Hand und fuhr mit der Straßenbahn linie

Fünf bis zum Langasser Tor, weil dort wie in Zoppot und Langfuhr
die Synagoge brannte. Die Synagoge war fast abgebrannt, und die
Feuerwehr paßte auf, daß der Brand nicht auf die anderen Häuser
übergriff. Vor der Ruine schleppten Uniformierte und Zivilisten
Bücher, sakrale Gebrauchsgegenstände und merkwürdige Stoffe
zusammen. Der Berg wurde in Brand gesteckt, und der Kolonialwarenhändler benutzte die Gelegenheit und wärmte seine Finger und
seine Gefühle über dem öffentlichen Feuer. Sein Sohn Oskar jedoch,
der den Vater so beschäftigt und entflammt sah, verdrückte sich unbeo-
bachtet und eilte in Richtung Zeughauspassage davon, weil er um
seine Trommeln aus weißrot gelacktem Blech besorgt war.

Es war einmal ein Spielzeughändler, der hieß Sigismund Markus
und verkaufte unter anderem auch weißrot gelackte Blechtrommeln.
Oskar, von dem soeben die Rede war, war der Hauptabnehmer dieser
Blechtrommeln, weil er von Beruf Blechtrommler war und ohne
Blechtrommel nicht leben konnte und wollte. Deshalb eilte er auch
von der brennenden Synagoge fort zur Zeughauspassage, denn dort
wohnte der Hüter seiner Trommeln; aber er fand ihn in einem
Zustand vor, der ihm das Verkaufen von Blechtrommeln fortan oder
auf dieser Welt unmöglich machte.

Sie, dieselben Feuerwerker, denen ich, Oskar, davongelaufen zu
sein glaubte, hatten schon vor mir den Markus besucht, hatten Pinsel
in Farbe getaucht und ihm quer übers Schaufenster in Sütterlinschrift
das Wort Judensau geschrieben, hatten dann, vielleicht aus Mißver-
gnügen an der eigenen Handschrift, mit ihren Stiefelabsätzen die Schau-
fensterscheibe zertreten, so daß sich der Titel, den sie dem Markus ange-
hängt hatten, nur noch erraten ließ. Die Tür verachtend, hatten sie
durch das aufgebrochene Fenster in den Laden gefunden und spielten
nun dort auf ihre eindeutige Art mit dem Kinderspielzeug.

(Glaube Hoffnung Liebe, pp. 163–4)

The Jewish toyshop keeper, who had been Oskar's friend, has
killed himself. Oskar, disguised by his childish outer shape, uses
the opportunity to steal a few drums, since supplies of drums seem
to be so threatened.

The most obvious irony comes from the tension between Oskar's
amoral stance and the horrors he observes with his child's eye.
Grass's condemnation of anti-semitism speaks with brutal irony
through the apparent coolness. The juxtaposition of 'unmenschlicher Tierquälerei' for example with the *Kristallnacht* brings
out not just the horror of the latter, but the almost incredible
combination of sentimentality and mindless brutality of good
citizens shocked by cruelty to cats yet enjoying cruelty to Jews.
The very notion of someone being expelled from the SA for

cruelty is ironic in the extreme. The use of irony allows the mentality of someone who finds nothing odd in this to be presented with shocking directness—that is the purport. The import of condemnation arises from the tension between the matter-of-fact style and what is actually being said. This is irony of the kind of Swift's *Modest Proposal*.

Beyond that again is the irony which arises from the tension between the point of view of the narrator Oskar and his earlier self, so that his apparent detachment and hence innocence are sometimes subtly, here fairly obviously, shown to be a kind of guilt. For who could remain detached at the sight of a pogrom and still be judged innocent? The narrator Oskar assumes here the stance that a child might have, as, for example, when he suggests that the SA-men have kicked in the window because they had not managed to write 'Judensau' neatly enough. A child would not realize what was going on. Such an exaggeratedly childish presentation is surely a bitterly ironic way of expressing disgust at his earlier irresponsibly selfish attitudes. Oskar may have remained detached from the Nazis, disgusted by the gross excitement of his petit-bourgeois father, Matzerath, who warms his hands and his emotions over the flames engulfing Germany's Jews. But he exploits his child's disguise to pursue his own interests and even manages to acquire some drums out of the *Kristallnacht*.

A further hidden import of the novel, expressed always with ironic indirectness, rises close to the surface here in the repetitions of the phrase 'Es war einmal ...', the traditional opening of fairy-tales. In the immediate context this phrase is clearly ironic in effect. It is a disgusted exaggeration by Oskar, the narrator, of his own earlier false naïvety, assumed to escape all responsibility. He apes his own childishness by telling this fearful tale as if it were a fairy-story fit for the nursery. But at the same time the phrase continues a series of fairy-tale motifs pervading the novel as a whole. Oskar himself is reminiscent of a changeling, a monster-child with an adult mind and destructive, magical powers. These fairly-tale motifs contrast incongruously with the otherwise realistic texture of the novel and so we may look in them for some ironically concealed meaning.

Oskar's attributes are fantastic; we do not 'believe' in him in a realistic way. He tells us, for example, that he was born fully developed intellectually and that he was totally uninfluenced by upbringing and environment. This biological and psychological impossibility is, in fact, an extreme kind of irony. Grass is surely implying the opposite of what Oskar would persuade us of: namely that no one, however intelligent, is completely outside of society and so free of responsibility. In Oskar, Grass is satirizing that type of German intellectual who assumed the stance of an irresponsible outsider. Far from being born completely detached from society, their alienation is symptomatic of a sick society and a further cause of the very evils which brought about their alienated condition in the first place. Oskar, by clinging to his false detachment helps, by sins of omission if not of commission, to further the moral collapse of German society.

But apart from this ironic commentary on the situation of the artist or intellectual in a sick society, Grass's novel contrives to include an ironic self-commentary, as it were, an indirect statement not only about artists but about art as well, and its legitimacy in an age of crisis and horror. The excerpt quoted above illustrates an incongruous mixture, continued throughout the novel, of conventional realism—the realistically drawn character of father Matzerath, for example—fairy-tale—'es war einmal ...', Oskar the changeling—and historical reportage—the real historical date of 9th November, 1938, known as the *Kristallnacht*. The novel fluctuates, as it were, between fantasy and history, the mean between these being realistic fiction in which fictional and factual truth coincide. We believe in the 'reality' of father Matzerath, for example, in a double sense. He is a credible though imaginary individual and a historically accurate portrait of a social type. Oskar, on the other hand, is an imaginary, incredible figure, while the *Kristallnacht* is not imaginary at all. The implication is that art can and should be true in a double sense. It should be internally consistent and aesthetically shaped, but it should also be true about life. The social and moral legitimacy of art lies in its capacity to tell human and historical truths, not pretty fantasies detached from all reality, like some of those Oskar beats out on his drum. But the irony is that it is precisely through the elements of fantasy that Grass has most 'told the truth'. When the truth is such horrors as the *Kristallnacht*, it is only perhaps through distancing devices such as the fantastic medium of Oskar that it can be told at all, that the shock of immediate horror can be sufficiently controlled as to avoid the pornographic. And yet it is surely important that such truth should be told and not forgotten.

Bibliography

I NOVELS

This list comprises only those novels from which quotations have been drawn in the text. All other novels mentioned will be found, with dates, in the index. Dates in square brackets are of first publication, except where indicated.

Gottfried Benn, *Roman des Phänotyp. Landsberger Fragment* [written 1944], in *Gesammelte Werke*, ed. Dieter Wellershoff (Wiesbaden: Limes 1958), Volume 2.

Heinrich Böll, *Haus ohne Hüter* [1954] (Cologne/Berlin: Kiepenheuer & Witsch, 1954).

Heinrich Böll, *Billard um halbzehn* [1959] (Cologne/Berlin: Kiepenheuer & Witsch, 1959).

Hermann Broch, *Die Schlafwandler* [1931–32], in Volume 2, *Gesammelte Werke* (Zürich: Rhein-Verlag n.d.).

Hermann Broch, *Der Tod des Vergil* [1945 in English, 1947 in German], in Volume 3, *Gesammelte Werke* (Zürich: Rhein-Verlag, 1958).

Hermann Broch, *Der Versucher*, ed. Felix Stössinger [from three unpublished versions written 1935–36, 1936 and 1950–51 respectively], in Volume 4, *Gesammelte Werke* (Zürich: Rhein-Verlag, 1954).

Hermann Broch, *Die Schuldlosen* [1949], in Volume 5, *Gesammelte Werke* (Zürich: Rhein-Verlag, 1954).

Elias Canetti, *Die Blendung* [1935, expanded version 1963] (Frankfurt a.M./Hamburg: Fischer Bücherei KG, 1965).

Heimito von Doderer, *Die Strudlhofstiege* [1951] (Munich: DTV, 1966).

Alfred Döblin, *Berlin Alexanderplatz. Die Geschichte vom Franz Biberkopf* [1929], ed. Walter Muschg (Olten/Freiburg i. Br.: Walter, 1961).

Alfred Döblin, *Hamlet oder Die lange Nacht nimmt ein Ende* [1956], ed. Walter Muschg (Olten/Freiburg i. Br.: Walter, 1966).

Lion Feuchtwanger, *Jud Süß* [1925] (Berlin: Th. Knaur Nachf., 1931).

Max Frisch, *Homo Faber. Ein Bericht* [1957] (Frankfurt a.M.: Suhrkamp, 1962 (Bibliothek Suhrkamp)).

Gerd Gaiser, *Schlußball. Aus den schönen Tagen der Stadt Neu-Spuhl* [1958] (Munich: Hanser, 1958).

Günter Grass, *Die Blechtrommel* [1959] (Frankfurt a.M./Hamburg: Fischer Bücherei KG, 1962).

Peter Handke, *Die Hornissen* [1966] (Frankfurt a.M.: Suhrkamp, 1966).

Hermann Hesse, *Der Steppenwolf* [1927], in *Gesammelte Schriften* (Berlin/Frankfurt a.M.: Suhrkamp, 1957), Volume 4.

Hermann Hesse, *Das Glasperlenspiel. Versuch einer Lebensbeschreibung des Magister Ludi Josef Knecht samt Knechts hinterlassenen Schriften* [1943], in *Gesammelte Schriften* (Berlin/Frankfurt a.M.: Suhrkamp, 1957), Volume 6.

Arno Holz and Johannes Schlaf, *Papa Hamlet* [1889] (Stuttgart: Reclam, 1968).

Franz Kafka, *Ein Bericht für eine Akademie* [1919] and *Kleine Fabel* [written 1920], in *Die Erzählungen*, ed. Klaus Wagenbach (Frankfurt a.M.: S. Fischer, 1961).

Franz Kafka, *Amerika* [written 1912–14], *Der Prozeß* [written [1914–15], and *Das Schloß* [written 1921–22], in *Die Romane* (Frankfurt a.M.: S. Fischer, 1965).

Elisabeth Langgässer, *Das unauslöschliche Siegel* [1946] (Reinbek: Rowohlt, 1965 (rororo)).

Heinrich Mann, *Der Untertan* [1918] (Hamburg: Claassen, 1961).

Thomas Mann, *Buddenbrooks. Verfall einer Familie* [1901] (Frankfurt a.M.: S. Fischer, 1965).

Thomas Mann, *Der Zauberberg* [1924] (Frankfurt a.M.: S. Fischer, 1966).

Thomas Mann, *Doktor Faustus. Das Leben des deutschen Tonsetzers Adrian Leverkühn erzählt von einem Freunde* [1947] (Stockholm: Bermann-Fischer, 1947).

Thomas Mann, *Bekenntnisse des Hochstaplers Felix Krull* [1922 and 1954] (Frankfurt a.M.: S. Fischer, 1954).

Thomas Mann, *Der kleine Herr Friedemann* [1897], in *Erzählungen* (Frankfurt a.M.: S. Fischer, 1960).

Robert Musil, *Die Verwirrungen des Zöglings Törleß* [1906], in *Prosa, Dramen, Späte Briefe*, ed. Adolf Frisé (Hamburg: Rowohlt, 1957).

Robert Musil, *Der Mann ohne Eigenschaften* [1930, 1933, 1943], ed.
Adolf Frisé (Hamburg: Rowohlt, 1952).

Hans Erich Nossack, *Das Testament des Lucius Eurinus* [1964]
(Frankfurt a.M.: Suhrkamp, 1965 (edition suhrkamp)).

Arthur Schnitzler, *Leutnant Gustl* [1900], in *Die erzählenden Schriften*
(Frankfurt a.M.: S. Fischer, 1961), Volume 1.

Martin Walser, *Halbzeit* [1960] (Frankfurt a.M.: S. Fischer, 1960).

Robert Walser, *Der Gehülfe* [1908] (Frankfurt a.M./Hamburg:
Fischer Bücherei KG, 1962).

Christoph Martin Wieland, *Geschichte der Abderiten* [1781] (Stuttgart: Reclam, 1966).

II SECONDARY LITERATURE

This list is selective. With one or two important exceptions, it
does not include literature on individual novels or novelists.
It is intended both to supplement the references in the Notes and
to suggest further reading on the theory and techniques of the
novel.

Helmut Arntzen, *Der moderne deutsche Roman. Voraussetzungen,
Strukturen, Gehalte* (Heidelberg, 1962).

Erich Auerbach, *Mimesis. Dargestellte Wirklichkeit in der abend-
ländischen Literatur*, 2. verbesserte u. erweiterte Aufl. (Bern,
1959).

Friedrich von Blankenburg, *Versuch über den Roman* [1774],
Faksimiledruck der Originalausgabe, mit einem Nachwort
von E. Lämmert (Stuttgart, 1964).

Günther Blöcker, *Die neuen Wirklichkeiten. Linien und Profile der
modernen Literatur* (Berlin, 1961).

Wayne C. Booth, *The Rhetoric of Fiction* (Chicago, 1961).

Richard Brinkmann (ed.), *Begriffsbestimmung des literarischen
Realismus* (Darmstadt, 1969).

David Daiches, *The Novel and the Modern World*, rev'd edn.
(London and Chicago, 1960).

Wilhelm Emrich, 'Die Erzählkunst des 20. Jahrhunderts und ihr
geschichtlicher Sinn', in *Deutsche Literatur in unserer Zeit*, ed.
Wolfgang Kayser, 2., durchgesehene Auflage (Göttingen,
1959), pp. 58–79.

Wilhelm Emrich, 'Formen und Gehalte des zeitgenössischen Romans', in *Protest und Verheißung. Studien zur klassischen und modernen Dichtung* (Frankfurt a.M., 1960), pp. 169–75.

E. M. Forster, *Aspects of the Novel* (London, 1927).

Joseph Frank, 'Spatial Form in Modern Literature', in *Criticism. The Foundations of Modern Literary Judgment*, ed. Mark Schorer, Josephine Miles, Gordon McKenzie, rev'd edn. (New York, 1958), pp. 379–92.

Rolf Geissler, *Möglichkeiten des modernen deutschen Romans. Analysen und Interpretationsgrundlagen zu Romanen von Thomas Mann, Alfred Döblin, Hermann Broch, Gerd Gaiser, Max Frisch, Alfred Andersch und Heinrich Böll* (Frankfurt a.M./Berlin/Bonn, 1962).

Käte Hamburger, *Die Logik der Dichtung* (Stuttgart, 1957).

Robert Humphrey *Stream of Consciousness in the Modern Novel* (Berkeley/Los Angeles, 1954).

Erich Kahler, 'Untergang und Übergang der epischen Kunstform', in *Die Neue Rundschau*, 64 (1953), pp. 1–44.

Wolfgang Kayser, *Das sprachliche Kunstwerk. Eine Einführung in die Literaturwissenschaft* (Bern, 1948).

Wolfgang Kayser, *Entstehung und Krise des modernen Romans* (Stuttgart, 1954).

Volker Klotz (ed.), *Zur Poetik des Romans* (Darmstadt, 1965).

Eberhard Lämmert, *Bauformen des Erzählens* (Stuttgart, 1955).

Lothar Köhn, 'Entwicklungs- und Bildungsroman. Ein Forschungsbericht', in *DVjs* 42 (1968), pp. 427–73 and 590–632.

Percy Lubbock, *The Craft of Fiction* (London, 1921).

Georg Lukács, *Die Theorie des Romans. Ein geschichtsphilosophischer Versuch über die Formen der großen Epik* [1920] 2nd edn. (Neuwied and Berlin, 1963).

Fritz Martini, *Das Wagnis der Sprache. Interpretationen deutscher Prosa von Nietzsche bis Benn* (Stuttgart, 1954).

A. A. Mendilow, *Time and the Novel* (London, 1952).

Herman Meyer, *Das Zitat in der Erzählkunst. Zur Geschichte und Poetik des europäischen Romans* (Stuttgart, 1961).

Günther Müller, 'Erzählzeit und erzählte Zeit', in *Festschrift für Paul Kluckhohn und Hermann Schneider* (Tübingen, 1948), pp. 195–212.

Edwin Muir, *The Structure of the Novel* (London, 1928).

Roy Pascal, *The German Novel. Studies* (Manchester, 1956).

Alain Robbe-Grillet, *Pour un Nouveau Roman* (Paris, 1963).

Allan Rodway, *The Truths of Fiction* (London, 1970).

Friedrich Spielhagen, *Beiträge zur Theorie und Technik des Romans* (Leipzig, 1883).

Franz Stanzel, *Typische Formen des Romans* (Göttingen, 1964).

René Wellek and Austin Warren, *Theory of Literature* (New York, 1949).

René Wellek, *Concepts of Criticism* (New Haven/London, 1963).

Benno von Wiese, *Der deutsche Roman. Vom Barock bis zur Gegenwart. Struktur und Geschichte* (Düsseldorf, 1963), 2 volumes.

Index

Index

Bold numerals indicate major topics.

DATE DUE